WALTZING
— WITH THE —
RAPTORS

WALTZING
— WITH THE —
RAPTORS

**A PRACTICAL ROADMAP
TO PROTECTING YOUR
COMPANY'S REPUTATION**

Glen Peters

John Wiley & Sons, Inc.

New York • Chichester • Weinheim • Brisbane • Singapore • Toronto

Published by John Wiley & Sons, Inc.
Published simultaneously in Canada.

Designations used by companies to distinguish their products are often claimed by trademarks. In all instances where the author or publisher is aware of a claim, the product names appear in Initial Capital letters. Readers, however, should contact the appropriate companies for more complete information regarding trademarks and registration.

The opinions expressed in this book are solely those of the author. In relating those views, certain identities have been created as a literary device, and the names of some actual individuals have been changed. This publication is designed to provide accurate and authoritative information in regard to the subject matter covered. It is sold with the understanding that the publisher is not engaged in rendering professional services. If professional advice or other expert assistance is required, the services of a competent professional person should be sought.

Library of Congress Cataloging-in-Publication Data:
Peters, Glen.
    Waltzing with the raptors : a practical roadmap to protecting your company's reputation / Glen Peters.
       p.   cm.
    Includes index.
    ISBN 0-471-32732-8 (cloth : alk. paper)
    1. Corporate image.   2. International business enterprises.
  I. Title.
HD59.2.P47   1999
659.2—dc21   98-31701

ACKNOWLEDGMENTS

There is an endless list of people without whose help the development of this framework would not have happened, and it is only possible to mention a few of them.

Luke Mulekezi, Lauren Goldblatt, and Amy Middelburg of PricewaterhouseCoopers had a large part to play in the development of the Reputation Assurance Framework referred to in the pages of this book. They handled the global complexity of numerous consultations with companies and nongovernmental organizations with great energy and enthusiasm. My thanks also to my fellow partners Larry Ponemon and Harold Kahn, who have added much-needed support, and to Ken Sicchitano for his sponsorship of the Reputation Assurance program.

David Bodanis's editorial assistance has helped position my writing style to appeal, I hope, to a wider audience than the average business book. Cartoonist Peter Henning, who happens to be an active member of Amnesty International, has been a pleasure to work with. Peter loved the image of the raptors and created Ronny and Rosy, the two amusing characters featured in this book.

Lastly, my long-suffering assistant Adele Burgess has had the combined job of proofreading and putting together the text in a coherent form. Without her help this book would not have been put together in the time available.

I am most grateful to the following companies and organizations for giving their time and input to the development of the model.

COMPANIES

ABN/AMRO
Bausch & Lomb
BP-Amoco
BT
Cable & Wireless
Co-operative Bank
Diageo
GE Capital
Heineken
Mobil
Normura
Northern Telecom
Philips
Reckitt & Coleman
Reuters
Rio Tinto
Shell

ORGANIZATIONS

Action Aid
Amnesty International
Business in the Community
CERES
Coalition for Environmentally Responsible Economies
Co-op America
Council for Economic Priorities
Drucker Foundation
Ethical Trading Initiative
Ethos
Fairtrade Foundation
Friends of the Earth
Greenpeace International

Human Rights Watch—Asia
Interfaith Center for Corporate Responsibility
Investor Responsibility Research Center
New Academy of Business
New Economics Foundation
Oxfam
RFK Center on Human Rights
Save the Children
Socially Responsible Business Unit, Department
    for International Sustainability
U.S. State Department
University of Leeds
University of Notre Dame
Warwick Business School
World Vision

*The views expressed in this book about any organization or individual
are those of the author and do not necessarily represent the views
of PriceWaterhouseCoopers or its partners.*

CONTENTS

Contents

INTRODUCTION

I feel I should clarify my interest in this introduction: I believe, as I hope that you my readers do, unequivocally in the power of business to build for us and our future generations a healthy and economically prosperous global civil society. Most business men and women, like me and you, the readers of this book, believe that we want to build and work in organizations that behave with a sense of responsibility toward all. Few of us would admit to wanting to consciously work for a company which systematically ill-treats people, pollutes our surroundings or trades on deceit and corruption. Equally, none of us would like our children to be starting out in life with companies who might unfairly exploit them, discriminate against their race, gender, or religion, or encourage them to indulge in corrupt practices.

It's easy to forget that good business is the cornerstone of a successful locality, country, and world. It's also easy to forget that a business functioning in a truly competitive environment provides more value for customers, better innovation, and perhaps, most importantly, the opportunity to afford the basic rights which we write about so eloquently. It is a salutary fact that the taxes that a single company like Exxon generates worldwide could pay to eliminate world hunger and illiteracy and have sufficient change left over to go some way to resolving third world debt; all in one year.

But from time to time we do get blindsighted. We forget some of the basic rules, which if ignored lead to bad business. We get caught up in fulfilling targets, achieving objectives, and meeting deadlines and forget to examine the wider consequences of what we are doing. This is not a fault of business people alone, for activists can be equally guilty of a narrow, single-issue focus to their thinking. Simplistic ideologies such as "all business is corrupt" abound.

The result can be modern guerrilla warfare. The corporation cannot get at the activists or defend against allegations and the well-intentioned activists cannot reach out to the faceless corporation. While my kids watched *Jurassic Park* one evening at home the image of the ferocious velociraptor captured my imagination. There seemed a certain similarity to the type of attacks to which we have seen corporations subjected. The raptors' speed, learning rate, and strike capability seemed to match an attack reported in the press at the time by two unemployed youths on McDonald's. An attack which seemed to do a lot of damage to the company and take its top management away from their regular day job.

Companies have begun to ask if there is a way to protect themselves from these attacks which seemed to occur without warning and come from nowhere. Traditional solutions such as massive injections of cash toward public relations seem to have the reverse effect. They make people more suspicious and cynical of the intentions of the company. Something else is needed—something that provides substance to the fancy value statements promoted by PR. Something that can be measured. Something that provides a structured way of ensuring management that their company is fundamentally a responsible one. Something that involves everyone.

Reputation assurance has been developed to respond to this need. It brings together a variety of management methods which my colleagues and I have previously practiced. You will see a good deal of quality management, plenty of risk analysis, a pinch of change management, lashings of auditing methods, spoonfuls of stakeholder analysis, a dash of project management and action planning, and a good dose of key performance analysis. It is this rich potpourri of management skills and resources which is needed to solve a problem as complex as reputation assurance.

We chose reputation as the reason why companies need to act responsibly because we saw its real value tied up in behavior to key stakeholders. As corporate value becomes more a determinant of intangible factors such as quality of innovation, word of mouth effects, societal and market image, and less of tangible assets such as plant, inventory, and real estate, reputation will need to be included as part of regular management process.

We began by researching many of the successes and failures in corporate reputation, and some of these examples are given in this book. We talked to company executives who were working on their own ideas of reputation assurance. We spoke to many activist and nongovernmental organizations who were trying to encourage companies to engage in a dialogue with them. And we scanned the huge proliferation of codes and standards that exist today. From this we developed the principles and framework of reputation assurance.

There appeared to be a number of common threads that we have pulled together. One of these is the five key stakeholder groups we have identified as common to most organizations: shareholders, customers, employers, society, and partners. Society represents a global civil society and includes a wide cross section of representatives ranging from formal bodies such as government to informal nonelected groups. Partners is also a catchall for suppliers and franchisees and other joint venture entities. Companies with good sustainable reputations try and manage these stakeholders together, often making trade-offs, but with due regard to the consequences.

Reputable companies also tell their stakeholders about issues which affect them and try to sustain an honest policy of sharing good news and bad. The Reputation Report in Appendix A is an attempt to suggest a format of reporting which might work for companies that wish to pursue a policy of transparency. Indeed, if I were a shareholder of Retail International, the hypothetical company illustrated, I would be most reassured if my company published such a report annually. A number of companies are now beginning to publish similar reports.

The framework in this book is not a static one. We began testing out the original ideas a year ago and have changed and adjusted our original proposals as we have held consultations with companies and nongovernmental organizations. We have tested the framework on ourselves and it appears to work well. We've been applying the framework to companies in North America and Europe and it appears also to work for them. Its immediate value is in helping a company to identify the critical principles on which it needs to focus its efforts. Users tell us that not only is it a good test of where a company stands with regards to best practice, but also later on it becomes an effective learning framework.

For global companies it provides a consistent format for reporting conformance with values and principles. Not long ago, corporate controllers were frustrated by their operating companies as they tried to make sense of the numerous different ways in which their far-flung entities reported their financial results. Today most corporations have a consistent way of reporting this information. We hope that the reputation assurance framework will become a way of bringing that degree of uniformity and consistency to values reporting.

I am aware that this book may be like a pebble tossed into the vast lake of thought on the topic of corporate responsibility and reputation. It is my hope that if even the faintest ripple of its content reaches the shore of ambivalence to corporate responsibility and causes someone to pause and think about these issues, it will have been all worth the effort.

WALTZING
— WITH THE —
RAPTORS

P A R T

I

THE
NEW
SETTING

Introducing Ronny and Rosy Raptor.

"How did we first meet? Ronny asked me for a waltz."

WHAT'S

CHANGED

Velociraptors were among the most deadly of dinosaurs. About as tall as humans, they could achieve speeds of up to 70 miles per hour, rarely failing to overpower their prey as they hunted in pairs. Their nine-inch long claws sank deep into flesh, wounding, disabling, and finally killing their prey. It was a painful death for the unfortunate quarry, all in preparation for the raptors' dinner.

When an asset stripper takes over your company, it too can be deadly. Companies are targeted like helpless prey being stalked for dinner. Their hidden value is much greater than is immediately apparent to their sluggish and complacent management. Vast acres of prime real estate, some potentially strong brands that haven't been nurtured for years, a good pipeline of research and development that has been hidden away under a shroud of corporate secrecy all appeal to the hungry asset stripper.

Asset strippers will stalk for months, scouring the world for potential targets, using scouts, searching public data, talking to suppliers and customers, and, yes, even consulting that seemingly friendly banker. Then they pounce. With the first swing of the mighty tail, the takeover brings the company's management to its knees. Then those long claws of restructuring, downsizing, rightsizing, and reengineering slash through.

Jobs that had been supported for decades are cut. The victims, without any alternative resources, skills, or sources of employment, might find themselves on the scrap heap for the rest of their lives. Communities can crumble overnight. Pride is destroyed. The raptor has its prey.

When activists target your company, they too can be deadly. They may have long dreamed about bringing some multinational to its knees. Capitalism equals greed. Business is essentially antisocial. Shareholder interests always come before all else: safety, education, conservation, or human rights. Corporations need to be taught a lesson; to be hoisted on their own petard of dishonesty or downright incompetence. Being the first to humble some lumbering corporation would bring recognition, more members, more subscriptions, and inevitably more resources.

The opportunity might lie with a disgruntled insider willing to discuss lax health and safety procedures with an activist. The activist network could mobilize around the world, with the allegations being disseminated first in a covert way to collect more evidence and then finally in a press conference to present the matter to the world.

Newspaper stories could appear on front pages everywhere. The activists could be more organized than your company. The autonomy of the different units in your company might make it impossible to get a handle on whether the allegations are real or fictitious. You have never bothered to monitor such issues in the past. Vote-hungry, publicity-seeking politicians might take up the cause without further investigation, inciting anxious citizens to boycott your company or even cause damage to installations. Sales begin to plummet. Investors withdraw their stock. The market value collapses. Your company is in tatters. The raptors have their prey.

But imagine a different world, a world where you engage the raptor. Instead of trying to outwit it or keep it penned in some high-voltage Jurassic Park, you find out why it wants to attack you. You provide alternatives that sate its hunger and placate its killing instincts. In a way, you provide the musical accompaniment of a calming Viennese waltz. The raptor wants to dance. The music is soothing. It too wants to engage, and before you know it, you are locked in an Ionesco's Theatre of the Absurd production.

Together you find that life seems simpler. While other organizations are still trying to outsmart raptors, you are streaking ahead with your partner-in-arms. This partnership is not only protecting you, but also putting you at an advantage while other organizations are being torn apart or maimed by the warfare. Whether you are a corporation concerned about protecting shareholder value or indeed an activist organization keen to protect the planet or the global civic society in which we live, you'll find this waltz helping you achieve each other's aims.

BP-Amoco is one of the biggest oil companies in the world. It pumps billions of barrels a year from gigantic oil fields in Alaska, Colombia, the North Sea, the Caspian Sea, and elsewhere. They process the oil in giant refineries around the world and transport it to service stations for our consumption. As consumers, we don't even see the fuel we pump into our tanks, or often consider the carbon monoxide we expel from our exhaust pipes in the name of transportation.

Before its merger with Amoco, British Petroleum (BP) painted its service stations green, and Greenpeace saw red. Here was a company releasing millions of tons of carbon dioxide into the atmosphere and rapidly growing its hydrocarbon reserves as its geologists and explorers got better and better at finding huge quantities of what many referred to as black gold. BP would be responsible for depositing more and more of those damaging gases into the finite precious air this planet has for its seven billion citizens. All from the company putting on a green face.

The raptors pounced. They boarded platforms in the North Sea, disrupted production, breached countless safety procedures, and scored a publicity coup. They came with the sophisticated media trappings any CNN team would have been proud of. BP responded by taking action through the courts to fine Greenpeace for every day they continued the occupation.

It was at about this time that BP's chief executive officer (CEO) John Browne decided to waltz. There were a series of consultations with Greenpeace and their fellow activists, Friends of the Earth, who wanted BP to get out of the oil business in 10 years. And do what? What of the 65,000 employees around the world? The endless array of competitors waiting to take their place? Wasn't energy part of the lifeblood of economic regeneration in this world we live in today?

Browne offered them a plan—an ambitious plan. He promised to create a $1 billion business in solar power over five years. Solar power, a renewable and nonpolluting source of energy, definitely has the blessing of Greenpeace. The cost of solar energy was the next big obstacle the oil company had to tackle; solar energy is about five times more expensive than fossil-fuel-produced electricity. BP, through its joint venture with Tata Industries in India, set up the production of solar panels where production costs were lower, and allowed Tata to create more jobs in a developing country. Solar power is still more expensive than electricity from the power station, but the costs are coming down.

BP-Amoco is waltzing. Greenpeace is waltzing, too. They're both getting something from the encounter. Browne was the first oil company CEO to address a major Greenpeace conference.

A REBALANCING ACT

We are seeing today the convergence of two significant phenomena. More value has been provided for shareholders in the past decade than at any time since the 1950s. Yet, we're also seeing the exponential growth and power of activist groups. Many of these groups are highly organized. Some, like Greenpeace, have more members and global organization than any political party. Often, their actions are based on perceptions, feelings, and frustration reflecting a societal pulse—a pulse that business cannot ignore.

In its 1998 strike, the autoworkers' union gave General Motors a reputation for "putting America last." This was quite undeserved given the investment data from the company; GM actually invested the bulk of its investment expenditure at home. But, few Americans want to drive a car from the company that supposedly put its country last. Greenpeace brought the Shell oil company to its knees over the sinking of a North Sea oil platform, again quite undeservedly when you look at the technical analysis in retrospect. But, nobody wants to fill up at a gas station that is dumping its waste in the sea. Nike says that activist groups claiming the company exploited factory workers have wrongly damaged its reputation. How many college kids want to be seen in sneakers that are suspected of having been made by young children?

Are we seeing evidence of a rebalancing going on? Are consumers feeling that corporate power is stifling their right to choose the food they eat? Is society tired of being continually asked to accept noise or air pollution? Are workers being asked too often to work for meager wages in exchange for the dignity of work? Are shareholders feeling the need to have more say in the organizations in which they invest?

> "Industry is the main player in society. . . . That's why we need to talk to them."
> —*Thilo Bode, Head of Greenpeace International,*
> Financial Times, *1996*

Many senior managers seem to agree this is happening. In 1998 Harris Research surveyed 160 senior managers from large global companies. These were all people who held main board positions. Harris asked them why they thought corporate responsibility was relevant to a wide constituency of stakeholders such as customers, society, employees, and suppliers, and whether it was strategic in building and protecting reputation. They rated change in societal expectations higher than differentiation or customer awareness, and put it at about equal pegging with image. See Table 1.1.

The reasons why society's expectations have been changing have been well covered in recent years. In summary, they are:

Table 1.1   Reasons Why Corporate Responsibility Is Important to Transnational Companies

Image and reputation	25%
Change in societal expectations	23%
Differentiation	11%
Customer awareness	11%

Source: PW/Harris Jan 98

- Governments today are less able than before to be the sovereign protector of the public's interests. As populations in the developed world begin to age, governments are beginning to struggle to keep up with old-style notions of how to provide for their citizens. Pension funds are running dry (see Figure 1.1). Health systems are going broke. Education is getting squeezed. Citizens are becoming disillusioned.

It is not surprising, then, that today's new recruits place tremendous value on education and the promise of transferable skills that enable employability. It is also not surprising that employees question the adequacy of the corporate health plan or that educational institutions are no longer coy about accepting sponsorships from companies for a library, a sports complex, or a special graduate program.

- Large, stateless global business organizations are continuing to grow in size and economic strength. Citizens are becoming more aware that just 100 corporations control $1.5 trillion of assets and a third of foreign direct investment—and they want companies to carry a proportionally greater degree of accountability than in the past.

The emerging view is that corporate responsibility begins where the law ends. All this in return for society's stake: access to markets of consumers with the economic means to buy products and services, a legacy of

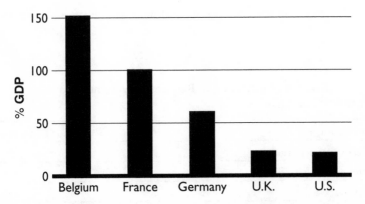

Figure 1.1 *Unfunded Pensions Liability as Percentage of Gross Domestic Product* (Source: *Daiwa*)

stable peaceful coexistence, infrastructure to enable communications, and a constitution that enables the whole system to work.

• Communications have also brought a common set of expectations to people around the world. Why shouldn't the Chinese peasant dream of driving that BMW seen on television targeted at a much richer market? Teenagers in Bombay have more interests in common with their peers in Boca Raton than with their parents, through viewing the same MTV music videos, Coke® and Levi's® ads, and pop publications.

• Today's global civil society is prepared to challenge the previously unquestioned authority of government, other traditional institutions, and large corporations. This is as if citizens were being allowed behind some Hollywood facade of a fancy Manhattan skyline to see only supporting beams and all the hidden paraphernalia of a film set. When ordinary citizens go backstage they see ordinary people like themselves: people who have the same frailties, watch the same soaps, and seek the same security and acceptance. Is the lawyer at $1000 an hour 200 times more valuable than the janitor who cleans the courtroom at $5 an hour?

Previously compliant German consumers now complain with impunity about poor service from Deutsche Telekom. Aggrieved employees the world over sue for victimization or sexual harassment and win huge payoffs in compensation. Communities affected by polluting companies seek redress and win. Shareholders oust sluggish management, precipitate takeovers, and pass resolutions against management's wishes at shareholder meetings.

Stakeholders are becoming more aware of their own powers and calling the shots. Companies ignore them at their own peril.

WHAT DOES IT TAKE TO WALTZ?

The complete dancing guide to waltzing has a number of useful tips for the beginner, but talk to most aficionados and they'll tell you there are three golden rules. The first of these rules is to listen to the music and to the rhythm of the "one two three, one two three" timing as the orchestra pours out those powerful melodies of Viennese magic. Good listeners impress their partners by keeping in time with the music for every step.

Successful organizations also need to listen to their constituencies and avoid making assumptions about them. The three golden rules of successful organizations are:

1. Listen to constituencies—and avoid assumptions.

2. Rely on self-assessment, not regulation.

3. Monitor and measure.

Listen to constituencies—and avoid assumptions

First, companies have a responsibility to listen to a wide constituency of the various institutions and people who inhabit their world. Until recently, senior executives have been comfortable taking management actions and making decisions in the belief that, as experienced managers, they can interpret the wishes of their shareholders, employees, customers, and the society in which their organizations operate. But, given the fast-changing, complex world in which corporations now trade, it is becoming dangerous to make these assumptions. John Drummond of United Utilities offers a helpful continuum on stakeholder consultation (Figure 1.2).

For example, Shell made the assumption that approval by the British government was sufficient for the company to proceed with the sinking of Brent Spar in the North Sea. Millions of Shell customers, made aware of the situation by activists, took a different view and forced the company to reconsider. Similarly, PepsiCo thought that by continuing relationships with the Burmese military government, the company had gained access to that country's markets. Kids on American campuses thousands of miles

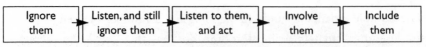

Ignore them	Listen, and still ignore them	Listen to them, and act	Involve them	Include them

Figure 1.2 *Stakeholder Consultation Continuum*

away didn't like the idea, causing PepsiCo eventually to reconsider. Companies will have to learn new ways of conducting a dialogue with both primary and secondary stakeholders that inhabit their world.

I remember the amateurish way in which most companies conducted their customer research not more than a decade ago. Many products were launched because the research and development (R&D) department thought these were good products that the market would gobble up. They were, in effect, solutions looking for a problem. Some made it through, like the adhesive that wouldn't stick, now known as Post-it® Notes, and the tape recorder that only played back, now famous as the Walkman.® However, many thousands of expensive product or service ideas were launched at the wrong time in the wrong place to the wrong people. The root cause: Someone hadn't listened to the customers or tried to understand them.

Then, techniques previously used by only the best consumer product companies, like Procter & Gamble and Coca-Cola, began to spread to other companies. Industries such as financial services, airlines, and health care, traditionally led by technocrats, began to learn from first-rate actuaries, zippy aviators, or world-class surgeons. Now, it's de rigueur to carry out detailed market research before a product launch. The whim of the CEO or product manager is not enough.

A company, too, will have to become accustomed to the idea that there are several stakeholders with which to keep in touch if it wants to succeed. The techniques that it uses to listen to these stakeholders are only just becoming understood, and stakeholders themselves are getting more savvy in their ability to communicate with companies.

In May 1998, in association with the University of Notre Dame, PricewaterhouseCoopers surveyed 140 of the world's most significant nongovernmental organizations (NGOs). Respondents included organizations like Amnesty International, CARE, Pax Christi, and many more. The main findings of our study were that little dialogue occurs between transnational corporations (TNCs) and NGOs, and that these interactions are frequently antagonistic. However, NGOs look to a future in which there will be more dialogue and relationships will be largely cooperative.

(The mission statements of many of these NGOs are given in Appendix B). See Figure 1.3.

But who are these NGOs? Do they really have teeth like the snappish raptor? Are they truly representative of the various constituencies we call stakeholders?

Over the past decade or so these agencies have mushroomed. It's difficult to say how many exist now: Some of them are large global organizations in their own right with millions of members. Others are minnows that are poorly funded but believe passionately in their cause. These organizations represent a valuable channel for companies to tap into to determine the potential risk to their reputation or to identify unfulfilled demand. If PepsiCo, Heineken, or Levi Strauss had discussed their investment plans for Burma with any of the human rights organizations they would have gained insight into the ruthless abuse of Burmese citizens by the military government. Would they have considered going ahead with the investment in the light of their consultations? Maybe not. Maybe they would have sensed people's anger and outrage about how innocent citizens are treated. Maybe they could have avoided an expensive mistake.

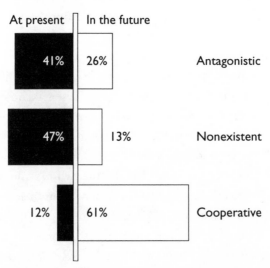

Figure 1.3 *How Nongovernmental Organizations Perceive Their Relationship with Transnational Corporations (Source: PW/University of Notre Dame May 1998)*

Many of the stakeholder groups with which a company deals are bound by contractual relationships. These contractual relationships are usually more complex than might at first be obvious. There is usually a written contract bound by law, but if you look behind this contract you may see a completely different picture. An investment institution holds share certificates representing its financial stake in a company, but who is the real investor? It is people like you or me—people who don't want to have to live knowing that the excellent pension they will receive in the future was made by the systematic exploitation of children, the evasion of health and safety procedures, or the production of goods that are known to harm or indeed even kill consumers. But companies do not listen to you and me; they listen only to the institutions. They have quarterly briefings, and one-on-one chats with buy-side analysts. That was fine until now, but it won't be enough in the future.

Likewise, many companies that previously were happy dealing with intermediaries and middlemen today are increasingly convinced that dealing direct is the way forward. In a world of increasing choice, listening to customers is an important everyday part of building reputation. For these are customers who instinctively distrust large faceless organizations, who are concerned that their health may be compromised for cost savings, and who are worried about the gradual encroachment on their privacy by aggressive selling techniques.

Employees used to be expendable. There was always a line of people waiting outside the door, dying to get a day's pay for a hard day's work. High turnover was fine in the days when workers were needed mainly to dig, build, assemble, polish, and paint. It is less so today. Alvin Toffler refers to our "brains not brawn" age. This is an age when service industries need highly motivated workers to deliver the highest standards of customer service and attention to detail. This underscores the need to listen carefully to employees, learn how to recruit and retain the best people, and determine what we need to do to continue to motivate them.

Suppliers were also expendable. Companies had thousands of them to ensure that they all killed for the job of supplying parts for General Motors, General Electric, or Ford. Times have changed. We've found out that suppliers killing each other is not the most effective way to source good-quality products—products that don't fall apart or have to be returned within the first week of purchase because the supplier had cut so many corners to keep within an impossible cost target. Now, partnerships are cool. Today's company has a few sustainable long-term relationships with suppliers and has to listen to them to understand the cost pressures they are under.

Of all these stakeholders, society is perhaps the most complex. As well as the stakeholders just mentioned, it also includes all the other groupings that do not have contractual relationships with a company. An organization may contract with a state's representatives, but these people do not necessarily reflect the entirety of the views of the society in which it trades. In some countries, the state represents a very small minority of society's interests. Civil rights groups, religious organizations, single-issue parties, and many more make up the rich and colorful palette of people you have to be listening to, in order to keep waltzing.

Rely on self-assessment, not regulation

Our waltzing aficionado's second golden rule in perfecting the dance and being in great demand is to know how to lead his partner: gently but firmly. She should know and trust the fact that you have every move figured as you glide across the room. The good leading dance partner takes the initiative and doesn't wait for his partner. My 80-year-old mother, who loved to waltz as a young woman, said that dancing with an indecisive male partner was like "dancing with a sack of potatoes." My second rule therefore for the company that wants to waltz is to take the initiative and not rely on regulation—rather, to develop self-assessment as a means of assuring its reputation.

Companies cannot look to external regulation as a guide to their codes of conduct. Regulation is cumbersome and expensive to implement, and has been shown to inhibit growth and prosperity. The best answer for companies that want to build sustainable reputations must lie in self-assessment. Companies have to take responsibility for safeguarding reputation by developing management processes which assure their stakeholders that they don't indulge in corrupt practices; they have respect for the environment; their products are safe; and they make a fair contribution back into society in proportion to the value which they extract. I believe that what the Total Quality movement accomplished in the 1980s could be applied with similar effectiveness in the development of these processes in the coming years.

Remember the bad old 1980s when Japanese competitors were knocking the hell out of U.S. companies, able to produce goods not only at a lower cost, but also of significantly better quality than their North American competitors? Tom Peters lambasted General Motors for the poor-quality cars and vans it produced. J. D. Power's customer satisfaction indicators put GM cars at the bottom of the class.

The folks at Xerox Corporation figured that they would be out of business before too long and hit upon the idea of importing the same quality management techniques that the Japanese had used to dominate the copier market. Also around the same time, Malcolm Baldrige was appointed by the U.S. State Department to set up a framework for measuring business excellence. Baldrige developed a mechanism for measuring the quality of management processes, previously difficult to quantify because they were soft, fuzzy, and intangible. Like quality, noticeable in its absence and very apparent when it exists, corporate reputation can be difficult to measure but we certainly know the companies who have a lack of it and those who have it in plenty. A process of self-assessment should be based on quality-like measurement processes, and we shall see later in this book how we can implement a system of reputation assurance based on some of Baldrige's ideas. In recent years Jack Welch of GE has led that company into quality management, and the company has continued to produce outstanding results where employees subscribe to the "get better or get beaten" byline.

But being self-assured is not just about self-assessment. It's also about being confident and bold enough to publish your results—to tell your stakeholders what you believe they think of you, where they want you to do better, and how you hope to achieve their aspirations, but also how you can't achieve some of the things they want you to do. Although John

Browne knows that Greenpeace and Friends of the Earth want him to be out of the oil business, he is clear that BP-Amoco, an oil company with other obligations to employees and shareholders, cannot do this. But it can begin to lessen its dependence on fossil-based fuels by investing in renewable energy sources.

Later we shall see how you can publish such results to your stakeholders, and in Appendix A there is an extract of a typical reputation report card based on self-assurance techniques developed in this book. You have begun to satiate the raptor's hunger. Your waltzing partner is impressed with your positive leadership. Rather than a sack of potatoes you are a magic carpet floating impressively in a clear, unambiguous direction.

Monitor and measure

The third golden rule of the waltzing aficionado, and by no means the least important, is not to step on your partner's toes. Every measured step you take needs care and should be in sympathy with your partner. Step too far and your partner will grimace in pain. Step too short and your partner will trip over you and curse. Successful waltzing organizations need to monitor and measure the steps they are taking to protect their reputation. Without measurement you may be stepping on toes, or worse, tripping up.

Cost-effective monitoring and measurement mechanisms are necessary to assure stakeholders that a company's good governance can be backed up by recognizable and verifiable measures. Good words abound in corporate literature on the highest principles of corporate governance, but few managers know how to implement these principles at the operational level or indeed how to measure their effectiveness.

For example, many businesses talk of fairly compensating their employees, but few actually benchmark these compensation levels to ensure fairness. Still fewer companies monitor attrition rates to see if compensation is a problem, and very infrequently is the relationship between productivity and compensation ever monitored.

Because most companies are made up of a number of different businesses in different markets, all with their own accountability in terms of profit and loss, you need a consistent system of measurement—a consistent system which allows you to measure the reputation achievement of the factory in comparison with the retail outlets (or the U.S. operation compared with the European business). Consistency can help you measure yourself against other companies and share best practices with them. It can also help your waltzing partner compare your skill with others on the floor. (Measurement is such an important topic that we'll come back to it at greater length later.)

DANCING ETIQUETTE

We have seen how to apply the three golden rules to becoming fabulous at waltzing, but there are also the other rules of behavior that our aficionados call etiquette. These are unwritten but extremely important, as they send signals of your good upbringing and your respect for your partner and the other dancers. There are rules of etiquette for asking for a dance, being gracious with your partner after a dance, exchanging polite conversation, not being seen as too possessive, and many more. The rules and their importance would vary slightly from, say, a ballroom in Vienna to the palace of Versailles to the ambassador's residence in Santiago. But you have to know them all to be the ultimate dancer.

Business principles—the etiquette of corporate reputation

Corporate reputation, too, has an etiquette that translates into how a company behaves with regard to certain common principles that build integrity and trust with stakeholders. These principles reflect the wider expectations of stakeholders (customers, society, suppliers, employees, and shareholders). The principles are not enshrined in any statutory code but do tend to have a certain consistency in the codes produced by various groups of people who get together to think about these things. The Caux Round Table, for example, is a group of such individuals, politicians and business leaders who met under the aegis of INSEAD, in Caux, Switzerland, and developed a code for corporate responsibility. You see striking similarities between this and other codes produced by, say, the International Labor Organization. These codes attempt to combine the different emphases on business, from North America with its strong stakeholder emphasis, to Europe with its respect for human dignity, to the Japanese emphasis of *kyosei*, the concept of working for the common good.

Looking at the way companies are beginning to tackle the business of monitoring their adherence to these codes, verifying them, and reporting on them, I can't help thinking that we are in the very early days of the development of some common international code for corporate reputation. The coming years may bring widespread acceptance, but today we have something approaching chaos. The overlapping in Figure 1.4 reflects some of this chaos.

There are corporate governance codes being developed all over the world: by Cadbury in the United Kingdom, by the Conference Board in the United States. These codes generally cover good practice by the top

Figure 1.4   *Overlapping Initiatives*

management of a company but frequently stray into wider areas of employee, environmental, or social governance. Then there are the environmental audit initiatives: every business seems to need one, whether its impact on the environment is zilch or gigantic. The boundaries of environmental audits also seem ill-defined. And then there are the social audits that we are only just beginning to become familiar with and which seem to cover almost anything that the auditors fancy. Add to these ethical auditing, supplier auditing, and employee audits, and you begin to see that we are facing a quagmire of confusion, diffused responsibility, and a lot of redundant effort.

Unlike waltzing with my friend the raptor, where all I need is a competence in waltzing and compliance with a few basic rules of etiquette in order to avoid a Raptor War, in the corporate world I'm still struggling to find out the rules of etiquette—the commonly applied principles.

It is with this in mind that we set out to define a framework of principles that could be commonly applied across any company, in any industry, anywhere in the world. We wanted the framework to sort out the confusion that currently exists between different types of audits and to establish a form of taxonomy that could be used to define terminology. This all seemed to be quite logical; surely no company could argue with the idea of being fair, honest, respectful. Surely no company could deny that all stakeholders require a fair return for their resources: be it investors for their capital, employees for their effort, or customers for their revenue.

We realized that many brainy people with thousands of years of collective experience working with these principles had exercised their intellect to establish codes that would be far superior to anything we could devise. So we looked at all the areas of similarity, tried to understand the differences and the omissions, and came up with a list of business principles that could conceivably be applied to any enterprise. We then tested them out on a number of companies, nongovernmental organizations, and academics and found that given some amendments we had a framework that was generic enough to accommodate any business.

Here's how the framework of common business principles looked:

Shareholders

Ensuring a fair and competitive return

What shareholder would want to invest in a company that didn't provide a fair return for the money invested? Capital today flows freely in world markets, and with the creation of bigger markets and exchanges such as the combined London and Frankfurt stock market, investors will be attracted to the companies that have the reputation for the best return. The challenge for most companies will be assuring their investors that future returns will be fair and competitive.

Disclosing relevant information subject to competitive and legal constraints

A company should disclose any information that shareholders have a right to know: information which might affect the value of their investment now or in the future. This applies equally to disclosing unforeseen abandonment or cleanup costs and to talking up the importance of some biotechnology stock beyond its real value. An oil company may have billions of dollars of costs to account for in decommissioning and cleaning up old refineries or abandoning offshore platforms. A chemical company may have a similar amount tied up in claims from users of its products.

Conserving, protecting, and increasing assets

Fraud, bribery, and corruption are all practices that undermine a company's ability to protect the assets of shareholders. A company like Exxon has strict codes in place to ensure that none of its employees anywhere in the world deviate from this principle. Even if a bribe is the socially accepted norm, Exxon would rather walk away from such deals than be seen to be accommodating corrupt practices. Reputable companies apply these codes universally irrespective of culture or location.

Respecting significant requests

From time to time shareholders will want a company to disclose certain information or will encourage management to change its policy on a certain issue. Many U.S. shareholders consistently made requests of companies to divest in South Africa; some companies obliged. Shell was asked by a minority of its shareholders to publish a social report, and the company obliged. Recognizing the strength of feeling and being able to comply with these requests are areas that many companies are still coming to grips with.

Customers

Meeting reasonable expectations

Reasonable expectations are those unwritten things we expect of companies that act responsibly. If we turn up at an airline sales desk and ask for a ticket to Atlanta, we would expect to be given the most competitive fare rather than the most expensive. I would expect my bank to give me the highest available interest rate on my checking account without me specifically asking for it. When I buy Windows 98 it is reasonable to expect the software to be compatible with Windows 95. When customers detect that a company is not meeting these unwritten rules they become disenchanted.

Meeting customer guarantees

Guarantees are usually the claims that a company makes about its products or services. If a company says that its prices are the lowest in the country, then it had better make sure that they are. If not, its credibility would soon be lost. If an appliance is guaranteed for a year, then a company should be prepared to honor this guarantee and not put obstacles in the way of customers to make it harder for them to replace defective products. Reputable companies not only meet guarantees, but they do so in a way that makes it easy for customers to exercise those guarantees.

Ensuring health and safety of products supplied

Products shouldn't harm customers, whether they are an exploding fuel tank on an automobile or breast implants with harmful side effects.

21

Companies need to assure their customers that their testing procedures are thorough and uncompromising and that any fears, no matter how ill-founded, are properly investigated. Monsanto will have to continue to convince food activists that genetically modified soya crops will not have irreversible side effects on the food chain and that its Food and Drug Administration (FDA) testing procedures are robust. Nestlé will have to convince campaigners that the marketing of their infant milk substitute in developing countries is compatible with living conditions and the un-availability of clean drinking water.

Showing respect in marketing and communications

When Benetton, the Italian clothes retailer, depicted an AIDS patient on his deathbed surrounded by family, the world was outraged. What was a clothes company doing with a dying man in its advertising? Equally, aiming alcohol or cigarette ads at children can be exploitative, as is the encroachment on our privacy by hard-selling telesales and direct marketing companies. Respect for human dignity is the hallmark of a company that complies with this principle.

Employees

Providing fair compensation

Every employee wants a fair compensation for his or her effort. In some parts of the world where there is an abundance of work this is less of an issue. In others where work is scarce, employers can easily exploit their advantage. A fair compensation means a living wage, one that allows employees to feed, shelter, and clothe themselves within the norms of the society in which they live. Paying your employees a few cents an hour to make products from shoes to footballs is not acceptable, not necessarily because of the significant markup you might enjoy but because of the fact that the paltry wage they receive won't be sufficient for them to live on. So, too, is the use of child labor. Wouldn't it be better to pay the parents a little more to allow their children the opportunity of some modest education?

Ensuring health and safety in working conditions

You should expect your employees to work in healthy and safe conditions. Certainly some processes are hazardous; but this is just even more reason for you to work harder at ensuring that your employees are not injured or killed on the job. A big issue facing global companies is the application of consistent standards around the world. It is not acceptable to get away with harming more of your Guatemalan employees than those in Wisconsin.

Being honest and open in communication

Employees expect a company to give them both good and bad news. They wish to be consulted on important decisions that affect their future, in ways they can understand, and to be encouraged to articulate a response. Many successful companies take their employees along with them every step of the way.

Taking suggestions and complaints seriously

Employees are your front line. They are seeing the day-to-day ramifications of your production processes, your customer service, and your supplier policies; in short they are a gold mine of potential ideas for improvement. Their complaints are just as important, be they about sexual harassment or workplace bullying. The Mitsubishi cases of sexual harassment showed how a company could suffer from ignoring complaints.

Respecting labor rights

All employees should be treated equally regardless of race, gender, or religion. Companies are often caught up in having to reverse decades or even centuries of inequality in the societies in which they operate. However, it can also be an area where they can be great agents of change. Examples include U.S. companies insisting on Catholics being given the same opportunity as Protestants in Northern Ireland, several Asian companies giving women more management opportunities than their peers in the West, and Disney promoting equal rights for gays and lesbians.

Showing sensitivity in dislocation

In the worst of cases, plant closures, restructuring, and relocation can leave employees with few options but to look forward to a lifetime of unemployment. The responsible company handles such dislocation with sensitivity, taking into account all that it can to help them maintain their dignity, and, if possible, find alternative employment. This does not imply, however, that a company must defy the laws of a market-driven economic system and provide for lifelong employment.

Fostering transferable skills and employability

The benefits of providing employees with transferable skills are twofold: facilitation of alternative sources of employment if your business does go belly up, and the added advantage of improving their productivity while in your employ.

Society

Contributing to the economic power of citizens

A company should put back into the economy something in proportion to what it extracts. If it extracts natural resources, it should contribute to regeneration. Alternatively, a company may wish to increase the local content of suppliers or reduce its dependence on expatriate employees. Many companies actually measure the increase in purchasing power of the citizens in the region in which they trade as a measure of their contribution. There is widespread agreement that business is one of the most important levers of economic activity.

Promoting human rights

Gradually a code of human rights is emerging, and many companies are being asked to sign up to it. Businesses can no longer afford to hide behind a policy of neutrality in political processes. Society sees that in many countries of the world a major investor like Shell, GM, or GE is infinitely more powerful than the countries in which it invests. The mere agreement to explore for oil or set up a plant or facility is a tacit recognition that the company is prepared to go along with the way that the host state treats its citizens. Conversely, unresolved questions remain about the need for engagement as a means of bringing about change. It is important that the company knows what its policy is regarding human rights and promotes it actively. The rest is for society and its stakeholders to judge.

Respecting local culture and law

Applying corporate codes on a global scale while at the same time respecting local laws is important in order to avoid allegations of cultural imperialism. Sensitivity to religion, traditions, and institutions are important for the company that wishes to maintain a sustainable reputation. However, this does not allow a company to turn a blind eye to corruption or bribery because "that's the way the locals do business." Look at the considerable damage to reputation suffered by the World Bank as it ignored the nepotism and corruption of Suharto and his family while he was president of Indonesia. The bank continued to give the country a favorable risk rating as nearly $30 billion of loans went sour. How long will it be before people are willing to believe the World Bank again?

Promoting fair trade

We've long known that competition is good for business, yet many companies try to stifle it. The 1980s were rife with "kill all competitors" talk. Companies that support initiatives to break up monopolies benefit society with better products, more innovation, lower prices, and eventually a larger addressable market.

Supporting sustainable development and conservation

The sustainable development movement has gathered much momentum in recent years. Companies should support this principle not only because it conserves finite resources and causes less damage to the environment, but also because in many cases a business may actually benefit from such programs. Many companies have initiated "more from less" campaigns and then found that they witness a drop in their operating expenses.

Rejecting illicit operations or corrupt practices

Just as a company must not tolerate corrupt practices by its employees, it should not accommodate corrupt practices in the society in which it trades. The U.S. Foreign Corrupt Practice Act has gained widespread acceptance, making it easier to implement these policies around the world.

Disclosing relevant information

The reputable company communicates with society using clear facts that it can verify and back up if requested. Surreptitiously hiding facts, hoping no one will notice them, doesn't endear a company to citizens. Good transparent communications can not only speed approval of new facilities, but they can also reduce operational problems from disruptive boycotts and delays. As in most cases, any company has to make trade-offs between the objections raised by a few and the benefits experienced by the majority. Truthfulness is by far the best means of getting stakeholders on your side.

Partners and suppliers

Fostering equitable relationships

Long-term relationships are vital to ensure the business future of your suppliers as well as providing your company with a secure pipeline of products and services. Long-term relationships also lead to better risk sharing, and we will see examples of how successful companies owe their success to these sustainable relationships.

Making sure suppliers have access to all the facts before they bid for work ensures that they are able to honor their commitments to the company. The better your reputation with suppliers, the better the grade of suppliers you attract—all helping to lower your costs and improve quality.

If you're a large, reputable company, or one in a powerful position, you don't use your size and muscle to squeeze your suppliers on costs to the point where you endanger their businesses. Also, you pay bills on time and don't shift the burden of inventory and working capital onto your suppliers unless they are fully aware and agree to you doing so.

Sharing in success in an equitable way allows you to choose the best partners. This is the essence of good partnership. How companies do this is an evolving practice. Marks and Spencer, the consistently successful British retailer, is famous for demanding high standards of its suppliers, but also for always rewarding them fairly—even generously—when product lines prove to be successful. As a result, many of the very best food and clothing suppliers are eager to do business with them.

Fostering responsibility

Choosing partners and suppliers that share similar values is vital to protect a company from its own reputation. Many of the allegations of sweatshops, child labor, and forced prison labor have come from suppliers and partners who have not shared the same values as the companies with which they trade.

Disclosing relevant information

The more your suppliers know about you, the better they can plan and match your current and future requirements. Great companies share their strategic intentions with their suppliers, as well as their investment plans, worries, and hopes for the future.

Respecting tangible and intellectual property

The more we create knowledge-intensive industries where ideas and concepts make up the true value of the company, the more we need to respect the intellectual property of the suppliers and partners with whom we deal. Proper compensation for these assets and verification of where they are used is vital to secure a good reputation.

The coming chapters will describe these principles in more detail, taking examples of how companies have either succeeded or failed to implement them and discussing the lessons we can learn. Then we will look at a systematic process by which an organization can apply these principles and publish progress reports on its achievement. We'll teach you not just to get by in waltzing; we'll endeavor to make you a great dancer.

P
A
R
T

II

HANDLING
ACTIVE
STAKEHOLDERS

"Now I can buy Ronny that new dishwasher!"

C
H
A
P
T
E
R

EMPLOYEES—

WORKING SMARTER

W e'll start with the simplest of all the criteria regarding employees from the framework of common business principles: the requirement to treat all employees equally. Failure to do that almost brought one of America's great corporations to its knees in the mid-1990s. It's an instructive story, recounted by Bari-Ellen Roberts in her book, *Roberts vs. Texaco* (Avon Books, New York, 1998). It all starts with a question of geography. Bari-Ellen Roberts and her husband had moved to Stamford, Connecticut, when they first got jobs in New York City. It's a beautiful town, only 60 minutes—and sometimes less—from Rockefeller Plaza in central Manhattan, where the Chase Manhattan Bank then had its headquarters. Roberts had graduated in the top five percent of her class from a graduate financial trust course at Northwestern University, and joined the master trust division at Chase.

By 1990 she was a company vice president, supervising accounts worth over $10 billion. Unfortunately, by 1990 her marriage was breaking up, plus Chase was moving her division to Brooklyn. She didn't want the three-hour daily commute that would entail, not with two teenage daughters at home, and so she started looking for something closer to Stamford.

Enter Texaco.

Its headquarters are in Harrison, New York, only 20 minutes from Stamford. The company had a good pay scale, and there might be the offer of international placements someday—which Roberts really wanted. Even though Texaco had the reputation of being a stodgy place, a good friend's husband who worked there at a senior job assured her it was changing.

There was something more—a challenge, almost. Roberts was black, and in the past Texaco had been known for being very white—not quite racist, but there were clear enough hints—interpretations she could give to the comments friends made—that the old Texaco wouldn't have been open to her. But now? What was exciting was that now this was changing.

A bit like that generation of American men born just a few years too late for World War II, she had been just a few years too young to take part in the civil rights actions of the 1960s. Like anyone who just misses out on crucial events, she'd always wondered how brave she'd have been if she'd faced the ordeals of the Freedom Riders or sit-in demonstrators she'd read about in the papers or seen on the TV news, sometimes beaten by white police, sometimes triumphing in arms-linked song. The students before her had opened the way, beginning to make it easier for blacks in America. She'd reaped the benefits, with only occasional trouble so far. So, there was an obligation to pay it back. And, so far, she'd done this. She'd shown initially suspicious executives at Chase that she was good, that a black woman could be analytical and responsible, and her performance really had changed their views. Even though she was leaving Chase, because of her the career paths there would be easier for younger American minorities who came after her.

It was almost like homesteading: Human optimism insists that challenges can be tamed, and indeed there is no shortage of optimism in the United States.

One week before Christmas, in the winter of 1990, she took the job. A few of her colleagues were difficult at the start. When she was first shown in, her boss's boss, the number two officer in the whole company's finance department, quizzed her a bit more harshly than needed about her credentials. Some of the junior dealers in the trading room piped up with similarly sarcastic comments when she was taken there. But, none of this was a total surprise; nor was it something Roberts didn't think she'd be able to handle. As a girl, she'd seen on television far stronger insults against blacks: Southern sheriffs loosing police dogs on children and unarmed adults. A few insulting comments and a few sharp digs were nothing like that. Also, she'd succeeded at Chase, and that was an institution that defined mainstream capitalism. Texaco was dated, but she'd known that. It just meant the changes there would have to be worked at a little bit harder than before.

As she'd hoped, it got better. As 1991 went on, Roberts was assigned to a high-level task force preparing the company's reactions to new federal banking legislation. In time she was called in to meet Texaco's chief financial officer. "We've been following your work," the CFO said, "and we like it. We like it very much." He probably shouldn't tell her, he went on in a friendly way, but she was actually on the company's high-potential list. That was where fast promotions and top jobs got offered. She left the meeting on a high, and told her friends. Even the boys in the trading room were coming around, it seemed.

And then, early in 1992, the director of human resources for her division asked Roberts and a few other employees to join an "excellence" team. It was designed to bring out employees' creativity, and make the new Texaco a better place. Her task—it seemed fair enough; it wasn't patronizing, but rather a recognition of how far she'd come—was to study best practices from other companies that could help Texaco extend its diversity. The presentation was going to be to John Ambler, head of human resources for the whole firm. It would finally be her chance to pay back her debt. She'd had it easy compared to the generation before her, and this was simply her obligation.

Ambler let Roberts and her colleagues start, and listened long enough to get the gist of what they were saying. Then he slammed his hand on the table. Who were they to impugn the company? Ambler demanded. He'd worked there for decades. He knew how things were done. If they thought Texaco was even going to consider their proposals, they were crazy. He wasn't going to have Black Panthers running down his halls.

She left the meeting not knowing what this meant but hoping Ambler was the only senior manager like this. Everything else in her life was going well—she'd become used to her separation from her husband and

loved the extra space it gave her. Life was expanding. She'd go back to doing her job, simply making sure it was even better than before. She'd work
so thoroughly and so conscientiously that there would be no way she
could be critiqued, even if Ambler did have a few cronies who started
looking for faults. And in mid-1992, that's what she did.

What Roberts didn't realize was that Texaco as a whole didn't appear
to want any new black hires. In the late 1980s the Office of Federal Contract Compliance Programs (OFCCP) had surveyed a range of firms to see
their hiring patterns. Texaco was one of the very worst, with virtually no
blacks in serious jobs. This had gone on year after year, even when comparable large firms were managing to find plenty of qualified minorities
from good universities for such jobs.

The federal report probably would have been filed away and ignored, except for Texaco's new CFO—the same man who'd told Roberts
she was on the high-potential list. He'd come from outside the company in
early 1990, and didn't want this bias to continue. From now on, he let it be
known, managers had to hire at least some minorities. In fact, that's why
Roberts had been hired just before Christmas. Her immediate boss had
told her it was for her vacation benefits, but it was mainly so he could fulfill his requirements and get one of these new hires on the damned books
before 1990 was out. It was not an attitude conducive to a warm welcome.

Everything might have stayed as it was after the meeting with Ambler, with Roberts warily avoiding him and trying other channels to advance within her new firm. But Ambler and his friends were in the
majority. The CFO didn't have a clue. The old boys began to fight back,
hard. Roberts wasn't attacked at first, but rather another senior minority
hire in the finance department started having his most competent staff
removed from under him; then he started getting lower evaluations.
Soon Roberts found that any special assignments she applied for were
"already filled."

It was creepy, invisible: like a small town slowly turning against you
in a Gary Cooper Western. And then—the final step—in January 1993,
Roberts's own annual evaluations were mysteriously lowered. Her evaluations, an embarrassed friend on the other side told her, were always going

to be marked down. It wouldn't matter what quality of work she did next (and in the finance department much of what you did could be objectively measured, since there were returns criteria that could be compared to those of similar firms).

The evaluation tool Roberts was judged by was called PMP (Performance Management Program). On the surface it seemed sensible. It had to be filled out by each person's supervisor once a year, so there would be no gaps, and there was space for extensive personalized evaluation. But it was entirely subjective! It didn't give any guidelines to the employees, recap their responsibilities, or say how they were expected to order their priorities.

Because PMP was so vague, misunderstandings were never brought into the open. Employees who'd been given a low PMP had no way to improve. They hadn't been given a clear list of tasks or told where they'd failed to measured up.

Performance Management Program was also surprisingly dangerous for supervisors. With a more clearly written ranking, supervisors would h‸ve had to bring their resentments out into the open. But, with PMP as it was, Texaco supervisors could just remain stewing, righteously holding a vague, generalized grudge, never having to undergo the discipline of trying to specify exactly where a new employee wasn't pulling his or her weight. If a supervisor tried that and saw that in fact the tasks were being achieved, there was at least a chance of changing one's mind.

(When John F. Kennedy was in torpedo boat training school early in World War II, for example, he said something to one of his fellow volunteers about how Jews were getting out of combat by joining the Quartermaster Corps rather than fighting units. One of his listeners, Fred Rosen, who happened to be Jewish, said, "Well, why don't we count?" So they did, polling the torpedo boat volunteers at their Rhode Island base. When it turned out there were quite as many Jews as Catholics there, Kennedy— who was utterly charming when it came to admitting defeat—thought it over, changed his views, and apologized, honestly, to his new friend.)

When Roberts was told that her PMP was always going to be marked down, that slammed a door. There's a huge difference between a partial filter, where you have to do better than others to advance, and a total filter, where it doesn't matter how much better you do, you are not going to be allowed to rise, and that's that. Roberts was now facing a total filter.

From the late 1960s, the promise of American society had been that no one would have to face a total filter again. There was a whole tradition from Roberts's cultural history describing committed blacks using their talent to prove this. The great football running back Jim Brown used to like to recount one of the canonical stories about this, from one of the first times he went out to play, facing a huge white defensive player. "You smell like shit, nigger," the linebacker muttered, looking right into his eyes. Brown said nothing. The ball was snapped, and Brown barreled over the defensive player, ran past or through the rest of the defenders, and made it to the end zone. He waited for the bruised defender slowly to stand up. "How I smell from here, m-----f------!" he yelled, waving the ball high.

Texaco was not going to offer this chance. It was an organism, and Roberts was trying to change it, and the organism had now rebuffed the change. It was simple homeostasis.

The rebuff might have worked before, but times had changed. Roberts was a proud American, and she was damned if she was going to be sent to the back of the bus.

Texaco was still immersed in the old attitudes, and saw just this one difficult woman—how could she possibly prevail against a huge corporation?

But Roberts wasn't alone, not in the mid-1990s. To start with, there was the Interfaith Center for Corporate Responsibility (ICCR), a church group active in shareholder interventions. It gave Roberts her initial support. Next, there were class-action law firms ready and willing to take on her case. Those firms can often hire the most motivated of law students, for their ideals sound good, and they can also keep more experienced (if cynical) law partners, for the rewards of winning a class-action suit can be stupendous. Roberts settled on Cohen, Milstein, Hausfeld & Toll. Mike Hausfeld had led the successful class-action suit by Native Americans against Exxon after the *Exxon Valdez* tanker spill a few years earlier. He was a powerful backer to have.

At first it looked like it would be easy for Roberts to take on her employer. To win her case, she just needed to get proof that there was discrimination throughout the corporation. Well, Texaco had a computerized database covering every employee. Roberts's team had a right to get such evidence, and could use that to check whether salaries and promotions were up to industry standard. Roberts would also need confirmation that a large number of blacks had been held back the way she had been. A longtime black Texaco employee with an outstanding record volunteered to phone around and use e-mail to quickly get that group connected. What he found was impressive, and disheartening.

Dozens of black Texaco employees, it now came out, had been getting grief for years. Lower-level employees got yelled at as porch monkeys, or orangutans, or n----rs; higher-level ones had faced vice presidents who dressed up as Little Black Sambo at company parties, or were told that they were uppity, or heard, "I guess we treat n----rs different down here." Throughout the company, their promotions were repeatedly held back. Isolated within the corporation, individuals hadn't realized how common this was.

It should have helped the case, for it was precisely the systematic evidence a class-action suit needs. But whoever said the balance of forces was now equal? Roberts herself was attacked, of course, with promotions being canceled and every detail of her personal life examined. But worse, the long-standing employee who started phoning around was fired, very publicly, with security guards marching him out. And then, worst of all, the key database that would give statistical proof to the charges was kept hidden away, with Texaco's lawyers even taunting the Roberts team that it would never get delivered. Months passed, then more months, and although Roberts's team even heard rumors of some sort of master book where all the employee data and promotion decisions were actually written down, the opposition lawyers just were not going to deliver it. By late 1995, it looked like Texaco's stonewalling would win.

And then—for although God gets distracted, He does have a satisfying tendency to return to business when we most need Him—one straight-arrow Texaco employee, a man Roberts had found as distant as any of her other white colleagues in the early days, phoned her lawyers.

He had some tapes.

At this point trumpets sound and petards start hoisting. The tape was of a meeting between the employee, Rich Lundwall, and Bob Ulrich, Texaco's treasurer. Lundwall had a minirecorder on to help in writing up the minutes later. No one else noticed it was on, which was pretty nice for Cohen, Milstein, Hausfeld & Toll, for what the two men were discussing was how to get rid of the master book—the document the Roberts team needed, since it's what contained the proof of systematic discrimination.

Ulrich: Boy, I'll tell you, that one—you would put that and you would have the whole copy. Nobody else ought to have copies of that.

Lundwall: Okay.

Ulrich: You have that someplace and it doesn't exist.

Lundwall: Yeah, okay.

Ulrich: I just don't want anybody to have a copy of that.

Lundwall: Good. No problem.

Ulrich: You know, there is no point in even keeping the restricted version anymore. All it could do is get us in trouble. That's the way I feel. I would not keep anything.

Lundwall: Let me shred this thing and any other restricted version like it.

Ulrich: Why do we have to keep the minutes of the meeting anymore?

Lundwall: You don't. You don't.

Ulrich: We don't.

Lundwall: Because we don't. No, we don't, because it comes back to haunt us, like right now.

There was also:

Ulrich: This diversity thing. You know how all the jelly beans agree.

Lundwall: That's funny. All the black jelly beans seemed to be glued to the bottom of the bag.

Ulrich: You can't have just we [sic] and them. You can't just have black jelly beans and other jelly beans. It doesn't work.

Lundwall: Yeah, but they're perpetuating the black jelly beans.

And finally:

Ulrich: I'm still having trouble with Hanukkah, and now I have Kwanza.

The *New York Times* published the tapes on Monday, November 4, 1996. It became the sort of week when public relations staff would prefer to suffer mass poisoning by E. coli rather than come in and have to face the phones. Texaco's stock dropped about $1 billion in value; columnists, even strongly pro business ones, were unimpressed; the comptroller of New York State hinted at a disinvestment campaign similar to the one that had been used against South Africa. But, Texaco still didn't want to settle!

The coup de grâce had to be administered by yet another American citizen, one who understood about discrimination from a slightly different perspective. Ted Koppel's family had barely escaped Hitler's Germany. As a Jewish boy living in postwar Britain, he'd been regularly bullied by the other boarders at his private school.

Koppel got Texaco's chief executive officer, Peter Bijur, on *Nightline.*

Koppel: I realize this is the kind of question that is probably going to make your lawyers cringe, but you know one way to put the old chapter behind you and to clearly signal the beginning of a new chapter is to say, "Clearly injustices were done; let's settle the damn lawsuit, get it out of the way, and move on."

Bijur: Clearly, Ted, injustices were done and we are exploring every possible opportunity to put this behind us and begin the healing process within our company.

Koppel: Well, if you're exploring every opportunity, one easy way to do it is to have your lawyers call their lawyers and say, "Let's make a deal."

Bijur: That's certainly one of the opportunities that we're looking at.

Bijur was caught off guard and nervously mouthed lawyerspeak. It was a bit like Dan Quayle trying to look statesmanlike.

Koppel: And, since you're the man at the top and you're the man who wants to put this behind you as quickly as possible, is that something you'd like to see happen?

Bijur: It is something that we are considering.

Koppel did not like evasions.

Koppel: You're not being directly responsive to my question. What I'm asking you is whether you'd like to see it happen.

There was a pause, then:

Bijur: Yes. I would like to see it happen.

And with that Texaco had agreed to settle.

THE LESSONS LEARNED

Lesson one
······················

Given a crisis of these proportions, many organizations go into denial and corporate IQ plummets. No one thinks, "What damage is this going to do to our reputation? What is the most honorable way out of this?" Instead, the tribal organization sounds its drums of denial, and the tribe begins to believe "Whatever it was, we didn't do it." All through the affair, in private meetings with Roberts, she felt that the Texaco lawyers were just as insulting and resistant as before.

Someone in the organization needs to be thinking about reputation. Clearly, Texaco's reputation did suffer in terms of public opinion, media comment, and a loss in investor confidence. If the company could screw up on something like this, what chance did it have of meeting far tougher business challenges such as growing new markets or withstanding a global assault of very low oil prices? If management had the continuing distraction of fighting lawsuits with employees, what chance did it have of fighting and winning a price war?

It was fair to expect Texaco to have someone concerned with overall reputation. Many companies have brand managers—people who have responsibility for protecting the brand from dilution in value or, even better, enhancing its image in the eyes of its customers. They give great attention to the way products and services are delivered. An airline brand manager would keep a watchful eye on how well the company was keeping to its schedule, the politeness of the cabin crew, the comfort levels on the plane. The brand manager of a grocery chain might monitor the satisfaction levels of shoppers via exit interviews, the queues at the checkouts, the general presentation of the stores.

Brands, the experts used to say, were about product attributes such as taste, smell, and content. Today experts say that brands are about more—about feelings, character, and recognition. But reputation takes the jackpot. In a world where we are bombarded with choice, reputation becomes *the* search engine. With dozens of service stations for motorists to choose from, all selling virtually the same product, Texaco could hardly afford to risk its reputation. Not many minorities or women who recognized what was happening to Roberts would be turning right to fill up at Texaco.

Lesson two

Why didn't anyone at Texaco recognize this? Well, in their private lives the managers probably would have. They lived in this changing America: Everything they saw on television, and the lessons their kids brought home from school, and how they divided up time with their spouses—all that was different from a decade or two before. The great engulfing amoeba of American culture just streamed right into their homes and lives. Slamming the front door does very little to stop it. Huge corporations, however, are less permeable. Their ongoing mechanisms and attitudes are too busy and too set to accept such intrusions. As a result, a lag between the company and its world builds up.

The intervention of external auditors early on could have saved Texaco much of its later trauma. I did sing the virtues of self-regulation in the earlier chapter, but self-regulation must be underpinned by an external check to make certain that processes to ensure reputation are being followed. We have to invite people whom we trust to be independent and fair to look over the company's method of self-assurance and to tell us how well we are doing.

An external check of the way Texaco was handling the principle of equality for all employees would have blown gaping holes in its procedures early on. It would have highlighted areas for immediate action and identified how far Texaco was off track. But who are these external auditors who are qualified to do this job? Louis Farakhan wouldn't work. We would need someone more independent, as we'll see in the discussion on the role of auditing later in the book.

Lesson three

Having a worthy statement of values is not enough. Boy, is it not enough! Texaco had a truly noble one, declaring its commitment "to treat each employee with dignity, to provide opportunities for development and advancement, and to maintain an environment where employees feel free to provide input into business decisions, to improve the system and to make a difference." But that's just like the thousands of mission statements that languish in corporate reception areas or the company values booklets that lie unread on managers' bookshelves.

"Sure, we have corporate values around here," managers might say when asked if the company has published a statement of the values it stands for. But ask them if they can quote from it and they get uncomfortable, saying they haven't quite had the time to read it, or can't quite remember it now. Values statements are worthless, simply vacuous proclamations by a company unless they are backed up by clear rules on how employees need to behave, or what it means for employees on the ground. Of course we would all sign on to the equal treatment of employees regardless of gender, race, and so forth, but translate that into realspeak. Show how smutty jokes or condescending comments offend, or imagine how it might feel to take orders from a minority manager, or ask what would you do if your top-performing salesperson was sexually harassing employees, and the issues come to life and they're memorable.

The weakness comes because the impersonal directive—"Hire more minorities"—was operating on the wrong target. Texaco executives were told to hire someone, and they nodded agreement, sent out the right letters, and even went through the hiring conferences. But did they really think about it? To an eager young MBA consultant, being able to check off items from an impersonal list is enough. Those with somewhat more experience of humans—with our rich capacity for grudges, hospitality, drive, or nerves—know that only if you delve into where our deeper attitudes exist do you have a chance of getting it right. The famous Total Quality dictum that "Only what's measured gets done," is perfect for our MBA's superficial list. The process of reputation assurance we will develop later will flip between these two views. Clearly, we need to measure how we stack up and whether we have systematically gone through the lists we need to go through. But, we will also see that we need to go deeper, and influence the underlying forces that affect how we behave.

Lesson four

Purely responding to regulations or federal pressure is not enough to assure your reputation—it's just one of those surface lists again. It feeds on numbers and statistics. It can't touch deeper behavior or feelings.

Note that what Texaco's CFO insisted on was accurately done. More blacks were indeed hired. But the finance department had no reason to do anything more. The impersonal directive said nothing about actively bringing the new hires onto the team. This was no fun for Roberts, but it was also bad for the staff already there. Any fearful expectations—that this new woman was incompetent, that she would want to hate them—were left to grow.

If you're dealing with people, it's not enough to find an index that can be measured. Unless it also incorporates inner world effects, it won't work. You have to influence deeper motivation as well; otherwise, you're stuck too far from the control switches that could really get your goals carried out.

Implementing a process of self-assessment helps you take control. It's something you do rather than have done to you. You control the setting of priorities based on real-world research and stakeholder interests. You allocate the resources and set the targets, the goals, and the milestones. Your employees all sign on. They take ownership. They understand why they're in the program and what they hope to achieve.

Lesson five

Recovering from a damaged reputation is a lot harder than preventing a crisis from happening in the first place. First there is the settlement to the wronged parties. Then there are the cost of the legal bill and the cost of management time and effort in dealing with the problem. Finally there is the damage to reputation, which can kill some companies while other luckier ones recover in time—a long, long time. Larry Ponemon, an ethics partner in PricewaterhouseCoopers in New York and a good friend of mine, says, "These incidents are so easily avoidable, yet companies do end up getting themselves into billions of dollars worth of trouble. There is a direct correlation between the quality of management of a business unit and the size of the pile of excrement they're in."

The framework and the assurance process we develop will not only allow a company to avoid such incidents, it will do more; when lapses do occur, the organization will be able to recover quickly.

Lesson six

Don't believe you can cover up anything. Own up. It's the best chance of an early recovery. People accept that organizations are made up of people who do make mistakes and who are subject to the same prejudices as society at large.

Companies are more open to scrutiny today than ever before. Employees leave, others join. We've accepted churn as a part of everyday life. The company is a place where people come to get skills, enhance their careers to a point, and then move on. It's like nomads in the tundra, setting up an encampment, taking from the land, and then departing. Organizations don't need only cradle-to-grave employees; they need the freshness of new blood, too, to vitalize staid practices.

These are conditions ripe for whistle-blowing. If someone sees or hears of something he or she disagrees with, you can be sure it will get out sooner or later. The closed Texaco tribal group was not as closed as it thought it was. It couldn't obliterate the evidence of wrongdoing. Sooner or later it would be found out.

PRINCIPLES AND ISSUES

Each principle described in Chapter 1 is made up of a number of issues that may be important to one group of employees and not to others. The issues that underpin the principle of fair compensation for workers on a Colombian coffee plantation may be very different from the issues affecting the software designer in Silicon Valley. The skillfully waltzing company engages and finds out those issues, establishes why they're important, and incorporates them into a principle.

The payment of wages below a living wage and the sweatshop

conditions of employment have been the issues of major concern to employees, nonprofits, and nongovernmental organizations in the developing world as Western-based companies look further afield for sources of cheap labor. And very welcome those jobs have been to the developing world, but not in all cases.

This is the story of Tumini, a young woman from an Indonesian island south of Java where the sea is very blue, the sand is white and unblemished around coves and inlets, and the air is nourishment itself. There is only one thing wrong with her island: There is no work. Eighteen-year-old Tumini comes from a family of seven children, all daughters, and on this island a young woman who comes from a family of seven sisters has very little collateral.

The country average for Indonesia's daily wage is about a dollar a day if you strip away all the propaganda and the obscenely rich compensation which the friends and family of the old Suharto government seemed to earn. On Tumini's island a dollar a day would be an excellent wage and it is very unlikely she would ever be able to aspire to it.

Tumini's parents need to find her a husband in the next couple of years or else she might remain a spinster all her life, a disgrace which no one would wish on a daughter on this island. But they have a problem: no dowry, no husband.

Tumini has one asset, though, a great asset. Fortunately for her, the island has a wonderful mission school run by Catholic nuns of an obscure order (but boy, are they good teachers!). At math and the basic sciences she scored well in her school leaving exams, and though she only has the language of her mother tongue she is fully equipped to look for a job further afield.

One day a man comes to the village. He is an agent of the personnel department of a large Western-based electronics company. He is looking to recruit young people for a two-year contract to work on the island of Batam next to Singapore, hundreds of miles away from home. This is Tumini's chance to go away for a few years, make some money, and, yes, maybe find that husband she so desperately needs to gain some respect in her community. She's never left the island in her life, but now may be her only chance.

She passes a short written test, proceeds to a quick interview, and at the end of that day finds her name pinned to the big pepal tree in the center of the village together with half a dozen other names, most of them ex-school friends. The news was received as if it had been feared she had some terminal disease and the results of the test now showed she'd live. Over a hundred of the inhabitants had taken the test, all fancying their chances, some just able to write their names on the answer sheet. She was one of the lucky ones.

Batam is dedicated to manufacturing. Dozens of factories with the names of some of the largest global companies on their rooftops are here. Tumini arrives by bus from the port area, having spent the better part of two days getting here. She is being checked in at the new intake reception area. The bus rattles along past the factories to a colony that looks like a concentration camp. There are long wooden huts that are the dormitories where Tumini will sleep, and then there is that 12-foot-high barbed wire fence complete with sentry boxes at intervals. The men are asked to get off the bus and go to one camp, and the women go to another, separated by that 12-foot-high barbed wire fence. "Are they trying to keep us in or are they trying to keep those guys out?" she asks herself.

Soon the deal becomes clearer. The work is easy enough; it's assembling bits of microelectronic circuitry to make boards that presumably go into computers, television sets, or VCRs. She has to work for ten hours a day six days a week. If she's not behind that barbed wire by six o'clock every evening, then she is locked out of the camp, and that is not something she wants to happen to her. Her meals are provided—not the sort of stuff that exactly reminds her of home, but it's food. On Sunday, her day off, she goes into the town along with the other women to stroll and chat and talk of home. All this, and a financial package of two and a half thousand dollars for the two years on Batam. That's just around 50 cents an hour.

Provided she doesn't spend a cent of her income, and she intends not to, she will have enough money to fund a good dowry, maybe even buy a small piece of land and build a home or start a small business. Her parents will be proud of her achievements. The community will revere her. She'll even have the pick of the potential husband circuit. How does the principle of fair compensation look here? You can begin to see how the key issues look very different to Tumini than they do to someone in Silicon Valley. The waltzing company keeps in time, it keeps listening, and it adjusts and moves accordingly.

It turns out that the barbed wire encampment, as daunting as it might be to Western eyes, is for the protection of the employees. She's thankful she can sleep at night without fear of being attacked or molested. Batam can be a frightening place at night with 25,000 single men and roughly an equal number of women all packed on the same island. This employer has a duty to protect the safety of its employees. She appreciates the safety, as draconian as it might seem.

And what of the other principles? The provision of transferable skills is nonexistent. Microelectronic circuitry assembly is specialized work and each company has its own methods. But neither Tumini nor her colleagues would like the idea of doing this work forever. They are here for a purpose, and training to continue their career as assemblers of electronic components is the last thing they want.

Refer to Figure 2.1, which illustrates the relative importance given to the aforementioned business principles by our assembly workers in Batam, Southeast Asia, compared with those in Silicon Valley, and you see some marked contrasts.

One of the main things that are dissimilar is that health and safety are very important to our workers in Batam. Employers there have a bad record of adequate provision, as life is regarded as being cheap, especially with regard to low-skilled, low-income workers. Employers frequently cut corners because legislation is nonexistent or poorly policed. Dangerous machinery may be unguarded from that accidental slip of the hands or the fingers as the anxious operative tries to keep up to a punishing piecework schedule.

In contrast, in Silicon Valley the law has protected employees for years, and anyway, software designing is not nearly as hazardous as a two-ton metal press which comes down with a thump every five seconds, inches from your fingers. But our Silicon Valley employees are concerned

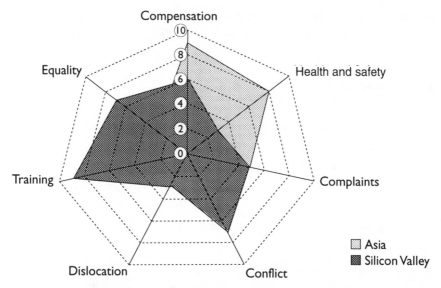

Figure 2.1 *Principles in Asia versus Silicon Valley*

about other principles such as training and skills transfer. They know that one has to stay abreast of the latest software tools and development environments in the rapidly changing, technologically chaotic world. They expect an employer to offer these transferable skills as part of the job.

Equality, too, might be high on an employee's list. The publicity given in the aftermath of the Mitsubishi sexual harassment case and other similar incidents would have heightened female employees' awareness of such issues. More and more female employees are asking their employers about their policies to ensure that harassment of staff is heavily discouraged, that there are efficient channels to hear complaints about such incidences, and that they know how the company hopes to discourage such incidents.

So we have seen how the importance of different principles and the issues contained within them can vary according to location, culture, and line of business. But, equally, the core values underlying each principle should not change. Fair compensation may be less important in one part of the world than another but it doesn't mean that we should compensate employees less fairly in some areas than in other areas. Human rights may be more important in China and less of an issue in the United States, but

49

we still need to respect those rights wherever we are. Good companies keep waltzing in time to their stakeholders, moving in step with every new issue as it emerges, and responding with leadership.

THEY'LL HAVE TO GO

Many businesses come to a point when they are hit by a downturn in their particular market, or a plant or infrastructure is no longer viable in the location where it was originally built. Sometimes it's simply that the company doesn't do that sort of thing anymore. Typical examples in the past have been coal mining, where the ease and abundance of oil and gas made coal extraction uneconomical, and shipbuilding, with Asians just beating the hell out of the rest of the world on price. Today the same thing is happening with automobiles. Worldwide car production is already far exceeding demand, and we could soon be producing 20 million more cars than we need.

Reputable companies that want to be in business several decades from now and need to downsize or restructure their activities will need to handle dislocation of employees sensitively.

I recall the days in the late 1980s when our business took a sharp downturn and we began to look grimly at a shortening order book. Monday morning meetings got more and more depressing as clients canceled projects, and several of our accountants, technology professionals, and business advisers were on the beach without a pipeline of work and consequently little in the way of income.

At first we put on a brave face and said that the best way was to market ourselves out of the problem, that the recession was a temporary phenomenon. We tried all manner and means of drumming up new business. We ventured into parts of the world we never dreamed of going into earlier. We also worked much longer hours trying to catch up on all the things we had never managed to get time to do because of client commitments.

And nothing changed. We had to face the facts. People had to go. We picked from a list people whose skills didn't fit the services clients wanted in the foreseeable future. When we told them, though, we gave them time and we gave them dignity. We counseled them on the problems of our business, showing that it was no fault of their own: that the economic cycle seemed to be working against their favor and that we would assist them in their endeavors to find alternatives. We tried to place them in alternative careers with clients or gave them time off for finding a job and career advice and training.

It was one of the most destabilizing things I have done in my career—like losing a close friend or relative. Going home one Friday evening and spending the weekend mourning the loss of loyal friends, I experienced a sense of failure, failure to make a business recessionproof, failure to succeed.

My only consolation today is that many of those people who had to leave in those difficult times are now clients. Some even now confide about the dignity with which they were treated. If we had devolved the job to some anonymous human resources department, it might have been easier but a clear abrogation of responsibility. The extra effort seemed to pay off, at least for some.

IN CONCLUSION

In concluding this chapter we might summarize some of the principles covered. We saw some complex examples of how fairness of compensation and health and safety are applied by a company in a region that has very different cultural values. We also saw the need to respect complaints and to ensure that labor rights are extended to all employees. The benefits of sensitivity in dislocation were also covered when it comes to difficult downsizing decisions. In these cases the need for providing transferable skills shows its true value. Above all, I hope we saw how it is best to adopt a principle of honesty and openness in communication.

Ronny discovers that being "green" sometimes means getting soaked!

C
H
A
P
T
E
R

3

SOCIETY—
ALL IS NOT
WHAT IT SEEMS

In this chapter we're going to take a look at a few examples of how easily companies today can get embroiled in difficult social conflicts, even without their realizing it. They plunge deeper and deeper into a quagmire of criticism and loss to reputation. I'm drawing my examples from some of the world's greatest companies of the 20th century because I want to show that these things can happen to anybody.

LOOKING FOR MR. RIGHT

My first example begins in Cleveland in the late 1960s. It wasn't the best place in the United States to be living at that time. The huge industrial growth that had propelled the country through the fifties and sixties was beginning to wane, and large industrial cities like Cleveland were taking the heat, with rising unemployment, poverty, and terrible racial tension.

Cleveland was a divided city—between rich and poor; between black and white. The rich white folks lived on the west side and the poor black folks lived on the east side. Racial tensions couldn't be higher following the assassination of Martin Luther King Jr. in 1968. Black activism was at its peak and the company to take the most public attack was McDonald's.

Here was the company, symbol of America, with thousands of restaurants across the country. Everyone remembers going to one, either packing into the family car or walking over. The service was always good, and even if a family wasn't wealthy, here was a place they could connect with the American dream, where they could be just like everyone else. The east side of Cleveland had about half a dozen McDonald's restaurants, but none of the owners were black. These restaurants were about to be subjected to a series of attacks that would soon make their businesses nonviable.

Activists persuaded fellow black citizens to boycott the restaurants. With vigilante-style tactics they patrolled the area to keep an eye on those who disobeyed the call. When that didn't work, they threw rocks through windows to shake things up. The campaign began really to hurt McDonald's.

The company thought it needed to bring in some tough professional management to turn the situation around. So it enlisted the help of one of its few black managers, who came to Cleveland to take over running the six restaurants and relieve the besieged owners temporarily of their responsibility. A police officer gave him a gun with the advice "Shoot to kill." That's how bad things had become.

And things didn't get any better. McDonald's began to negotiate with the leader of the activist group. It transpired that the activists weren't quite as representative of the black community's interests as had been previously supposed. This was no ordinary activist group. This was a highly organized protection racket in the making. The group wanted to be appointed as a vetting committee to select, for a fee, potential candidates as franchisees. Clearly, this "commission" might not stop at the selection of the candidates. No company could sign on to such an agreement.

Then a well-known public figure and physician spoke up. Dr. Kenneth Clement was passionately committed to the advancement of his community, and to him the unfolding events of corrupt practices were abhorrent. He called for McDonald's to find appropriate black franchisees but slammed the tactics of the activist group. The black restaurateurs were found and the activists' ringleader was subsequently convicted of blackmail.

Lesson one

Anticipating problems before they occur can be a lot easier than trying to fix them when you have a full-blown crisis on your hands. This is a message that occurs repeatedly in this book, and I do not tire of emphasizing it. If McDonald's had anticipated the changes going on in the United States with the civil rights movement and kept in step with the demands that society was making of the company, the Cleveland crisis might not have happened.

Lesson two

Know whom you might be waltzing with. McDonald's began to negotiate with the wrong group, a group whose interests were entirely selfish. If the company had courted Dr. Clement earlier, it would have been able to find appropriate black franchisees far sooner. But a company that is not used to waltzing won't know the partners that it's good to dance with and those with whom it's positively dangerous.

MCDONALD'S VERSUS THE FRIENDS OF SIXTY-SIXTH STREET

Our second example is also one from McDonald's, but one that revolves around a company gaining the license to operate from society. No company can assume that it has unrestricted access to operate in a community without the community's approval and consent. Sometimes that consent is a formality because the authorities involved in granting approval represent the interests of that community. But, there are other instances when those authorities do not have their finger on the societal pulse.

This was never truer than in 1974 at the junction of Lexington Avenue and 66th Street on New York's Upper East Side. McDonald's would have killed for a site in this fashionable neighborhood. The company had virtually ignored urban America in the first decade and a half of its breakneck expansion, but now it was building restaurants all over New York City to cash in on rich pickings from wealthy city dwellers. But, in fact, what was about to happen would do more to kill shareholder value than any previous incident.

This time the activist group that reacted in raptor-like rage was the Friends of Sixty-Sixth Street, a group of highly influential writers, lawyers, media people, and all the great and good of Manhattan. This McDonald's construction site may as well have been on top of a nuclear silo with the President's hand on the "fire" button. And yet the company continued to maintain that the land had been legally acquired, that it was properly zoned, and that no one could stop McDonald's building a restaurant there if it wanted to since doing so was all clearly within the law. The company even refused to meet the negotiators.

The Friends of Sixty-Sixth then began to use their contacts, and the media barrage began. Television news covered protest marches with famous names inveighing against the restaurant. Respected newspapers began carrying comment, opinion, and editorials about the blot on the landscape they were about to witness, the litter, the noise, and the undesirable behavior the site would encourage. The effect on one of the most attractive parts of Manhattan was stressed, as indeed was the poor nutritional value of the food. The *New York Times Magazine* ran an article entitled "The Burger That's Eating New York," which was a damning attack on the company as though it were some mutant parasite. Questionable accounting practices, exploitation of youth wages, environmental destruction were all laid at McDonald's door. Who on earth wanted such a company in their midst?

A respected brokerage house downgraded McDonald's to a "sell" recommendation and took the stock off its list in the belief that the company could no longer cope with the difficult urban expansion program and thus its future revenue growth would be stunted. How many Friends of Sixty-Sixth could McDonald's take on?

And still McDonald's didn't want to waltz.

Then came the final lunge of the raptors' claws: an article written by a respected professor of accounting at New York's City University. The professor argued that the company was using questionable accounting methods and overstating its profits. He cited two examples: its use of "pooling," a technical term for a way of accounting for acquisitions, one that he didn't approve of; and not properly expensing stock which Ray Kroc, the CEO, had given to his pet employees. Despite these methods having the approval of the Securities and Exchange Commission, that guardian of virtuous business practice, this was the straw that broke the camel's back.

On the day the article was published, the stock fell off a precipice by a fifth of its value. The raptors of Sixty-Sixth had their prey.

McDonald's decided to retreat. The company called off construction of the restaurant in exchange for a truce, and today a boutique called The Forgotten Woman stands where a restaurant should have been. The company learned a lot from both examples. It went on to be the most successful retailer and restaurateur in the world.

Lesson three

Your stakeholders can be much more powerful than you give them credit for. Don't be arrogant and believe that the might and power of corporate muscle can overcome the guerrilla tactics of activists or nongovernmental organizations. "Ignore them and they'll go away" doesn't work, either. And don't for one moment believe that staying within the law is your license to operate.

WITH FRIENDS LIKE THESE . . .

The next two examples take us to a wider international setting, and they both come from one of the foremost global companies, Royal Dutch/Shell Group. I have the greatest respect for Shell and know a number of its senior management. I would put the company in the highest category of corporate social responsibility. And yet we see in these two examples how an organization in the recent past—it has since shifted its habits considerably—got itself into an awful lot of trouble when it dealt with government on the understanding that it represented the best interests of society.

Shell's engagement with Nigeria reminds me of the man in the Casbah asking the way to the airport and being told that "There are many ways to the airport but not one starting from here." Nigeria in the 1980s looked like rich pickings for Shell. There were nice large reserves of oil, a government very keen to get much-needed petroleum dollars for a desperate economy, and Shell executives so well positioned as to walk away with an operator's agreement that made competitors green with envy. Shell did this so well. Its ability to gain the confidence of governments, being seen to be a long-term player in a country, had long been cited as being one of the firm's key competencies. In fact, it continued to beat British Petroleum at this game. Britain, the kings of colonization, couldn't produce the magic combination that Shell, the Anglo-Dutch company, conjured up.

But by the end of the 1980s ordinary citizens in the developed world were beginning to revolt against undemocratic, military regimes. There was Tiananmen Square in the People's Republic of China, mass demonstrations in Burma, and the East Timorean uprising in Indonesia—all ruthlessly suppressed. And then there were the Ogoni tribespeople in Nigeria who objected to the Port Harcourt regime's corrupt practices and in particular to Shell's "occupation" of their lands. Shell, a major investor in Nigeria, was seen as being a friend of the government. If you can't hurt the government, hurt its friends. And Shell began to be hurt. There were bombings and other attacks on Shell personnel and infrastructure.

In 1990 the division manager of Shell's operations in a place called Umuechem, close to the Ogoni people's homelands, got worried about the prospect of an imminent attack on Shell's installation there. He wrote to the local police for help to protect the installation and put in a special request for the mobile police (generally referred to as the "kill-and-go mob"). These weren't your average Keystone Kops; they were feared as serious killer cops intent on causing grievous bodily harm as a minimum.

The following day a group of youths staged a protest at the camp. There was none of the expected violence; the presence of the mobile police seemed to have been a good idea. Just for good measure, tear gas was used to disperse the demonstrators. But the kill-and-go mob had not had their share of fun, so they returned the next morning at dawn to arrest a few suspects and killed 80 people and destroyed 500 homes.

Was Shell now in the Casbah or what?

There followed a sequence of other allegations of Shell funding the Nigerian police and security forces and corporate funds being directed at supplying arms to them. In the meantime, the government became more and more corrupt with a significant percentage of Shell's petroleum royalty payments ending up in government officials' accounts in the banking capitals of the West.

Then, when it looked like the heat was beginning to die down, Ken Saro-Wiwa, an Ogoni author and environmental activist, was arrested along with eight other dissidents. They were convicted by a special military tribunal and sentenced to be executed. The world held its breath. Here was the chance that Shell had been looking for to redeem itself. Wasn't it a friend of the government? A major investor? Surely now it could save this man and his colleagues.

Despite Shell's attempts, days later Ken Saro-Wiwa was executed along with his colleagues. A ruthless regime was using ruthless means to defend its indefensible position, and Shell was being seen as supporting it every step of the way. Could Shell's international reputation get any worse?

That's when the company decided to waltz. Shell began a long process of consultations with human rights groups, decided to include human rights in its statement of business principles, developed guidelines, and published its first social report in 1998. All future investments would be thoroughly evaluated for their social and environmental impact, and today Shell is developing a new competence—stakeholder management. Pax Christi and Amnesty International, both leading nongovernmental activist organizations, paid Shell the ultimate compliment in 1997 when they said, "For the first time, a major company has expressed responsibility for human rights. . . . Shell has showed openness and a declared determination to fully implement the new commitment."

Shell's road map toward building its corporate responsibility goes at least a decade into the future. But many other organizations haven't even begun to make the journey. Will they all have to undergo a similar baptism of fire before they begin to waltz?

SHELL VERSUS GERMANY

This example is of a very different kind. It deals with societal concerns about the environment.

In the early 1990s, Royal Dutch/Shell Group had a problem on its hands as the owner of a huge, outdated, and quite unusable oil storage platform. It was called the Brent Spar, it was cluttering up the North Sea, and the question was how to get rid of it. In the very old days there would have been no problem at all. Local regulators were easy to deal with, and some other firms would just leave the hulk bobbing in place until a storm wrecked it. In more recent times, though, Shell knew this was changing. Oil companies couldn't bribe national governments, and anyway, this was not the way Shell operated.

Specialists worked out that the safest thing to do would be to tow the rig out to very deep water and sink it there. That sounds an easy enough conclusion, but it conceals a great deal of work. Shell's engineers prided themselves on always getting the top solution. They spent three years going over 13 possible solutions before they reached that conclusion. Dismantling the structure on shore was one possibility, for example, but they computed that would have taken 360,000 man-hours of work. With that much effort, the chances of there being a fatal accident to some worker started rising into the danger zone.

By 1993/1994, it was becoming clear that when you added up the pros and cons of each option, sea disposal came out the best. There were more studies, the United Kingdom's Department of Trade and Industry (DTI) approved the plan, and then, just to be sure, Shell contacted all the governments facing the North Sea. To be surer than sure—for who wants bad publicity when you can avoid it?—Shell went further, and contacted all the governments that had signed the Oslo Convention, where international standards for such disposals were fixed in law. All the countries accepted the Shell plan.

Shell executives thought they were doing fine, and had all positions covered. Weren't all the potential government legislators taken care of? But although the world of the mid-1990s looked similar to what they were used to, the underlying mechanism of consumer activism had altered. At first no one at Shell could spot the difference.

That soon changed.

The DTI's approval of Shell's plan came in February 1997. But during the previous months Greenpeace had been having intense internal meetings, really divisive ones. One faction at Greenpeace felt that the organization was losing the wild spontaneity that had made it so effective in its early years. What it needed, this old-guard faction insisted, was a return to its roots: to more of what had made it great. A separate faction, priding themselves on their greater maturity and their greater awareness of what the real political battle was like, didn't want to have anything to do with that. Their organization was just beginning to get serious respect: to be listened to, and its counsel taken, rather than to be disparaged as a bunch of eco-activists who had to be guarded against but clearly couldn't be taken seriously. The two factions argued, and some long-standing friendships were broken. The final vote came. The old guard won.

They were very, very good. They set up a media center in Frankfurt, fast, and then they started attacking the Brent Spar storage platform as it was being towed out to sea—literally attacking it, with dinghies and helicopters. Even if an ordinary pilot, a tight-lipped professional, had been flying the helicopter it would have been story enough. But Greenpeace had a photogenic young woman bring the machine banking down from the sky, trying to fly in and land.

The media loved it. Why was a huge corporation spraying water cannons at a harmless woman? She was in a fragile helicopter. Didn't they realize the water jets could hurt her? And then, as the television footage Greenpeace conveniently took was transferred to local TV stations, Greenpeace's spokespeople raised the campaign. How dare Shell go ahead and sink this monstrosity in the North Sea? they asked. Don't they realize that doing so could pollute it?

Shell, of course, was flummoxed. They had spokespeople tell the TV cameras that sinking it, carefully, was the best way out. There were references to the three years that had been spent studying it, the slow mineral transfer rates in the deep-sea environment, and the fact that the ecosystems closer to shore were far more fragile. Anyway, what better solution did the nonprofits have? Shell asked.

It seemed a logical question, but only by the previous rules of the game. The nonprofits were against every possible disposal method that Shell proposed. Popular opinion in Europe backed them up. From inside Shell headquarters it seemed the world had gone nuts. But, had it really? Years later, after the storm had cleared, Mark Huxham, from Napier University in Edinburgh, pointed out that Shell had been thinking only in terms of what might be called first-order effects. Oil storage units are small, on a global scale. The North Sea is vast. If you sink one empty storage unit in that great expanse, you will have only a minimal effect. But if you go beyond the individual act and think about the precedent you're setting, you've now entered a deeper realm, that of second-order effects. The 1958 Law of the Sea is actually written in such a way that individual actions, once approved, can set such rolling precedents. The ordinary public wouldn't have known about the 1958 agreements, but Greenpeace's filming showed an overwhelmingly powerful corporate machine on the loose. It was in the process of sending one huge metal device out to be dumped in the sea, and who knew when there might be more? The popular awe at corporations—the belief that they really are very, very powerful—made this seem quite possible.

And then there had been the decision to have the main media center in Germany. This was brilliant. It's no pleasure traveling around Europe if you're a German, because you suspect, as the conversation gets late, and you're settling back with colleagues, that somehow, in the back of everybody's mind, is the topic of World War II. Sometimes your foreign colleagues will bring it up, but usually they won't and you're just left wondering what they think. This is especially unsettling when it's a Dutch business colleague or friend you're meeting with. From many other countries, there's a sort of resentful anger at Germany, covered over by whatever degree of politeness there might be. With the Dutch, though—so close to Germany in many respects—it's different. There's a much quieter disapproval, a disappointment almost. It's never spoken, but it's always there, and it drives Germans nuts. Now, finally, there was the chance to turn the tables. Royal Dutch/Shell's governing body is split between British and Dutch members. Attacking Brent Spar's disposal allowed Germans to feel morally superior to the Dutch, and that was a wonderful feeling indeed. It also allowed them to feel justifiably offended at the British for damaging their North Sea, but that didn't compare with the pleasure of lording it over the Dutch.

There were boycotts of Shell service stations by earnest—surprisingly buoyant—German citizens, and there were street protests, and, around the edges, there were scattered firebombings in Hamburg and even reports of shootings in Frankfurt. Shell's gasoline sales in Germany dropped about 30 percent, with the slack easily taken up by competing oil companies. Other countries were more restrained, but when a burning or besieged Shell service station appears on your TV screen, the message suddenly seems very immediate, even if the image is identified as coming from afar. At one time there would have been a last-ditch defense a multinational such as Shell could have used. Weren't nonprofits like Greenpeace dangerously left-leaning? This had worked fine against many antinuclear protests a few years earlier. But by the 1990s no one could disparage the pressure groups as being secretly pro-Soviet, for there were no longer any Soviets around to be pro. And then it was found out, from one of the government documents, that there was atomic radiation on the storage platform. Shell might as well have bought harmless little bunny rabbits and started eviscerating them on camera; the publicity would have been no worse. It didn't matter that all oil has some radioactivity, as do most natural rocks, and that the levels were not much different from those in ordinary homes. A multinational is dragging giant metal structures into our Sea, and assaulting female helicopter pilots, and opening the path for hundreds more rigs to be dumped, and now it's pouring in atomic radiation as well.

On June 20th, British prime minister John Major, with the impeccable timing for which he was renowned, informed Parliament that he backed Shell unequivocally. But Shell couldn't take it. A few hours earlier, Shell had decided to give up and tow Brent Spar back toward shore.

Lesson four

What Shell had missed was the huge popular reaction against governments. Who trusted them anymore? Even before the yuppie era, leftists had said big governments weren't trustworthy. Then, all through the 1980s, Ronald Reagan and Margaret Thatcher had been repeating that message for the right wing. Now that message had percolated through. The result was that when Shell spokesmen forlornly declared that they were following government regulations, that they had consulted with every relevant agency, they were just making their position worse. Although the nonprofits weren't always logical—they even ended up, a little later, once the publicity ceased, privately agreeing that deep-sea disposal was the safest option—theirs was an illogicality that the public accepted. Government was no longer a sufficiently protective blanket, an impregnable barrier you could trustingly settle within. New sorts of nonprofit organizations, boycotts that seemed to spontaneously synchronize, and suddenly disrespectful mass media: those somehow were now greater powers, able to reach you and judge you, wherever you went.

> "We were ill-prepared for the public reaction to plans to dispose of the Brent Spar offshore storage buoy."
> —*The Shell Report 1998: Profits and Principles*
> —*Does There Have to Be a Choice?*

It seems unfair that Shell of all firms had missed the change, but the reasons it did so are instructive. Royal Dutch/Shell had actually been renowned in the oil business for its deftness at dealing with relevant outsiders. It was the down-home American companies that had spent decades being the uncouth ones, believing that they could just go out and do what they wanted. In the United States, because the background of stable law is so trustworthy, it's possible to ignore the fact that it's there. Taking care of a few local politicians is often enough. But Shell had spent decades operating overseas, in one strange, or exotic, or strange *and* exotic land after another. Shell's lore was full of accounts of multilingual executives who were adept at working out local mores and discerning—with the deftest precision—with whom the true power in a kingdom was to be found.

That was their downfall. Shell people knew you had to work with local governments; they even knew that which governments it was would always vary. They had a slot ready for that, as we saw with all their checking with the DTI and other governments. But they didn't question the assumption that it was governments or other official organizations with whom they had to negotiate. That was their fundamental mistake. And that's what an honest concern with reputation would have helped with, for it would have forced Shell to pay attention to *all* the diverse entities on the receiving end of its operations.

ENVIRONMENT

Another example of letting the outside filter in comes from looking at British Airport Authority, the company that runs Heathrow

Airport. Since there had been substantial public opposition to its privatization in the mid-1980s, BAA has to be the sort of good corporate citizen that no one could criticize. It helped fund an organic garden for the homeless, and, in a nearby borough, a sensory garden for the profoundly disabled. There's a wildflower meadow that members of the local community can walk through; there's a wet weather shelter for local schoolchildren, facing nicely reclaimed grasslands and ponds; and staff are encouraged to tutor reading in local schools.

Many of these actions are good in their own right, but they also build up an attitude of responsibility to the community in further areas. To lower smoke residues, fire training is done with liquid petroleum gas instead of the usual kerosene, while pressure release valves on the big fuel storage tanks cut down on evaporation of fuel vapors, and their choking odor. These considerate attitudes, plus a correspondingly consultative management style, got noticed. When Australia started privatizing its own airports, in the mid-1990s, BAA's track record at home helped it win the contract to take over the running of Melbourne's airport. This was an especial coup, given that its partners in the bidding consortium included financial groups from Sydney, and if there's anything that gives Melbourne officials satisfaction in life, it's finding some way of blocking Sydney money from coming anywhere near them.

A few months after BAA took over, it had to submit a master plan on the future of the Melbourne airport. There were 18 requests for emendations from local groups. At Brisbane, there were 4200. Although most of those were from a single orchestrated pressure group, at least 200 were genuine, and ones which Melbourne, too, might have had to slog through if a different approach had been used. After the Melbourne contract, BAA won another contract—from municipal and state governments to work on reorganizing the airport near Naples, Italy. A company known for brute-force management, or provoking strikes, would not have got the deal.

IN CONCLUSION

In this chapter we have seen how contributing to the economic power of citizens and promoting human rights in advance of legislation can avoid a backlash. Respecting local culture could have avoided the battle with the Friends of Sixty-Sixth. Other principles covered were sustainable development and conservation and disclosure of relevant information. In an era of increasing global trade, the principle of promoting fair trade is becoming increasingly important as well.

"It got busted and I want a refund!"

VALUING

THE CUSTOMER

MEETING GUARANTEES

Doris Peachey had worked for London local government for 25 years, ever since she left school. She didn't have a great job, just a simple nine-to-five routine sort of job doing the payroll for the maintenance department. Evenings were spent by the TV and weekends were with her aged mother. Doris seldom missed a day's work and quite looked forward to Monday mornings, which nicely broke the boredom of the weekends with her demanding mom.

Doris could only work for another 15 years, or maybe less if she were offered early retirement, a prospect she did not look forward to. "Take up a hobby or something, darling," her mother would often say. "You may meet someone nice. You never know."

"Maybe I should," she thought. This isn't to say she was into husband hunting at her age. It was more to have something to occupy herself on that fateful day when she couldn't catch the bus to work and might have to stay home. It would be then that the evening classes in watercolors or the summer school in archaeology might pay off.

Then one day she read an article in her Sunday newspaper written by a government minister who extolled the virtues of the portable pension. He argued that traditional pension funds were going bust and that in a couple of decades' time neither the state- nor employer-managed funds would be able to sustain their commitments to future pensioners. He spoke for the then Tory government of Margaret Thatcher by leaking the news that the government hoped to make it easier for employees to come out of these sluggish good-for-nothing employer-managed schemes. The portable pension went with the portable job and the portable health plan.

Her retirement in 15 years was a long way off and Doris wasn't interested in the idea of a portable job—things were too comfortable in nine-to-five land—but it would be quite nice to have the extra pension if it didn't cost more and only involved signing a few bits of paper. Who knows, with the extra money she might be able to buy that time-share in Spain or afford to run a better car. But, Doris didn't take it further. Quite contented with her lot, she settled in for another 15 years of catching the bus to work every weekday morning, seeing mom on the weekend, and starting the cycle all over again.

Several months later she received a telephone call at home one evening while watching *Eastenders*, the popular London-based soap. No one phoned in the evening. A few months earlier a couple of heavy breathers called, so now her number was unlisted and no one called (except last week when it had been a wrong number). "Mrs. Peachey? You don't know me, but I'm a financial adviser and I've been given your name as someone who may be interested in increasing your pension at, I might add, no extra cost to yourself."

"Oh! I'm not sure right now," said polite Doris, too genteel a lady to say, "Piss off, buster, and get my number off your Rolodex."

But the caller persisted. "Oh, no, Mrs. Peachey, I just wanted to know if you were interested, that's all. It's part of a survey, you see."

The old survey trick worked with Doris. No one had ever surveyed her, or asked her opinion of anything. When researchers stood outside her grocery store doing exit polls they never stopped her. When people with clipboards seemed virtually to accost passersby on Saturday mornings in her local shopping mall, they never seemed to go near Doris. "Wouldn't it be nice if someone asked me what I thought," she would muse as she positively loitered around to see if she would catch their eye. But no one noticed.

And now at last someone was actually asking her view. This nice man. "Well, yes, I suppose I would be interested," she began, hesitantly at first, then more confidently. "Of course I wouldn't want to fill out any forms or anything. Can't be bothered with all that. Oh, yes, and I would definitely want to be guaranteed that I wouldn't lose anything in the transfer, and then, oh, yes, my employers would have to agree—" All along the caller had been offering the odd "hmm . . . yes . . . of course . . . I understand." Then came an intervention that appeared to conclude the survey. "Well, Mrs. Peachey—Doris. May I call you Doris? You have been most helpful to us. Can I thank you on behalf of the company for your time? There is one more thing. Would you like someone to call to see you about transferring your pension? I think you will find that most of those requirements could quite easily be met and without any cost or obligation to yourself. Our advisers are very professional and knowledgeable and have been working with many hardworking people like yourself who do not want to be losing out on the great stock market boom going on. They can call at any time, evenings or weekends. There is also, I believe, a special Spanish dream villa drawing for anyone agreeing to see our advisers. Chance to catch up on some of that sun we've missed out on all year."

The rest was easy. In days Doris was signing forms to transfer her pension from her employer over to one of the biggest pension funds in the country. Although with her current pension she was guaranteed 60 percent of her leaving salary, she was trading this in for the "almost" assured certainty that she would be better off in 15 years' time.

She had been duped, like thousands of other Dorises. A few years later, when the new Labour government came to power, it would emerge that they had been duped to the tune of some $18 billion. And the companies involved in what has now come to be known as the great British pensions misselling scandal will remain with a tarnished reputation, which will be a huge advantage to their newer upstart competitors.

Lesson one

Corporate values and the reality of operational values did not match up here. The sales force and their marketing network of so-called independent financial advisers were not even on the same planet regarding the principles under which these well-established centuries-old institutions operated. And, of course, corporate values statements abounded with "We value our customers . . . respect their rights . . . believe in standards of excellence." The marketing team was breaking every rule in the book: obtaining contact lists through illicit means, invading a person's privacy, misrepresentation.

The reputational values of the organization were not communicated in a way that would be understood or used in the everyday running of the business. What did "We value our customers" mean, anyway?

Lesson two

There were no incentives or disincentives in place to accommodate appropriate corporate behavior. Salespersons had targets to meet. These were pure sales targets. The marketing team had targets to meet in terms of qualified leads. Remuneration was based on commission, and the fatter the commission the more the killer instinct reared its ugly head for a spot of mis-selling. Failure to convert a qualified lead would have probably counted against the salesperson that visited Doris in her apartment one Monday evening. Those who consistently failed to convert leads were given poorer and poorer leads—a sort of vicious circle until you spiraled right out of the pattern and were asked to give some other organization the benefit of your great selling skills.

Lesson three

No one seemed to check that the product on offer had passed the reputational values test. Could its claims be corroborated? Was the literature and advertising honest? Could customers be deceived? When should the company say no?

Each new product or service is a journey into the unknown. Some fit really well in continuing to promote reputation; others fail miserably. If we test products for quality, consistency, and usability, shouldn't we also be testing them for reputability? The framework for reputation assurance in this book is a good process to adopt to test new products for reputability.

NEW PRODUCT REPUTABILITY

A bank we worked with was about to launch a new service, a sort of micro bank within a large chain of grocery stores. The idea was that when you turned up to purchase your groceries, at any time of day or night, your friendly micro bank would be there at your service—not just the glowing screen of an automated teller machine (ATM) welcoming you in some impersonal way, but also a warm friendly real person who would deal with your queries, maybe help you set up a savings account or carry out some transaction you couldn't do or didn't like to do on an ATM. The micro bank would guarantee to offer you the best lending rate and the best interest rate on your checking account, plus, of course, the convenience of the warm friendly person for the lonely, technologically phobic customers.

We used the reputation assurance framework to run a reputability test. One of the key principles this bank had to be assured of was that it was able to meet customer guarantees and expectations. Offering the best interest rate was the key guarantee which the bank had the resources and the ability to fulfill. But, there was no clear communication of the guarantee in any of the literature or signage around the bank. If I wanted to know I'd have to ask. Then there was very little in the way of communication of this guarantee in the employee training program. The bank had in its very efficient way thought through the training in terms of operations of each of these micro outlets, but so far it had missed how it might actually deliver the guarantee. There was also no clear procedure for how the bank might track its performance with regard to the assurance that it would be offering the best interest rates to borrowers and lenders. This was potentially a very dangerous omission. If you tell your customers that something is bigger, faster, lighter, stronger, better than anything else on the block, how does the consumer know that it is? You have to prove it.

Here's how the micro bank's reputation might look in a year's time through the eyes of a reporter writing for some consumer page of a national magazine.

It's the first anniversary of Microbank's debut in a brave new venture that was heralded as this decade's big idea in bank retailing. The idea seemed compelling. You're down at the local grocery store to top up the refrigerator with more food and drink for hungry mouths and while you are schmoozing in between the broccoli and the French beans you spot Microbank's friendly frontage welcoming you to check it out. You do. There's this very friendly bank assistant who tells you all about the convenience of the bank within a store, of how whenever you need to come to the store she or her colleague is there to assist you in meeting all your day-to-day banking needs. I ask her about the terms of the checking account, and she mentions that the bank guarantees to offer the best rates for borrowers and lenders.

So far so good. But what if my own never-to-be-beaten bank which loves to say "yes" subsequently offers me a better deal? How might Microbank respond? "I'd have to get back to you on that one, sir," is her response. Does she have a record of the interest rates on checking accounts over the past six months? "Not at the moment, sir." And what about transaction costs—how do they compare with other banks? But I have stopped asking.

Frankly, Microbank's new business, which combines the convenience of shopping with the availability of banking, is a good idea for the consumer who can never find time to pay those bills and review account details, but as a good deal for its customers, the jury's out.

After a year of trading, this report card would be a damaging side blow to Microbank's reputation. Putting Microbank through the reputability test reduces the risk of our bright enthusiastic investigative reporter finding a story where there isn't one.

MEETING CUSTOMERS' EXPECTATIONS

Meeting customer expectations is the unwritten requirement of a customer-supplier relationship. The following example is a lighthearted illustration of this principle.

At a recent computer expo (COMDEX), Bill Gates reportedly compared the computer industry with the auto industry and stated: "If GM had kept up with technology like the computer industry has, we would all be driving twenty-five-dollar cars that got a thousand miles to the gallon."

In response to Bill's comments, the following was circulated on the Internet much to the enjoyment of all:

If cars had developed like PC software:

1. For no reason whatsoever your car would crash twice a day.

2. Every time they repainted the lines on the road you would have to buy a new car.

3. Occasionally your car would die on the freeway for no reason, and you would just accept this, restart, and drive on.

4. Occasionally, executing a maneuver such as a left turn would cause your car to shut down and refuse to restart, in which case you would have to reinstall the engine.

5. Only one person at a time could use the car, unless you bought "Car95" or "CarNT." But, then you would have to buy more seats.

6. Macintosh would make a car that was powered by the sun, was reliable, five times as fast, and twice as easy to drive, but would only run on five percent of the roads.

7. The oil, water temperature, and alternator warning lights would be replaced by a single "general car default" warning light.

8. New seats would force everyone to have the same size butt.

9. The airbag system would say "Are you sure?" before going off.

10. Occasionally, for no reason whatsoever, your car would lock you out and refuse to let you in until you simultaneously lifted the door handle, turned the key, and grabbed hold of the radio antenna.

11. GM would require all car buyers to also purchase a deluxe set of Rand McNally road maps (now a GM subsidiary), even though they neither need them nor want them. Attempting to delete this option would immediately cause the car's performance to diminish by 50 percent or more. Moreover, GM would become a target for investigation by the Justice Department.

12. Every time GM introduced a new model car, buyers would have to learn how to drive all over again because none of the controls would operate in the same manner as the old car.

13. You'd press the "start" button to shut off the engine.

GIVING THE CUSTOMER THE BENEFIT OF THE DOUBT

In the 1980s several retailers pioneered the ideology of the customer always being right. "Rule No 1, 'The customer is always right;' rule No 2, 'if in doubt read rule No 1.'". These were the rules that governed successful retailing, and many customers told apocryphal tales of how well they had been treated at their local Nordstrom or L.L. Bean.

I remember the summer vacation when I went to Maine to learn to fly floatplanes on Sebago Lake. One evening I visited a local folk festival near Freeport, home of the famous mail order retailer L.L. Bean, and happened to drift into the festival beer tent as if propelled by an unknown force. There were magnificent local beers, the likes of which I had never known existed. When the brisk talk of hops and barley and specific gravity had waned, someone asked the question, "Have you been to L.L. Bean yet?" To which I replied in the negative. As if in some Rodgers and Hammerstein musical, the entire cast went quiet. The only audible sound was the gentle whoosh of beer being poured. And then, on cue, the chorus: "You must go to L.L. Bean." Surely these were employees all keen to have another customer spend the rest of his life savings. But they weren't. They were just very enthusiastic customers.

Apart from the friendly service, L.L. Bean offers more. It is one of those retailers that has pioneered the art of always giving the customer the benefit of the doubt. If the zipper jammed, sure, they'll replace it, no questions asked. If the shoes pinch a little, no problem—they'll give you your money back.

I wonder how many damaging class-action lawsuits going through the courts today could have been averted by giving customers the benefit of the doubt. Retailers have the advantage of being close to the end consumer. They feel and breathe customers. Ray Kroc was never far from one of his McDonald's restaurants. Marcus Sieff of Marks and Spencer spent most Saturdays visiting his stores unannounced. Ben Cohen and Jerry Greenfield made ice cream and dispensed it to customers themselves in the early days of setting up the business in Vermont.

Contrast that with companies which are much more removed from their end consumers: Dow Corning, Exxon, Shell. How do these companies give their customers the benefit of the doubt that their concerns are valid? Sticking to the old attitudes can be very expensive. Remember what happened with Exxon's mammoth oil spill in Alaska.

The *Exxon Valdez* was the supertanker that ran aground in Alaska, seemingly due to human error of a sort that the courts—and public opinion—thought Exxon should have been able to foresee, and so could be held responsible for. The ship hit Bligh Reef in Prince William Sound early on March 24, 1989. Over 11.2 million gallons of crude oil leaked out, and there was extensive television footage of dead and dying seabirds and other damage to the ecosystem. Although Exxon paid $2.5 billion directly for cleanup, it was indicted on five criminal counts, and faced countless separate civil lawsuits. In 1991, it settled with the federal government and the government of Alaska for $900 million, to be paid over 11 years. (Its stock market value went down by $3 billion, or about 5 percent, over the next month.) Yet, how much of this could have been avoided if senior executives had simply been willing to show up at the scene and publicly apologize? In the ethos of most oil companies at the time, however, that was something you did not do. Saying sorry was not part of the corporate vocabulary; executives didn't feel the need to make the effort to view matters from the ordinary citizen's perspective.

Johnson & Johnson executives did better; they showed that they knew something about the concerns of end consumers, when at great expense the company withdrew all Tylenol from drugstores and all potential outlets for the painkiller. The mere suspicion that contamination might be of concern to consumers seemed reason enough to protect the company's reputation. Perrier did the same when the minutest traces of benzene were found in their bottled water.

The story of New Coke illustrates how important this can be. It's a saga that begins in 1985 when Coca-Cola's CEO, Roberto Goizueta, decided that the company's hundred-year-old classic drink must be replaced. It was time for a change. Very detailed research on a new formula was carried out in a hundred test sites and focus groups all over the United States. The results were positive. Compared to Pepsi the results looked favorable, in fact so favorable that translated into real sales, Coke would be making $800 million more in revenue.

So the stage was set. New Coke was launched with the entire fanfare and razzmatazz that a $100 million advertising budget could manage, and the result was a flop. Even worse, it began to get dangerous for Coke employees as consumers voiced their protest. Calls to the company hot line were up to a thousand a day with comments such as, "I don't think I would be more upset if you were to burn the American flag." People pleaded with Goizueta when they saw him, "You're not going to take our Coke away?"

What Coke had not properly tested in its extensive research was how consumers would feel if the company took away their beloved Classic Coke, that symbol of their youth, their country. One might say it was a reasonable expectation of customers to believe that a company that had

78

kept a product on the shelves for a hundred years would continue to do so and not withdraw it overnight. In fact, when consumers had been asked the hypothetical question in one or two focus groups, the response had been abusive: "What do you mean you're going to take away our f---ing Coca-Cola!"

But despite Goizueta's five-year attachment to the idea, despite the great expense of the ad campaign, and despite the face-saving that the management team would need to endure, they abandoned the idea. Just over 10 weeks after the initial launch, the company announced to the world that Classic Coke was coming back. So relieved were consumers that TV stations interrupted favorite programs with the news that Coke was back.

The Coca-Cola Company had restored to consumers the principle of meeting their reasonable expectations. They were waltzing with the raptors once again.

UNLEASHING CONSUMER POWER

Angry consumers can be as dangerous and uncontrollable as the raptor when they're aggrieved. Consumers are escaping from their own electrified pens of anonymity by unleashing the power of affordable communications and the Internet, a power and a force that seems almost impossible to tame. For a few dollars anyone can set up their own page and tell the world about how they've been treated, and there is not much a mighty corporation can do. Legal threats just make matters worse; the letters get published on the Internet. The world then thinks that there is some truth in the allegations, and the corporation stands accused of bullying. No one wants to do business with a bully.

If ever there was a case for waltzing there is one now.

Drew Faber was a fitness freak. Being in good condition was important to him, and there was no way better to keep in shape than a regular workout at the local Bally Total Fitness health club. There was only one problem: Faber, a photographer, had to travel regularly and needed to work out just as regularly while he was away as while he was at his home base. So Faber decided to cut the company a check for the upgrade to use the chain's Chicago club. All Faber got in return was a few more months' extension to his existing membership. The reason: His plan didn't cover him for the upgrade.

Hopping mad, Faber went on the attack. He set up a web site and called it Bally Total Fitness Sucks. Visitors to the BTFS site were confronted with a corporate logo with the word "sucks" all over it. It wasn't the best greeting for potential customers wishing to find out more about the company and its facilities. He told reporters, "I thought a web site would be the easiest way to get a response from Bally. If I wrote, they would just ignore me. They couldn't ignore the World Wide Web."

Gradually more and more dissatisfied customers of Bally Total Fitness health club sent messages of support or accounts of their own negative experiences to the BTFS site. These Faber prominently published, giving extra credibility to his isolated experience. One raptor had been joined by a herd. And Bally Total Fitness began waltzing. The company now monitors the Internet for aggrieved customers and contacts them to see if their problems can be fixed.

Ed Goldgehn was proud of his new shiny Ford Ranger. There it stood parked in his driveway for all the neighbors to ogle at. But then one afternoon (the day after Thanksgiving in 1995), Ed watched his beloved car just burn up into a charred and twisted shell. When, according to *Computerworld*, Ed and his wife Debra learned that Ford Motor Company had already recalled Canadian vehicles after they appeared to burn up in similar conditions—apparently due to faulty safety switches—they felt they had been misled.

They too resorted to a web site, in this case with the address flamingfords.com, and the site began to attract the attention of other Ford Ranger customers who claimed to have experienced similar incidents. Soon after, Ford initiated a massive recall of millions of cars and trucks, which probably cost the company a few hundred million dollars. Full marks to the car company for the scale of the recall, but the media attention in flamingfords.com was an unwelcome smear for Ford on an otherwise good reputation. Neither the Goldgehns nor their Internet friends are going to be looking too closely at a Ford for some time.

When John Bunt took his car through the car wash of a BP service station, it came out clean but different. Bits were missing, mangled in the brushes of the cleaning gear, and this made him mad. Several calls to BP's offices got him tied up in the usual telephone tag large corporations are famous for. When he did speak to someone, the representative gave him little joy. BP could not be held responsible. The bits that were missing were bits that had no business being in a car wash.

So he did what Faber did. He set up a web site with the words British Petroleum. The oil company's own address was simply BP. What visitors to the site saw initially were the company logo and then the word BASTARDS; the small-time consumer getting his own back on the mighty corporation.

Internet-based consumer activism covers a wide spectrum from the ludicrous to the serious: GTE Sucks; the I Hate McDonald's Page; ToysRUs Sucks; I Hate Bill Gates!!! I Hate Microsoft!!! I Hate Windows!!!; the Official Packard Bell Hate Page; Why America Online Sucks; and at least a dozen anti-Nike sites.

Nike's troubles of late may have some links with the Internet-based criticism the company gets for alleged labor abuses in Southeast Asia. Nike CEO Phil Knight has also begun to waltz. His firm has initiated independent monitoring of the Nike manufacturing sites, and publishes reports on the company's web site.

Waltzing seems to be the answer. Old-style confrontations won't do. Provided a protester doesn't infringe a company trademark or copyright or be seen to confuse people by pretending to represent the company, legal action is out of the question. This medium is only beginning. As its use spreads to more and more consumers, you can expect that the only recourse to refute these allegations will be a great reputation, one that can be verified and is available for all to see.

THE HEALTH AND SAFETY OF CUSTOMERS

On the surface, Flight 592 from Miami on May 11, 1996, was like any other flight. There were the deadpan announcements that the flight would be boarding and could people needing special assistance come forward. Then there was the rush of the infrequent air travelers wanting to be first on, and only after them came the more seasoned air-weary who had waited until the bitter end to minimize the time in those uncomfortable seats. The engines start up, the aircraft pushes back, and then there's the taxi to the holding point. At no time could any of the 110 passengers have known that danger of fatal proportions lay smoldering in the deck below.

Finally the clearance for takeoff, the trundle down the runway, the liftoff into the climb—and then the explosion; one that sent the aircraft plummeting into the swamps of the Everglades. Four years of compromises on safety were finally taking their toll. The crash wiped out everyone on board as well as the company itself.

The reasons: negligence, a poor safety culture, inadequate documentation or shipping papers for the hazardous materials being carried, an identical occurrence on the ground two years earlier in California not being acted upon. The jet had been carrying 37 lethal chemical oxygen generators on board, generators which could release oxygen to make a smoldering fire burn with all the vigor of a furnace. These could well be unmarked bombs wrapped in bubble wrap. One wonders if anyone in ground handling cared.

ValuJet Airlines was an organization whose founders had put up a million dollars of their own investment to create the Wal-Mart of airlines. They succeeded in getting Wal-Mart prices by cutting costs and corners, but they also got banana boat safety, with the problem that their customers were at 35,000 feet, not at sea level with life rafts. (Southwest Airlines also offers good prices but safety is not an afterthought with them.) Rather than dispose of the oxygen generators in Florida, ValuJet was shipping these dangerous canisters back to Atlanta where they were reputedly $7 cheaper to dispose of.

Safety is something that customers don't usually ask about but assume is in order. They'll ask if this plane's going to leave on time, or if there's a hot meal on board, or if it's a nonstop service. But they never ask if the engines have been maintained recently, or if there are any hazardous materials on board that could explode any minute. They trust that the airline takes care of that.

Women customers trusted that Dow Corning's breast implants wouldn't leak or damage their health, but when they felt that trust was betrayed, it cost the company $3.2 billion for its 170,000 claimants. When customers lose trust, you lose your reputation. What happened was that in the early 1980s, anecdotal evidence began to appear about health problems with those implants. The greatest impact came when Connie Chung, on CBS, devoted a program to moving accounts from women who insisted their ill health came from these implants, and no one had warned them about possible effects. By 1991 one individual had been awarded $7.3 million in damages by a California jury on such grounds. In early 1992 the FDA blocked further sales of the implants, and soon Dow Corning stopped making them. By late 1994 Dow Corning faced thousands of lawsuits, and had a $4.2 billion overall settlement offer rejected. It filed for bankruptcy reorganization in 1995 even though Dow Corning manufactured almost 5,000 products, very few of them directly related to the implants. Only in 1998 was there a final settlement.

The main legal charge was simply that in the mid-1970s, when the breast implant market boomed, Dow Corning had quickly developed new silicone-based implants and marketed them even though there had been serious scientific concerns about safety. It also didn't help that Dow Corning's public relations had been poor, that it had shown little remorse or concern, and that Dow Chemical itself was infamous for having produced Agent Orange. By the mid-1990s evidence began to appear suggesting that although there might be health effects, they were a lot less common than the media had reported; but the cold initial response by Dow Corning executives had done its damage. When customers lose trust, you lose your reputation.

CAUSE-RELATED MARKETING

For many years companies have resorted to cause-related marketing in an attempt to highlight a particular social issue and in the process obtain some commercial advantage. A retail chain might provide computers for local schools rather than give discount vouchers. Every hundred dollars you spend at the store gets you a small fraction of a computer for your school. That keeps you loyal and gives the local school much-needed technology that the state can't or won't provide.

Procter and Gamble Italy and the United Kingdom–based relief and development agency ActionAid agreed to collaborate in a humanitarian mission that raised over a million pounds for health centers and water projects in Africa. An in-pack leaflet asked purchasers of the soap powder Dash to donate to the ActionAid program. About 170,000 consumers responded to the joint promotion with an average gift of 10,000 lira, and Dash sales volume rose 5 percent. The company commented, "Our joint promotion with ActionAid in Italy was a very effective branding exercise for our product Dash. With a well designed promotion we were able to defend our leading market position."

British Airways has had a campaign for years called "change for good." Every passenger who travels on a BA flight is asked to put any spare foreign coins into special envelopes that are provided, and the airline claims this has provided millions of dollars for children of the world. Steve Jobs got Apple Computer into a form of cause-related marketing by offering deep educational discounts and locking in many millions of Apple addicts early in life.

Activists remain cynical about these initiatives because in some cases they see companies concentrating on only the issues that give them a marketing advantage; other times they just feel that companies are trying to do what governments should be doing.

I can see only good in such initiatives, however, provided all the principles we discuss in this book are not compromised. Imagine how a sports shoe company's fortunes might be transformed if, say, for one experimental year, the company decided to redirect sponsorship money from the likes of Messrs. Jordan and Woods to the labor force that actually manufactures the shoes. Table 4.1 shows how the sums add up for a $70 shoe. Only $1.66 goes to labor costs, so if a dollar on each $70 shoe went to increasing the wages or benefits of the people who made the shoes, the

Table 4.1   Typical Breakdown of Sports Shoe Costs

Retail price		$70.00
Store costs, profit	$32.20	
Wholesale price		$37.80
Nike's transportation costs, profit	$22.95	
Ex-factory price		$14.85
Subcontractor profit	$1.19	
Subcontractor administration, overhead	$2.82	
Materials	$9.18	
Labor	$1.66	

Source: The Wall Street Journal

funds being redirected from traditional sponsorship marketing to cause-related marketing would greatly increase the workers' quality of life.

ISSUES TO WATCH FOR IN THE COMING YEARS

It's important that organizations look to the future to anticipate how changes might affect their reputation, and develop policies accordingly before a crisis occurs. Customers will trust reputable companies to maintain their principles of responsibility. These are examples of some of the issues that companies will have to look out for in the coming years:

• Respecting a customer's privacy of data could begin to be more important as the use of technology expands past data warehousing, advanced expert systems, and Internet tracking tools. The movie *The Net* gives us a glimpse of what we can look forward to. "They knew everything about me," the character played by Sandra Bullock bursts out in hysterics, "the school I went to, the food I eat, the cigarettes I smoke, the contraceptives I use, my Social Security number. . . ." The age of one-to-one marketing is upon us, and companies will have to watch its implications for their reputation. Already we hear that companies' records on customers are giving them an increasingly accurate profile of the way we behave and how they might react to us when we use their services or complain about poor service. Labels for customers such as "obnoxious boor" or "frequent complainer" or "charming manipulator" are being given to customers without their knowledge. Every time you deal with a company you are treated according to your label. Rather like the "no reason" given to people who are turned down for credit or for a bank account, we have records being kept about us without our knowledge or understanding.

• The increasing intensity of food production is giving rise to concern about the food we choose to eat. Monsanto markets a genetically modified strain of soya crop that is resistant to infection while it is being grown. This reduces the amount of pesticide needed to keep yields up and, says the company, produces a lower-cost product more efficiently. But soya ends up in most of the processed food we buy, and some consumers don't like genetically modified anything being forced upon them without their knowledge. They want labeling to show clearly when the soya has been used, because they don't trust Monsanto's testing methods. Should consumers get what they want? In 1997 more than 30 million acres of commercial farmland worldwide were planted with genetically modified seeds—10 times as much as the year before. Consumer concern about whether companies can unleash the most powerful tools of modern biology says much about the cultural and philosophical differences between pragmatic and risk-ready America, where genetic technology that focuses on food has largely been accepted, and the far more reticent people of Europe. Europeans are terrified about the abuse of genetics. To them the potential to abuse genetics is no theory. It is a historical fact. Someone will work out a way of waltzing to their tune.

• Health care, too, will be a sector under constant pressure to meet customer expectations. For years customer expectations have been high and the health maintenance organizations (HMOs) have managed to respond well. But now with populations aging right across the Western world, boomers need more care what with those expensive Viagra tablets and the hormone replacement therapy, the hip and knee replacements, and obesity. Health costs are rocketing, yet the advent of managed care keeps forcing those costs the other way. Companies will have to work hard at changing customers' expectations in order to continue to maintain their reputation.

IN CONCLUSION

This chapter covered the principles of fulfilling reasonable expectations and meeting customerz guarantees. We also saw the importance of ensuring the health and safety of products and respect in marketing and communications.

"After you, partner."
"No, after you!"

PARTNERS

IN SUCCESS

WHEN HARI MEETS CONSUMERS

Hari was seven when his father died of tuberculosis and the entire family of three brothers and two sisters plus his mother became the property of his uncle. His uncle was the last person in the tiny Indian village able to support another six souls, having four of his own and an income of less than a dollar a day. But there it was: 10 people to look after. It was definitely an entry for the *Rough Guide to Living.*

Then Hari's mom committed suicide by drinking a strong pesticide, adding yet another statistic to the death toll that put female mortality 70 percent higher than that of men in her state. After the cremation, one of the village elders, seeing the plight of this new extended family, offered to send Hari and his nine-year-old brother to work for an acquaintance in the nearby town. It would at least get two of the boys off the uncle's hands, and he would also receive a little income to contribute to the upkeep of the rest of the family.

So Hari and his brother were taken to the town, two days' walk away. They found their future home, a corrugated shed on the outskirts of the town, amid a mountain of litter, stray dogs, open sewers, and all the trimmings which tough city kids were supposed to endure. In the shed at least 10 other boys of similar age squatted on their haunches on the bare earthen floor having their evening meal, which seemed to consist of a bowl of what looked like rice. One solitary dim lightbulb illuminated the interior just enough to reveal piles of handbags made of leather and others in different stages of preparation.

Their "carer," reclining on a low rattan bed called a *khatia*, beckoned from a dark corner. He was the first plump man Hari had seen and to him seemed to belong to a different species of human. Their carer eyed the boys and asked the uncle if they had any ailments or disabilities. The uncle shook his head. He asked the boys if they were prepared to work hard, very hard just like the other boys in the room. They nodded in silent agreement. He then eased himself off the *khatia* and asked the uncle to come with him outside. That was the last Hari and his brother ever saw of their uncle or any member of their family.

The next day at sunrise the entire shed was instantly transformed from dormitory to workhouse. The handbags were brought out from the piles, and covers were taken off treadle sewing machines. The workday had begun.

The handbags were all without labels but their construction, the quality of leather, and the closeness of the stitching all seemed to indicate they were destined for the fashion capitals of the world—the chic designer outlets in Milan, Paris, or New York. They seemed incongruous in these surroundings.

In their first couple of weeks Hari and his brother were given all the simple chores, like starting on the bottom rung and moving their way up: unpacking, cleaning, making cups of highly sweetened tea that provided both calories and liquid nourishment to the young workers and their carer throughout the day. There were no breaks or siestas or pauses in the day. They worked from dawn to dusk when the failing light made the stitching and the cutting hazardous and increased the rejection rate of the finished items.

The sanctions were severe for those that made mistakes or took their time over what they were doing. The simplest punishment was a night without that bowl of brown rice. The harshest, though, was a flogging for significant violations affecting productivity. But the carer preferred to restrict the number of floggings because they usually took the victim out for most of the next day.

Surprisingly, no one ran away. Either they felt too intimidated by the inhuman carer, who would easily be able to seek them out, or they felt that life outside the shed was worse. The 12-hour, 7-days-a-week routine was harder on the older kids, but the younger ones seemed to take it in their stride. No one was older than 14 and the eldest and longest-serving boy had been in the shed for just over four years. None of the boys knew where the elder boys went. One morning when they woke up a boy would be gone.

Then one day the children were told they would be having the day off and could play by the garbage dump next to the shed. Most of them had forgotten how to play and they ended up ambling around, talking to each other as if they were waiting for something to do. A few men and women came to the shed and began to work; none of them had been there before and they could only go through the motions pretending to cut a piece of leather here and sew on a piece there.

Then came a silver-haired white man in a jeep, with a couple of minders who acted as his interpreters. He spent about half an hour at the shed, talking to the men and women and the carer, looking around at the desperate surroundings. He appeared glad to leave as he shook the hand of the carer and drove off in a cloud of dust. In minutes the men and women were leaving the shed and the children were being called back. That night they were given an extra bowl of rice and sweets, which some of them had never tasted before.

Life got back to normal with Hari and his brother as they continued to climb the bag maker youth ladder. Hari was a few rungs higher than his elder brother because his small hands could sew the finest detail on the handbags whereas his brother's bigger hands were better for cutting and rough stitching. It would soon be the anniversary of their initiation to the shed, although to them time meant nothing as the routine of each day just made life an endless string of stitching and sleeping. Village life seemed another life away, a dim recollection of a previous incarnation.

And then one afternoon when the temperature hit 112 degrees and the shed began to resemble an oven rather than a factory, there was a terrible commotion outside. The carer was flinging his hands about in a rage at a television cameraman as he tried to make it to the shed with a woman carrying a boom mike. He got through for long enough for the camera flood to catch the children at the sewing machines and Hari at a bench doing that intricate stitching, and then the carer brought the cameraman down with a blow to the head. The woman hit out with the boom and there was one hell of a row.

Soon there were sirens and the police. The carer was arrested, the cameraman and the woman were nursing their wounds and, as is usual in any Indian town, a huge crowd had gathered. There were lots of people without much to do, very interested in the unfolding of a real-life drama.

That night the children went to bed without the carer and without their bowl of rice. What would become of them now? The next day as if on autopilot they awoke to begin their daily routine in the hope that the carer would return and life would get back to normal. But it didn't, and by nine o'clock half the world's TV personnel seemed to be at the shed with satellite dishes beaming the pictures to people in those faraway cities of Milan, Paris, and New York who bought those fine bags, the fine bags that Hari and his brother and the rest of the 9-, 10-, and 11-year-olds made every day, and for which they didn't receive a penny.

Government social workers took the children away, but within days they were back on the streets of the big city trying to find a living and perhaps start the whole wretched cycle all over again—to find another carer, perhaps start on a higher rung of the bag makers' ladder.

Lesson one

If you were one of those branded goods companies selling Hari's handbags at $500 a throw and pictures of the children in the shed of misery were beamed all over the consumers markets of the West, where most of your customers were, your reputation would be rock-bottom. And yet, every year billions of dollars worth of merchandise are sold at premium prices without the retailer, the distributor, or even the owner of the brand knowing that many of the products were made in conditions similar to those just described.

These companies are laying themselves a long fuse connected to a large bomb in the foundations of their organization. Just as fur went out of fashion when we saw how the animals were caught and clubbed to death or trapped in painful snares, your products could be history overnight when Hari gets on the tube. Ask Nike, The Gap, Adidas, Dutch-based clothing retailer C&A, and a dozen more.

Picking partners that share similar values is important if we want to be sure of the goods we use, the food we eat, and the clothes we wear. Global sourcing has become de rigueur, and it is quite normal to search the world for plentiful supplies of good quality, competitively priced products. It also behooves the reputable buyer to ensure that the suppliers are just as reputable. Reputation can fall with just one weak link in the chain. Like quality or cleanliness or hygiene, you need consistency down the entire supply chain. There's no point telling the patient that the scalpel you picked off the floor to make an incision was "previously" sterilized or the passengers on a jet that the engines are "generally" serviced every thousand hours or the automobile buyer that "most" of the 20,000 components in the car are quality-assured.

Selecting suppliers that share similar values may sound simpler than it really is. It's fine if you're making auto parts in some advanced factory in Malaysia or Mexico, but it's harder if it's sneakers or soccer balls in Pakistan or China. In the latter case it is quite normal for products to be handed down long supply chains of intermediaries, either to disguise the identity of the eventual manufacturer or to minimize the risk of copying.

To tackle the problem, standard setting, monitoring, and verification bodies are being set up, either to establish auditable health, safety, and employment standards or to ensure compliance by local manufacturers with Western codes of conduct. The Council on Economic Priorities' social accountability standard, SA 8000, is a pioneer in this field, although only a few companies—such as Avon Products—have so far declared their intention of adopting it. Good practice in this area hardly exists yet, and inspections can sometimes be as superficial and useless as the one at the shed. The inspector's arrival was probably announced, he couldn't verify anything himself, he didn't speak the language, and he didn't get to talk with the real employees.

WHY EDUCATION WORKS

Table 5.1 shows an example of the inverse relationship of literacy rate vis-à-vis infant mortality rate and child labor.

More and more companies have found that working with suppliers to get them to act more responsibly can be better in the long run for building a long-term relationship, as well as for the society in which these suppliers operate. Normally the sheds are closed down if they failed an inspection.

Table 5.1 A Comparison of Two Indian States

	Kerala	Andhra
Total literacy rate	90%	45%
Female literacy rate	87%	33%
Population growth rate	1.3%	3%
Infant mortality rate	16%	72%
Child laborers	68,000	1,754,000

Source: CRY

But what becomes of Hari and the other children? Will they end up back out on the streets to beg or to get involved in drugs or prostitution, or back in another version of the shed?

Perhaps the sustainable solution is to set up alternative education facilities for the children so that they can have access to a basic education. In Colombia, for example, children go to school in three shifts—morning, afternoon, and evening. They might work for their parents during the day when they aren't at school. That subsidizes their school fees. In Bangladesh, 30,000 children were laid off because of a threatened U.S. bill to ban all imports from that country if child labor continued. Children's rights organizations have traced only about 6000 of those children. The other 24,000? They're almost certainly back working in nonexport industries like brick making, where conditions are worse. Sledgehammer regulation rarely works. Some companies have set up crèche facilities so that women can go to work and children can do what children do elsewhere in the world. These suppliers aren't just some forgotten entity thousands of miles away; they're partners, part of the success of the enterprise and its other stakeholders.

The C&A code of conduct for supply of merchandise

- We specifically require our suppliers to extend the same principle of fair and honest dealings to all others with whom we do business.

- We will always comply fully with the legal requirements and intellectual property rights of the countries in which we do business.

- We have specific requirements relating to employment conditions based on the respect for fundamental human rights. These requirements apply not only to production for C&A but also to production for any other third party.

- The use of child labor is absolutely unacceptable. Workers must not be younger than the legal minimum age for working in any specific country and not less than 14 years of age, whichever is the greater.

- We will not tolerate the use of forced labor or labor which involves physical or mental abuse or any form of corporal punishment.

- Wages and benefits must be fully comparable with local norms and must conform with the principle of fair and honest dealing.

- Suppliers must ensure that all manufacturing processes are carried out under conditions which have proper and adequate regard for the health and safety of those involved.

- We respect the freedom of employees to choose whether or not to associate with any group of their own choosing, as long as they are legal within their own country.

- All C&A suppliers are required to make their subcontractors aware of and comply with our codes of conduct and are required to authorize our auditing company to make unannounced visits to any manufacturing facility at any time.

OPEN PARTNERSHIPS

Some of the best partnerships that provide for profitable relationships are those which come from freely sharing information and respecting each other's interests. For our next example—a great example—we look at how British Petroleum (BP) and Mobil, two oil companies, forged a joint venture to deliver one of their most successful periods in the marketing and distribution of oil and its related products.

The marketing and distribution of fuel oils—such as gasoline, heating oils for your home or office, the lubricants that make your engine run so smoothly, and the kerosene that propels the jets we fly in—is a tough business. It's tough because these industries have been around for decades, fuels have become a commodity like coffee or orange juice, and there has been virtually no innovation in these businesses. While the oil companies have put plenty of thought into locating oil, with fabulous new computer systems for unraveling seismic data to find oil in the oddest places, they have not been very inventive or clever in marketing the products that pour out of their refineries. In short, these businesses, which are called the downstream businesses, have for many years gobbled up all the juicy profits they make upstream.

This was the situation in Europe, where the U.S. oil company Mobil and European-based BP competed head to head in a sluggish and highly competitive market. Then they decided they might get married; create a joint venture. They had eyed each other for a long time and thought their values were similar. Although they had much in common, their service station networks and other outlets had minimal overlap and therefore gave them better coverage. Together they would stand a much better chance of taking on Shell and Exxon, the two biggest players in the market.

But how do you put together two large companies like these that have different cultures and capabilities and create something bigger than the two separate entities? This is where they came up with a really ingenious solution.

The downstream business fell into two rough categories, fuels and lubricants. Fuels required good operational know-how to keep costs low, minimize disruption to supplies, and be on the lookout for new potential sites, particularly in the growing markets of Eastern Europe. Lubricants needed good marketing flair, persistent selling of the product, and lots and lots of innovation to continue to differentiate it from the competition.

What if BP took over all the running of the fuels business and Mobil took over the running of the lubricants business? The more they thought about it, the more it seemed like an excellent idea. BP not only had a more extensive network in Europe, but its distinctive European consensus culture would lend to running, pardon the pun, a well-oiled machine. The Mobil American culture was more aggressive in marketing and had already established a strong lubricants brand. Why try to create a single culture when the market actually needed two different cultures?

And so they carved out two distinct European segments. BP ran one and Mobil the other, each one respecting the other's culture. All there remained to do was to agree on the way they cut the financial cake. And the results were fantastic. While other competitors struggled to maintain profitable operations in Europe, BP and Mobil with their creative and trusting joint venture delivered to their shareholders some of their best years' returns.

CHOOSING THE WRONG PARTNER

Our next example shows how choosing the wrong partner can destroy all your dreams of a happy business marriage.

In the early 1990s, Kimberly-Clark was interested in investing in China. This was the new market for the future with its billion consumers, lots and lots of people who needed paper towels and hopefully other related products. The company studied everything you would expect them to: markets, costs, locations—the whole thing. It even tried to be careful about the main problem good strategists are aware of when it comes to investing in a potentially huge market: There will be lots of competitors racing to get in alongside you, all determined to establish enough market share to get a good base. That was okay. You can take that into account: Estimate capital needs, have contingency plans, prepare ways to establish a unique position—again, it's standard stuff.

Now, in almost all business expansion plans in the United States and Western Europe you can count on much enthusiasm from the local governments when a big company is waving investment dollars around. Jobs are great. They produce taxes, bring about useful contracts, and please voters. It's so much a part of the mind-set that playing off one local government against another to get the best possible tax advantage has almost become a part of the game in the final stages of deciding where a factory should go.

In China also, initially at least, this appeared to be so. Executives on fly-in visits were treated with enormous banquets ("death by duck," as it has come to be known by the seasoned China hands).

But the initial wining and dining was soon to give way to quite a lot of indigestion. Kimberly-Clark managed to get started, sinking money into a paper towel factory in the north. It even knew that it was wise to have a local Chinese manager/partner, but this, too, was still consistent with their previous mind-set: In many parts of the United States it pays to have a local partner who can show you the ropes and clear away some of the minor obstacles. What happened in China, though, was that the local manager did more than clear away minor obstacles. He started clearing away the raw materials that were being brought in to the factory. He put them in trucks, and had them driven to another factory that also was going to make paper towels. Only this was a factory he and a few friends owned.

Kimberly-Clark's Western managers were livid. How could he do this? There wasn't even any pretense of hiding. The second factory wasn't located somewhere far away. It was right next door! Kimberly-Clark took their case to court. The court ruled against them. Then they appealed to the local government, the one that had been so welcoming when they'd been first considering coming in. This did not get them very far. The local government officials were friends of the stealing manager.

It was, of course, a trap. The local government officials had seen these rich foreigners stumbling around, and knew that if they said the right words, they could get them to come back, en masse, and this time loaded with money all ripe for the taking. The local government had never considered that there would be a mutual benefit from having the first factory, operating under normal rules, in their location.

Who could have told Kimberly-Clark's hard-driving executives what they were in for? None other than those soft-hearted representatives of prisoner's rights organizations who spend so much time and effort badgering companies about their investment decisions. The dissidents, as well as many other local Chinese citizens, knew only too well how arbitrarily the power of local government officials could be used, once you were within its grasp. The conclusion isn't that outsiders can't do business in China.

Several huge firms have, and most successfully. But when they started, they had enough prudence to take on board all these information sources, including seemingly extraneous ones. That's what enabled them to outmaneuver these problems before they arose.

Lesson two

When entering new markets or areas unfamiliar to you, it's wise to take professional advice on markets, finance, taxes, and so on. It can be even wiser to speak to the organizations who are pressing for change. Get their views. You might be surprised by what you hear.

WHO IS SCREWING WHOM

My early professional life was spent as an engineer managing large infrastructure energy projects. The rule was get the job done on time and within budget. Invariably the budgets we had to work with had significantly underestimated the risks and the true costs of material and construction in order to get through the investment expenditure committees. When we came to issue contracts for construction and for the procurement of the major items of expenditure, our bosses had one target in mind: to get the job done for the money we had available.

The only way possible was to screw the suppliers. When we received the quotes and proposals for the work to be done, we eyed the estimates, picked the lowest one, and then immediately began to negotiate hard to get the estimate reduced further. Our head of purchasing actually got remunerated on the effectiveness with which he reduced the contract sum.

But of course the suppliers were smarter. These were hard-bitten, seasoned old hands. They, too, had only one way: Screw the client.

Contracts would be negotiated, the head of purchasing would be pleased, and everyone would feel very smug. But then the job would begin, and written letters notifying us of extra work due to unforeseen scope would begin to arrive. By the end of the contract these were piled high, ready for the lawyers and negotiators to haggle over. The extra claims were often several times the value of the initial contract. By the time we sorted

99

it all out we might as well have awarded the job to the highest bidder, who knew the real value of the work but didn't want to be screwing clients.

The cost of the management time in screwing each other was enormous. The contractor had a whole floor of tough legal negotiators who had a copy of the contract under one arm and the relevant legal case law under another. We spent most of our scarce resources running around trying to pretend that we could outwit them. It was probably the most inefficient way to run a project.

Then we began to learn a better way. What if we selected one of the contractors, say the one with the best reputation for quality and consistency, worked with that contractor through the design and the estimating stages, and then got them actually to do the job. How would that work?

Well, it worked like a dream. The estimates were higher but the investment committee was getting wiser and now wanted a contractor to underwrite the estimates before they would approve them. But the best result of this new way of partnering with the contractor, of sharing information freely and of sharing in success, was that the work got done under budget. We shared the underspend 50–50 and we all had time for golf on a Friday afternoon.

Lesson three

A trusting relationship with suppliers is far more productive for both parties than one of distrust. But moving toward a trusting relationship requires changing behaviors of both your organization and the supplier. You also need selectivity. You can't date someone new every night of the week and be believed if you tell one that you're not serious about any of the others. Similarly, you can't play off numerous suppliers against each other and get them to take you seriously.

SUPPLIER SOLIDARITY

HarperCollins, one of the world's leading publishers, has some very important suppliers: its writers. These are the people who toil at their word processors for months, sometimes years, to come up with the words which make books which make its profits which sustain its reputation. But one incident in 1998 had its key suppliers, names like Fay Weldon and Doris Lessing, all lining up to take their words elsewhere and with them Harper-Collins's reputation.

The person they were putting themselves on the line for was Chris Patten, a man of much integrity. He was the last British governor of Hong Kong and later responsible for ensuring Northern Ireland was governed peacefully. Patten had made some sort of a spiritual connection with Hong Kong in the last remaining days of his governorship. He had fought hard to bring some semblance of democracy before the handover to the People's Republic of China, suspecting that Hong Kong's citizens would not have the same freedoms they had previously enjoyed. And he thought he might like to write about it.

He found in HarperCollins an enthusiastic commissioning editor who said that the work was the best he had ever read by a politician. That's quite a plaudit coming from an editor of a big house like HarperCollins. But then things started to go wrong.

Patten had been critical of the People's Republic of China, and the publisher's parent company, News International, had significant interests in China. News International's venerable leader, Rupert Murdoch, apparently let it be known that he was unhappy with the decision to publish the book.

Here we had a perfectly average everyday dilemma: one stakeholder compromising the interests of another stakeholder—in this case, an author compromising the relationship the company had with the government of a country in which it had a great deal of interest, far more than the potential revenues that Patten had to offer.

Patten was told that his book was below the accepted standards. One British newspaper carried a leaked diary excerpt claiming that the work had been too boring to publish. That's when the solidarity of the other writers who heard about the treatment of Patten kicked in. They spoke about wishing to review future relationships with HarperCollins, and competing publishers began the process of seducing the best talent away.

Patten's book *East and West* was eventually published by Times

Books. HarperCollins may take some time to recover its reputation as a result of the episode. Clearly, writers will be wary of renewing future contracts, and readers will begin to see future books from the publisher as being associated with bias and censorship in a way that readers do not associate with quality brands.

Lesson four

Coercion doesn't pay. Patten should have been told the truth and offered a deal. "Your book compromises the company. We screwed up, because we didn't know you were going to be so critical of one of our key stakeholders. Let's do a deal." Telling him his work was poor could be seen as bullying, and no company wants to gain a reputation for bullying suppliers.

OUTSIDE-IN PARTNERS

We have seen that some of the most successful companies of the past decade owe their success to great partnerships with other companies that become part of the corporation, not as wholly owned entities but as comakers, part of a virtual organization. This has never been more striking than in the success of Dell Computer, the personal computer (PC) maker that outsources most of its activities to third parties who look, act, and behave like parts of the Dell organization.

Coca-Cola similarly owes much of its success to the close relationship with its bottlers, many of whom have their own products to bottle and distribute. The strategy is simple yet highly effective. Coke handles the marketing and makes the concentrated syrup, and its bottlers do the rest—add carbonated water, fill containers and bottles, and distribute them. The bottlers like Coke because it extends their capacity and adds revenue from the world's number one brand. Coke likes the bottlers because they act both as outlets for the syrup and as a source for investment.

These relationships have flourished because they are true partnerships. The bottlers are consulted on all major aspects of strategy, new product introductions, and investments. Nothing succeeds unless the bottlers sign on to the idea and see the benefits to themselves. Likewise, Coke demands that bottlers share with them every detail of their business—weekly sales data and the effectiveness of campaigns.

Many outsourcing contracts go sour because companies get what they set out to achieve from the start. These contracts were initiated merely because companies wanted to shed staff, not end up with world-class processes. They achieved their goal, but the service suffered. Outsourcers were kept at arm's length, so they were outsiders rather than insiders. Employees hated them because they killed their jobs.

The ValuJet disaster was blamed on poor safety procedures. SabreTech was a company to which the airline had outsourced its refurbishment work, allegedly for cost reasons. With poor supervision, not enough checks and balances, and the main client more concerned about costs rather than safety, this was a relationship doomed from the start.

Lesson five

For outsourcing to succeed—and there is no reason why it shouldn't—clients and the providers of these services need to engage in a new spirit of partnership which takes on some of the principles that have made Coke, Dell Computer, McDonald's, and many more succeessful.

IN CONCLUSION

In this chapter we have seen how fostering equitable relationships with partners is important in protecting reputation. Equally, fostering responsibility with suppliers to ensure they share the same values was covered in the example of how suppliers who don't share your values can wreck your business venture. Showing respect for intangible and intellectual property of partners has great importance to partner relationships as well.

"I see cardboard boxes are up."

C H A P T E R

6

SHAREHOLDERS—

LOOKING AFTER

NUMBER ONE

This book has been written with a capitalist market-driven idea of the way business and commerce work at this point, the beginning of a new millennium. Of course there are other models around, and many have been tried, some more extensively than others. Marxism is the most extensive 20th-century experiment in alternative economic models that has been tried and then dropped.

A friend of mine, a very bohemian antiquarian book dealer, gave me a copy of a book called *The World Next Century*. It was written in 1898 and featured a group of writers that included George Bernard Shaw and William Morris. It was breathtakingly accurate about the events to come in the first half of the 20th century and about the widespread adoption of Marxist ideals and all variants of them. This is because there were plenty of clear indications at the time that Marx and his disciples were propagating an alternative model. And there was a receptive audience waiting to listen and try out Marx's ideas.

Today things are a little different. There is no alternative economic model staring us in the face. Europe looks like it's consolidating its financial markets into one big board to rival the New York Stock Exchange (NYSE). Governments have been privatizing all their state-owned nationalized industries, and only the most stubborn hang on while their privatized peers float off into the distance leaving them behind. U.S. boomers have record sums of money in stock, and around 45 percent of Americans have some element of their future income dependent on corporate performance.

Britain's Labour government, once a bastion of Marxist idealism, now has a bold plan for citizens to buy stock with their groceries, up to $75,000 worth, in an effort to encourage the masses to invest in companies. Even conservative Germans rushed to buy stock in their national telephone company, Deutsche Telekom, oversubscribing the issue by five and a half times, quite exceeding any analyst's expectations.

In adopting any stakeholder model of corporate reputation assurance, we can't duck the issue of who has primacy. Who is number one? It's true that our company could not exist without its employees, its customers, or its suppliers, but there is one stakeholder whose interests need to be looked after first or all else fails—the investor. John Browne, CEO of BP, puts it bluntly: "Corporate responsibility is only affordable after we have delivered our shareholders an adequate return." Without investors wanting to invest in a company there would be no jobs, no new products for customers, no contracts for suppliers, and no taxes for society.

I have argued in this book that the most efficient way to sustain shareholder value is by a balanced portfolio of stakeholder interests and not by the selfish short-term blindered interests of one stakeholder. But the shareholder carries as a minimum the casting vote, and at best the power of veto.

Although shareholders may be number one, for many companies they have been arguably the most ignored, the least listened to, and communicated with as an afterthought. But that's not how some of the more activist shareholders have been behaving of late. Despite previous years of great performance, in later years the board of AT&T handed out to Robert Allen millions of dollars in compensation for lackluster performance. No more. For years, managements like Barings Bank have turned a blind eye to the corrupt practices of rogue traders like Nick Leeson. No more. The raptors are out of their cages.

THE DEVASTATING HAND OF CORRUPTION

A number of factors seem to fan the flames of corrupt practices in organizations today. The first of these is declining organizational loyalty. Increasingly, companies represent to employees just a temporary stage in their career when there is some mutuality of interest. The attitude is that the company needs me now, but when they don't, they'll spit me out; I need this company, but when I get something better, it's adieu. It used to be like that with salespersons; meet your targets and we're nice to you, but miss them and it's been nice knowing you. Now it's like that with many more jobs, including trading, where each trader can be taking huge positions.

There's nothing wrong with this highly focused performance culture except that companies have not equally stepped up their emphasis on the rules of staying within the law, of avoiding deception, of engaging in squeaky-clean, noncorrupt practices. They have not sufficiently ensured that the message is understood: You need to ensure the reputability of our current performance, or you're out.

The second reason is the shroud of anonymity that technology has brought to our companies. What goes on in those cubicles is anybody's guess. You can put in all the controls an army of math PhDs from M.I.T. could dream up, but the brightest and most devious brain could still cover one's tracks for long enough to have brought down the corporation.

Corruption has been the shareholder's nightmare. External gloss and the patronage of the Establishment are no guarantee. There was Barings Bank; the Queen of England banked there. And why not? It had been around for 350 years. Surely this alone was evidence enough that the organization's managers would ensure that the enterprise ran according to the most reputable criteria in keeping with the quintessentially English standard of "my word is my bond."

But it wasn't so. One of the bank directors said after the event, "Ninety percent of us don't know what's going on 90 percent of the time." What they did see was a seemingly high level of profitability coming from young Leeson in Singapore. "Good chap Leeson. Give him some more to play with. Yes, that billion should do the trick. And yes, of course, a few million for his bonus. Oh, what? Discrepancies? Bit of a rogue? Now come on, my good fellow—the man's making money, making our investors very happy. Let's look at that one when we do our Far Eastern trip. Another Port Fortesque?"

107

And then the collapse. The young aggressive Leeson could no longer hide the forged signatures, the secret accounts, and the many bank policy rules broken. The $1.7 billion fraud should be a lesson to all. But Barings was not alone. Decades of corruption at Sumitomo Bank in Japan brought down that national institution. The Bank of Credit and Commerce International (BCCI) and savings and loans are other examples where corruption has afflicted companies, some terminally.

Lesson one

The only way to reduce corruption is to change something fundamental about how we give rewards, modify behavior, learn, work together, and communicate our success.

> **An Excerpt from The Shell Report 1998:**
> *Profits and Principles—*
> *Does There Have to Be a Choice?*
> - Shell managers are regularly offered bribes. . . . They are assured that they will not be penalized if they lose business if they choose not to compromise Shell's principles.
> - The policy and procedures are part of a strong anti-corruption culture within Shell.
> - One such policy is that we declare all gifts and those above a certain value are declined.
> - Last year we detected 23 cases of staff soliciting or accepting bribes. Every case resulted in termination of employment.

COMMUNICATING VALUE

A French speaker goes to a Club Med in Mauritius. He doesn't need to learn a new language to get a date. Then he goes to a Club Med in Morocco and finds the same. So too in Quebec, the South Pacific, and all the other places where the French have had an influence through their days of colonization.

Shareholders, too, prefer to have a common language that communicates the current and future value of a company. This will be especially important as more and more companies follow the lead of SAP and the other newly listed foreign stocks on the NYSE. What shareholders want is something they can understand and can relate management strategies to. The language used to be earnings per share (EPS), the profit the company made after interest and tax payments, divided by the number of shares. It was an easy formula; the only problem was that it was difficult to relate directly to the future value of a company as a long-term play.

Then some companies, probably led by the best value creator of them all, Coca-Cola, began to educate their shareholders, and in particular the more analytical and rigorous ones, that there was a more powerful language, the language of cash flow. The late Roberto Goizueta, who as CEO of the company for 18 years presided over a 3500 percent increase in shareholder value, was a strong advocate. He was a master at simplifying the complex. He would tell his audiences about Coke's simple philosophy. "We raise capital to make concentrate, which we sell at a profit. We use that profit to pay the cost of capital. Shareholders pocket the difference."

It's this simplicity of communication translated into strategy that gave investors a very warm feeling about Coke: the partnership with bottlers to fund expansion and keep down the cost of capital; the intense scrutiny of cash generation to pay the cost of capital; not pursuing growth by sacrificing the efficient application of capital; limiting diversification to focus on the core business; and the "Coke is it" slogan emphasizing this focus.

GE's Jack Welch, another titan of value creation, has also been in the "cash is king" camp for years. Here again investors know how the various levers of cash generation are being operated and can make good value judgments about the company.

Lesson two

Decide how you want to run your company, tell your investors why this is the best way, and then consistently report along those lines. Your investors will reward you handsomely.

RISING INVESTOR ACTIVISM

Look what's happening on the investor front. For a start, investors are demanding more accountability and more information about their investments. Any when they don't get what they want, things can get ugly. No longer will they trust boards to look after their investments well; there have been too many instances of incompetence and lack of accountability and professionalism. Investors are bypassing boards and dealing directly with management, pushing for spin-offs, initiating mergers. No management wants to be told how to run its business.

Activist pension funds are now on the loose, rampaging across America and Europe, charging into areas they previously just accepted.

There is one fund that has made its name famous. This is where the killers assemble. The California Public Employees' Retirement System (CalPERS) fund, for example, has a $100 billion investment portfolio managing the assets of some one million individuals. These funds are so significant that even a gradual pullout from an individual company can send that company's shares plummeting. CalPERS cannot help but begin to nose around in a company's business if it feels the management isn't performing. In fact, when companies' stock is purchased by CalPERS, studies show that their performance begins to improve. (See Figure 6.1.)

CalPERS trustees are slightly different from those responsible for other funds. There are a good number of union officials on board, and these are mostly white-collar officers who rose high in their organizations. They have the motivation, and the habits, often to take in more than the private-sector trustees they're working with, and that means their opinions get listened to. Plus, whenever so many words and reports have to be consumed, it's easiest to try to lump things into categories you're used to. People fall back on their previous assumptions. A strain of "let the guys on top get a taste of their own medicine for once" is strong in unions throughout the world, and these Californian officers are no exception. They're generally only too happy to see firms squirm. And then there's the New York City Teachers' Retirement Fund. Californians can be resentful—*Grapes of Wrath* was centered there—but for good old-fashioned class warfare you're always going to do better turning to the East Coast. Imagine a room of fast-talking New Yorkers, with an attitude, and a union commitment, and lefty antecedents. Now imagine they're given a few billion dollars to work with.

But this slightly tongue-in-cheek description of these public funds trustees shouldn't minimize the fact that they have been at the forefront of setting codes of corporate governance and corporate reporting. No CEOs like being told how to run their company, and this emerging form of shareholder activism is not always welcomed in the boardroom. But as with other stakeholders groups, where voices are being raised and concerns are being expressed, investors are no exception. There are rumblings of similar activists in other countries, as with the Pensions and Investment Research Consultants (PIRC) in the United Kingdom.

Who wants these guys to come and get you? If they're justified, you're in trouble, and even if they're not, those journalists are always looking for a scoop, and you're going to be in for some rough handling. It's far better to ward them off, to somehow appease the marauding beast, to retarget the roar-accelerating homing missile.

This is what's happening at Pfizer, which has a vice president exclusively for corporate governance. His job is to go beyond PR spins, like leaks to the financial press. He's the point man for setting up systems to link executive pay to performance, to create a governance committee that could recommend new board members without the old CEO or his friends getting in the way. But just as importantly, the other part of his job is to communicate all this to the big institutional investors.

You can succeed in this, for in several key respects, Pfizer's openness has worked. Think again what their VP is entrusted to do. Come right in, he says to the lunging raptor. Do look around, he says to the fast-accelerating missile. The reason they're hurrying in is that they have a serious attitude problem—often, alas, based on fact—about how trustworthy any corporation in their path is likely to be. Pfizer could print up the most

Figure 6.1 *CalPERS Core Principles and Governance Guidelines, April 13, 1998*

CORE PRINCIPLES

A. Board Independence and Leadership
1. A *substantial majority* of the board consists of directors who are independent.
2. Independent directors meet periodically (at least once a year) alone, without the CEO or other non-independent directors.
3. When the chair of the board also serves as the company's chief executive officer, the board designates—formally or informally—an independent director who acts in a *lead capacity* to coordinate the other independent directors.
4. Certain board committees consist *entirely* of independent directors. These include the committees who perform the following functions: Audit, Director Nomination, Board Evaluation and Governance, CEO Evaluation and Management Compensation, Compliance and Ethics.
5. No director may also serve as a consultant or service provider to the company.
6. *Director compensation* is a combination of *cash and stock* in the company. The stock component is a significant portion of the total compensation.

B. Board Processes and Evaluation
1. The board has adopted a written statement of its own *governance principles*, and regularly re-evaluates them.
2. With each director nomination recommendation, the board considers the *mix of director characteristics, experiences, diverse perspectives and skills* that is most appropriate for the company.
3. The board establishes *performance criteria* for itself, and periodically reviews board performance against those criteria.
4. The independent directors establish *performance criteria* and *compensation incentives* for the CEO, and regularly review the CEO's performance against those criteria. The independent directors have access to *advisers* on this subject, who are independent of management. Minimally, the criteria ensure that the CEO's interests are aligned with the long-term interests of shareowners, that the CEO is evaluated against comparable peer groups, and that a significant portion of the CEO's total compensation is at risk.

C. Individual Director Characteristics
1. The board has adopted guidelines that address the *competing time commitments* that are faced when directors candidates serve on multiple boards. These guidelines are published annually in the company's proxy statement.

GOVERNANCE GUIDELINES

A. Board Independence and Leadership
  1. Corporate directors, managers and shareowners should come together to agree upon a uniform definition of "independence." Until this uniformity is achieved, each corporation should publish in its proxy statement the definition adopted or relied upon by its board.
  2. With each director nomination recommendation, the board should consider the issue of continuing director tenure and take steps as may be appropriate to ensure that the board maintains an openness to new ideas and a willingness to critically re-examine the status quo.
  3. When selecting a new chief executive officer, boards should re-examine the traditional combination of the "chief executive" and "chairman" positions.

B. Board Processes and Evaluation
  1. The board should have in place an *effective CEO succession plan*, and receive periodic reports from management on the development of other members of senior management.
  2. All directors should have access to *senior management*. However, the CEO, chair, or independent lead director may be designated as liaison between management and directors to ensure that the role between board oversight and management operations is respected.
  3. The board should periodically review its own size, and determine the size that is most effective toward future operations.

C. Individual Director Characteristics
  1. Each board should establish *performance criteria*, not only for itself (acting as a collective body) but also *individual behavioral expectations* for its directors. Minimally, these criteria should address the level of director: attendance, preparedness, participation, and candor.
  2. To be re-nominated, directors must satisfactorily perform based on the established criteria. Re-nomination on any other basis should be neither expected nor guaranteed.
  3. Generally, a company's retiring CEO should not continue to serve as a director on the board.
  4. The board should establish and make available to shareowners the skill sets which it seeks from director candidates. Minimally, these *core competencies* should address: accounting or finance, international markets, business or management experience, industry knowledge, customer-base experience or perspective, crisis response, or leadership or strategic planning.

beautifully designed PR packages or offer the most graceful of high-tech video presentations. But who's going to believe that? It's only if you show inquisitive investing around that you have a chance of appeasing the raptor. Honesty works.

In 1997, for example, Pfizer's vice president managed to convince the activist New York City Teachers' Retirement Fund that a poison pill configuration the company wanted to set up should be allowed. Now, if anything is going to raise a pension fund's suspicion, it's when a company tells you that it's going to set up a poison pill. A poison pill makes an outside takeover difficult by setting a trap which would force such a buyer to unload its new shares at embarrassingly low prices to the current shareholders. In theory it can be used sensibly, to keep destruction specialists of the ilk of James Goldsmith away, but it often simply ends up as yet another way to entrench mediocre management. A bad guy couldn't buy and kick them out, but a good guy couldn't either. Pfizer's VP, however, showed all the investment visitors that the firm was writing in a provision to guarantee that the poison pill would have to be reviewed by independent directors in three years' time. The investors were appeased and let Pfizer go ahead, undisturbed by shareholder actions or any recommended withdrawal of funds.

Companies need such twists, because suspicion is high. One academic study found that firms with activist shareholders, even if there are relatively few of them, are more likely to vote against a poison pill defense—even if it really is for the good of the firm. Pfizer's open viewing approach is likely to spread, simply because it's one of the few ways to get around that suspicion.

Lesson three

In Europe, for example, banks and governments play a large part in providing equity-based financing, and corporations run their organizations according to the rules and dictates of their investors. So do the family-based organizations of Asia and Latin America. The important point is that the reputable company needs to find out what constitutes good governance among its investors and react accordingly. However, there is strong reason to believe that there is a global convergence going on in the most efficient way of organizing equity ownership, and it would be fair to say that the world appears to be moving more toward the American system of open equity markets.

BOARD DIVERSITY

Boards that run like cozy clubs are bad for shareholders. Everybody agrees with everybody else because they don't want to offend the management, and of course there is one's reputation; you don't want to be known as a troublemaker or else you don't get invited to sit on someone else's board.

You see them at cocktail parties held, say, to celebrate a well-known chairman or CEO's retirement. They turn out in droves. It reads like a list from *Forbes's* or *Fortune's* hall of fame. If by some freak incident you get invited to one of these events and you are on the outside of this cozy club, a quick exchange with anyone is rapidly terminated with a "must circulate." By the end of the evening the same old cliques have assembled. The lucky ones have picked up a directorship or two, and it's on to the next cocktail party to look for more.

If diversity is good for employees, why isn't it good for the board?

Percy Barnevik, former CEO of ABB, the European engineering conglomerate, who had some experience with improving corporate performance, waited a long time before doing anything when he took up his position as chairman of the Wallenberg family's holding company. (The Wallenbergs own most of the bits of Sweden which Saab unaccountably left over.) Then, to the world financial press's intense gaze, he announced his first key changes. They were nothing about particular strategy, or reorganization, or funding. They were board changes. Sony's president and CEO went on the Electrolux board; Helmut Werner of Mercedes-Benz went on the SKF (an engineering firm) board. "You can't have 10 Swedes sitting around a table talking Swedish and going hunting together on weekends," he explained to a *Wall Street Journal* reporter.

Cadbury on Board Governance

In 1992 the Cadbury committee drew up guidelines on corporate governance in the United Kingdom.

- The board must meet regularly, retain full control over the company, and monitor executive management.
- There should be clearly accepted division of responsibilities at the head of a company to ensure a balance of power and authority. When the chairman is also chief executive, it is essential that there should be a strong independent element on the board, with an appointed leader.
- Nonexecutive directors should be of high caliber and respected in their field. They should bring independent judgment on strategy, performance, executive pay, resources, and standards of conduct.
- The majority of nonexecutive directors should be free of business connections with the company; terms should be specific and not more than three years. Reappointment should be only by shareholder approval.
- Executive directors' pay should be decided by nonexecutive directors.

WHAT ARE THEY WORTH?

When a CEO delivers billions in shareholder value, turns a company around from the brink of extinction, and gives employees hope for a secure future—that's probably worth a bit. If a CEO presides over years of underperformance, low morale, and sliding reputation—what's that worth? Executive remuneration is what gets noticed most about corporate governance, and reputable companies are sensitive to how much they pay their executives in comparison with the rest of the workforce.

Many companies have installed independent remuneration committees with external members to ensure that the CEO does not put overt pressure on the committee to accept excessive remuneration packages. But even with these independent committees, shareholders can find themselves voting for recommendations they have no way of understanding. Never has this been so evident as in the case of Computer Associates, where in 1998 the business press reported that three executives took $675 million in compensation and thereby transformed a $200 million profit to a $480 million loss.

Sure, there was a compensation committee made up of independent outsiders, including the chairman and CEO of the New York Stock Exchange, and sure, the recommendation went to a shareholder vote and got through by 78 percent in favor. What was wrong was that not many understood the complex proposal.

Boiled down, the proposal was to reward the executives by giving them 20 million shares if the stock stayed above a set level for 60 days over a period of a year. This was the largest pay allowance for any public company and was 43 percent of the company's total income for the previous three years. But shareholders didn't see through this. They trusted their management, only to find subsequently that the company they had invested in would lose its market value by 40 percent in one day. With the company's reputation in tatters, it was unlikely they would recover for some time.

Lesson four

Keep shareholder communications simple if you really want to know what they think. If Computer Associates had known in real terms how much they were going to be rewarding their executives, they would never have backed the deal.

IN CONCLUSION

Standards are still in a process of evolution on the best way to organize corporate governance. The Conference Board is actively pursuing this agenda in the United States and Europe, and governance guidelines of CalPERS, Cadbury, and Hampel have been published. In essence, a company needs to stay close to the promise to shareholders of protecting their investment, giving them a competitive return on that investment, and respecting significant requests from them.

APPLYING REPUTATION ASSURANCE TO YOUR OWN FIRM

"Don't worry, Rosy. I got a star for framework in fourth grade."

C
H
A
P
T
E
R

7

THE REPUTATION

ASSURANCE

FRAMEWORK

The U.S. Federal Sentencing Guidelines of 1991 reduce liability in ethics cases if "reputation-maintaining" procedures are in place. There's a truly baroque measurement system. The "goodness" of a company is measured on a scale of multipliers from 0.05 to 4.0. If a company can show it deserves to be at the most lenient, left-hand side of this scale, then any fine it has to pay gets reduced by that multiplier. A $1 million fine gets shrunk to $50,000. The way it gets to be on this left-hand side is by being able to have its lawyers explain to a judge that the firm has long had programs in place to improve its awareness of current ethical concerns—training courses that have to be attended, promotions that include reference to how well such standards are followed, and so on. If the company doesn't have the suggested systems in place, it can get hammered by being stuck with the maximum multiplier of 4.0. A $1 million fine becomes $4 million, and the official maximum fine of $72.5 million becomes $290 million.

In one respect the guidelines worked near perfectly. In early 1991, before they came in, fewer than 30 percent of U.S. firms had formalized codes of ethics. By 1994, the number was over 80 percent. But how worthwhile is a forced conversion? The evidence from within the firms that have made the switch is mixed. Sometimes there's resistance; sometimes it's redundant. The whole thing may seem too huge—the effort to have every employee go through the same forms and follow the same, externally imposed rules. If it's not supported from on top, and even more, if it's not carried out with some additional feeling—some extra factor—it doesn't seem to really affect the way jobs are done.

We have said before that reputable companies seek to act responsibly regardless of whether laws are in place to justify their actions. A reputation assurance program certainly allows you to satisfy the essence of the sentencing guidelines, which is that errant companies who take reputation seriously are less likely to be harshly penalized under the law. But reputation assurance actually goes further. It's not just an externally imposed rule or procedure. Rather, it is a process that sets the foundations for a better-run company: It minimizes major risks and enhances reputation with a very wide constituency of stakeholders. Your company gets known by word of mouth as being trustworthy, fair, and considerate, and as providing leadership in all these areas. This is 21st-century marketing. It brings you an advantage that advertising dollars can't.

In Chapter 1 we saw how Malcolm Baldrige, with the help of a number of leading industrialists and academics, set out a standard for a quality-led organization. It was a framework of best practice, a code, a way of guiding a company to winning the quality war. It was a means of self-assessment that told you how you could see how your business stacked up against the framework of quality behavior. But perhaps most importantly, it did not prescribe how you achieved the objectives set out in the framework. Instead, it allowed each company to come up with its own innovative means of achieving a set objective.

If one of the quality objectives was "understanding customers," then whether a company, for example, engaged a market research company, an opinion polling organization, or actually went out and talked to customers themselves, in each case it would be achieving the same objective. Companies that devised innovative, low-cost schemes to understand customers, such as opening free telephone hot lines or reply-paid coupons integrated with product packaging, got ahead of their competitors by achieving the same objectives more effectively.

Quality management taught us how to measure processes, those fuzzy things that lead to well-being, to success, and to long-term survival. *This is exactly how we need to approach the management of reputation.* We can measure outputs, such as carbon emissions and the percentage of waste recycled, and the number of legal actions taken against a firm, but the true assessment of a company's reputation is if it actually acts responsibly.

Quality management has also taught us that self-assessment can be an important tool in the hands of employees, so long as they believe that the organization is serious about continuous improvement. Acting ethically is something we must want to do rather than have done to us. If government sets down rules and tells us what we need to do to be legal, then we'll comply. It doesn't mean that we do those things because it's for the good of society or the community we live in. Paying taxes is keeping within the law, but it doesn't mean that when people pay their taxes they feel that they are fulfilling their obligations to put something back into the society in which they operate.

People deride self-assessment on the basis that unethical organizations can make an evaluation look good and cover up the cracks. In practice this doesn't happen very often, so long as the initiative is seen as a genuine improvement tool and that there is some degree of external oversight. When I carry out assessments of staff performance, I usually ask staffers to first assess their own performance according to certain preset criteria and then meet to compare this with my perceptions. It's very rare that we get widely differing assessments.

Management processes such as those espoused by self-assessment systems bring structure to the achievement of goals. They help us to look in the mirror and evaluate our performance and to observe the reality of our actions. Philosophers from the ancient Greeks to recent times have had much to say about the measurement and the observation of reality. In Book 7 of *The Republic*, Plato proposed that observing reality was like sitting in a cave and watching the reflections of transmitted light from the exterior fall on its walls. Thinking you are doing well can be very different from the reality of what's going on below the surface. A good self-assessment system brings in some of that underlying reality. Stop a male colleague and ask him if he thinks he behaves in a sexist way toward his female colleagues and you would most probably get the answer, "No." Get the same person to answer a few more specific questions: Do you crack smutty jokes about women in their company? Do you make assumptions about male and female roles? Have you ever done the dishes at home? It might soon become evident that in fact he does have sexist attitudes.

To assess our true compliance with the principles of corporate behavior, we have developed a process of questioning that is based on what we know about quality management. These are the fundamental things you always need to do in order to implement any principle. Experience has taught us which ones work. For example, we need to set specific goals and measure our achievement. If we don't have goals, we don't quite know what we are trying to achieve. It's like saying you want to become fit and healthy. When will you know that you are feeling fit? When you have lost 20 pounds and stopped panting every time you climb a flight of stairs? If so, will you be weighing yourself to see how your fitness program progresses and will you be walking up that escalator now and then to check your heart palpitations?

Now we are going to see how we can apply some of those fundamental quality processes to measuring our achievement in reputation management.

THE REPUTATION PRINCIPLES

Earlier in this book we described the scope and content of some of these principles. In Appendix C we list them within a structure we have begun to call the Corporate Accountability and Responsibility Evaluation framework. The framework has been helpful for two reasons. It structures the assurance process, which we will discuss over the next few pages. It also serves as a knowledge exchange on best practice and benchmarks.

NOT ALL PRINCIPLES ARE EQUALLY IMPORTANT

The principles that populate the Corporate Accountability and Responsibility Evaluation framework are not equally important to every company. For example, we may not be very concerned that a software company will damage the environment in comparison to, say, a petrochemical firm. A consumer credit financing operation may have little to do with protecting human rights, but safeguarding customer privacy may be a primary concern. A retailer may need to be highly vigilant when sourcing from subcontractors, while a pharmaceutical company may need to put great emphasis behind protecting the health and safety of its customers. So, along with the basic assessments, we also need a process for arriving at which principles are more important than others.

The weighting of a principle begins with determining if it is important to your stakeholders. Let's imagine that you have acquired a company located in a region such as Northern Ireland. Ninety-five percent of your employees are Protestants, but the community as a whole is made up of roughly equal numbers of Catholics and Protestants. When considering the principles of diversity, you will be caught in the dilemma of discharging your responsibility toward the society in which you operate while also reflecting the priorities of your current Protestant employees. The Catholic community may also have a wider community of interest thousands of miles away in the United States, where millions of Irish-Americans would have a deep interest in ensuring that the Catholic community in which you operate is given a fair share of opportunity for jobs. So, you can see how a seemingly local issue begins to have a global dimension and how without appropriate dialogue with the various constituencies you will be making decisions without due regard for all the forces acting on your organization. Only you can judge the importance of the principle concerned, and to do this you'll need to weigh the relevant degrees of concern to your primary and secondary stakeholders. (See Figure 7.1.)

To rate an issue in terms of importance, consider the issue descriptors in Figure 7.2 when in dialogue with stakeholders.

THE POWER TO CHANGE

There will be examples of principles that we find to be important to our stakeholders but that are difficult to influence. An example might be found in compensation for employees. If wage levels of employees are agreed to by some national negotiating body, then the power of an

Stakeholder Analysis
Primacy of Stakeholders

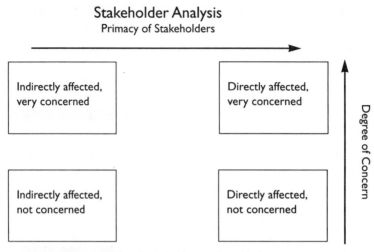

Figure 7.1 *Stakeholder Analysis Matrix*

individual employer to bring about change at a local level is significantly diminished. From air traffic controllers to truckers, there are several instances where aside from making representations to negotiating bodies, the company has little power to effect significant change.

The more barriers there are to effecting change, the more difficult it becomes to implement a principle. If one of your principles is not to employ subcontractors that use child labor, you may find that by applying this principle you cause enormous social upheaval in the community affected. Children not employed in the factory might be left to fend for themselves and become involved in drugs or prostitution. Therefore, simply applying rules and sanctions will not bring about the required change. In this case you have to change social attitudes, create educational facilities for children, and improve working conditions for the adults. It will require more resources to apply this principle than the mere writing of codes of conduct or rules of good governance.

SO HOW DOES THIS PRINCIPLE RANK?

Arriving at whether a principle is important to assuring our reputation is a matter of combining these two characteristics into a hit list of action

0–4 Little Concern Shown	
Clarity of issue	Not represented by clear stakeholder view.
Organizational status	Company perceived as having a limited impact on issue, no calls for action.
Ethical status	Potential contravention of widely accepted local legal or social norms.
4–7 Moderately Concerned	
Stakeholder profile	Of concern to local, national, and international stakeholders.
Clarity of issue	Clear majority stakeholder view, unfocused/indirect public campaign implicating company.
Organizational status	Perceived as having significant influence on issue, calls for long-term action by company.
Ethical status	Potential contravention of widely accepted local, national, and international legal or social norms.
7–10 Highly Concerned	
Stakeholder profile	Of concern to local, national, and international stakeholders.
Clarity of issue	Clear majority stakeholder view, well-organized/concerted public campaign directed at company.
Organizational status	Seen as major influence on issue, consistent calls for action.
Ethical status	Likely contravention of widely accepted local, national, and international lega or social norms.

Figure 7.2   *Stakeholder Rating Guide*

plans and resource-allocating initiatives. We have to decide whether we want to tackle a few principles that are very important to our stakeholders and require substantial resources to solve or we want to take on a more even spread of principles to ensure that we cover all aspects of the framework.

Some companies, like Shell, have decided on the former strategy. In their social reports, Shell executives openly admit that there are some areas in which they have to improve, but there are others where they have been doing quite well. For example, they have been tough on corrupt practices and on meeting environmental concerns and put much effort into achieving these principles. Now they have turned their efforts toward meeting social concerns.

A similar example is that of Denny's restaurants, hit by a class action brought for racial discrimination. Here was a business faced with a crisis arising from a string of allegations of discrimination among its own management and employees, and against its customers, particularly its African-American diners. Denny's had to prioritize business principles that related to these concerns high on its list of important areas to get right if it was to survive another devastating blow from the full force of the law. It had to ensure that all its employees were treated fairly and that all its customers' expectations of being provided the same levels of service and courteousness were met. Assuring these principles was crucial to delivering shareholder value. Without them, Denny's 2000 restaurants would be history.

Or, take California-based ICN Pharmaceuticals, hit by a series of allegations of sexual harassment of female employees by its CEO Milan Panic. The all-male board apparently never considered making the reduction of harassment a key principle for the organization, despite these events taking place for over a decade. Instead, they continually sought to defend the actions of their CEO, settling claims out of court and rewarding their leader handsomely for adding shareholder value by many times more in monetary terms than the claims brought by the women. Will ICN's reputation suffer in the long term? With female employees it certainly will. That's half the potential workforce from which this company has to draw. Will the rising numbers of women in management positions who deal with ICN as customers favor other competitors? Only time will tell.

As we proceed through the evaluation we shall become more aware of some of the resource implications of addressing these principles of corporate behavior.

THE THREE LEVERS OF REPUTATION ASSURANCE

We have borrowed three levers of reputation assurance from the experience of Total Quality management. They are the *approach* adopted, the *deployment* of the principle, and the ways of *monitoring* the success of the initiatives. (See Figure 7.3.)

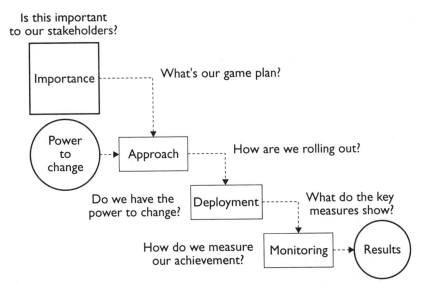

Figure 7.3 *The Assurance Processes*

Approach

To faithfully apply a principle we have to ask ourselves a number of questions about how we hope to approach the successful application of that principle. These are the questions that numerous studies of good and bad practice have taught us. In summary, they are as follows:

  • *Have you conducted a stakeholder analysis that includes the primary and secondary stakeholders and their levels of concern?* The thoroughness of your analysis will reflect how well you have considered stakeholder concerns.

One of the most thorough examples of this I have seen was when Shell consulted with over 200 stakeholder groups during its evaluation of a major multibillion-dollar oil and gas production project in Peru, one that it has decided not to pursue. In order to exploit the reserves of oil and gas, the company would have had to set up facilities deep in the jungle. The risk of environmental disruption to both humans and nonhuman species was great. Shell's consultations with the many varied groups got the company to understand that if it were to exploit these reserves it would have to follow a plan that minimized this disruption and ensured benefits to the community of increased economic activity. Shell's exploration and evaluation activities were carried out with sensitivity. It treated the site like a platform in the North Sea or the Gulf of Mexico. The sea was the jungle and the platform was the exploration site. Helicopters flew in personnel and matériel just as though the operation was conducted at sea, minimizing the disruption to the natural habitat of thousands of species of wildlife and the home of local indigenous people. This raised the cost of exploration, but Shell took the view that preventing a potential negative impact on its reputation would in the long run preserve its return on investment. No longer do responsible companies want to suffer the long-term disruptive and value-destroying effects of litigation, local militia, citizen activism, or consumer boycotts.

To begin to address its problems of acute discrimination, Denny's had to conduct extensive focus groups with its customers and its employees. Denny's had to understand the frustration of minorities in the organization who saw not one of them represented in management, and the anger expressed by customers who when given tables at the back of the restaurant believed that they were being discriminated against. Many of these grievances had gone unnoticed by the company. Denny's signed an agreement with the NAACP (National Association for the Advancement of Colored People) to expand employment and management opportunities for minorities and increase its business with minority-owned suppliers.

• *Have you established policies and procedures with codes of conduct and clear goals of where you want to get to?* Take diversity, the great buzzword. It means different things to different people depending on who is asking the question. To minorities it may mean giving them a fair chance within the organization. To others it might mean accepting diversity of thought and competencies to enrich innovation and continuous improvement. A policy statement would clarify where the company wishes to focus its efforts. Suppose its primary focus is to implement sexual diversity. Goals would be set regarding where the company wants to be in, say, the next five years regarding the mix of male versus female employees at all levels in the organization, or by when it hopes to introduce benefits for gays equal to those enjoyed by heterosexual employees. It also means that your stakeholders begin to have confidence in your expressions of concern and feel that you take the achievement of these principles seriously.

Denny's set clear goals of increasing its share of minorities in management; it also wanted to dramatically reduce the number of calls from customers who felt they were being discriminated against. It established policies and procedures in great detail on how staff should treat customers and how staff should respond to complaints of discrimination. Staff was told to always apologize when a complaint was made, and to assume the customer was always right. Denny's target of generating $1 billion in wages for minorities by the year 2000 was to be achieved by maintaining black employment at 20 percent of the 120,000 workforce, raising black managers from 4 percent to 12 percent, and increasing the number of black franchises from 1 to 55.

To combat sexual discrimination, many organizations have begun to establish codes of behavior. For example, dating between coworkers is permissible, but dating between an employee and a direct supervisor is not. Touching someone in an overtly sexual manner is prohibited and so are lewd jokes in mixed company. The legal obligations of employees and managers have to be clearly spelled out. A manager, for example, is liable for all discrimination carried out by his supervisors. Employees are obliged to raise their complaints with someone in authority.

• *Have you allocated people with responsibility to implement these policies?* Do they have defined roles, reporting relationships, authority to exercise their responsibilities, and prior experience to qualify them for the role? These are just a few of the things we frequently forget to do when we give people the responsibility but omit to give them the authority to exercise their roles. At BP-Amoco, CEO John Browne has assigned reputation management to a main board director who has the role incorporated into his performance contract. The responsible officer, Chris Gibson-Smith, has a network of regional directors who report to him with their sole purpose in the company being to manage

131

the company's reputation within the areas of geography in which they operate. (See Figure 7.4.) These regional directors integrate all the various corporate activities within a region to present a common face to government and community representatives. Chris and his team share a common passion for corporate responsibility. Many of them have campaigned for years within the company to elevate the importance of the issues they now manage.

• *What resources in terms of finance and materials have been committed to implementing the principle?* Implementing some of the principles will go beyond assigning people; funding for education, research, or the setting up of facilities may also be needed. Providing equal opportunity for men and women, for example, might entail setting up crèche facilities for mothers with young children who may have previously had to interrupt their career to stay at home and look after their young offspring. Reducing gas flaring, cutting leakage of oil from pipelines in environmentally sensitive areas, and other related programs cost millions of dollars that have to be allocated. Resources equal commitment.

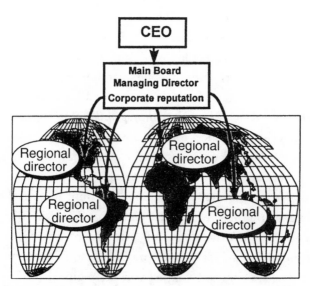

Figure 7.4 *How Authority for Safeguarding Reputation Flows at BP-Amoco*

- *How would you engage in a plan of continuous improvement and innovation to achieve the principle set out?* These would include the management processes you wish to address, the milestones you wish to achieve over a period of time, and how you would benchmark best practices in other organizations. While you begin to implement your program, societal expectations don't stand still; neither do your competitors. You need to continue to find how these expectations keep changing and match them with action. Some companies, for example, have been working hard at minimizing any offense given by their advertising. They have set new goals for lowering complaints from the public. They continue to ensure that the marketing function and their external ad agencies work in accordance with clearer accountability to stakeholder interests.

Deployment

The effective deployment of a principle will require rolling out the policies, procedures, and ideas covered in the approach. But deployment is the bit which we often stumble over. It's easy enough to define an approach. Consultants can do that. Getting the approach bedded down, however, understood and accepted by stakeholders is often the process that gives us the most difficulty. The number of fine policy manuals, elegantly contrived mission statements, and eloquent speeches given by senior executives significantly outweigh the number of well-deployed programs of corporate responsibility.

In the Florida city of Boca Raton recently, lifeguard Beth Faragher claimed that she and several other women were regularly harassed by their male supervisors. She charged that these men regularly asked for sexual favors, would fondle them sexually, and make vulgar references to them. The women complained to a police lieutenant of the city police who responded that the matter was none of his business. In awarding damages to the women, the judge ruled that although Boca Raton claimed to have a nonharassment policy in place, it had not been able to demonstrate an effective means of disseminating and enforcing that policy.

These are the questions which well-deployed programs answer:

• *Is there an effective stakeholder communication program in place to solicit opinions?* Great examples of a well-executed program include clear communication of the principles being adopted so that all stakeholders understand the rationale of a policy and have the opportunity to comment. The stakeholder communication program would consider style, content, accessibility, and frequency. An oil company may use its service station network to distribute leaflets of its environmental policy to its customers who fill up. Call center staff handling hot line inquiries could remind callers of the company's guarantee of product or service quality. Communications should match the stakeholders affected; there's no point in having English-language-only call centers when all your employees are Hispanics who speak only Spanish. Web pages and Internet-based communication may be better suited to customers who are wired than the paper-based media alternatives.

Denny's CEO Jerome J. Richardson featured in 60-second television commercials together with other minority employees pledging to treat all customers "with dignity, respect, and fairness."

• *How do we raise awareness and educate our stakeholders?* Employees may be reminded to say "switch off the lights" before they shut down their computer at night. Ben Cohen of Ben & Jerry's tells the story of how one of the firm's smaller local suppliers—Greystones, who made biscuit brownies—struggled to meet supply quotas. This had begun to cause extra work for the ice cream maker's production staff. The company had a strong policy of keeping its sourcing within the locality of Vermont to contribute to strengthening the immediate economy. In order to get Ben & Jerry's staffers to appreciate why they were being asked to put up with substandard product, they were encouraged to visit the supplier to understand its problems. Likewise, the supplier visited the ice cream maker to appreciate the difficulties its customer was experiencing. This two-way dialogue gradually helped to ease the problem. By contrast, a glossy brochure detailing a company's business principles may languish on coffee tables in reception areas but never get read by the people who need to be informed. One representative once told me that she believed the expensive production style of a social report was inversely proportional to the quality of the company's corporate responsibility program.

For a few of the principles, education programs that involve classroom-based learning may be necessary. Some companies running diversity-based programs today organize sensitivity workshops, getting managers and staff aware of the actions that sometimes offend. Male managers need to be aware that seemingly innocent gestures or comments to female colleagues may be misinterpreted. In Europe, for example, male executives use terms of endearment such as "sweetheart," "luv," or "darling" with impunity when addressing their female peers or subordinates. These women, who tend to be less prepared to take issue with these comments than their U.S. counterparts, may not appreciate the level of familiarity. Cultural and racial diversity needs also to be understood. At the 3Com factory near Chicago the company employs a majority of immigrant workers from dozens of different countries. Indians, for example, don't have conventional words for "please" and "thank you" in their vernacular, and their direct English-language requests such as "do it" and "give" don't fit comfortably with locals. Foremen and supervisors have to be made aware that their staffers are not being rude in their interactions.

When Denny's rolled out their race sensitivity programs, many of their white employees were surprised to learn how certain behaviors might offend minorities. Some might hurriedly put customers at a table that hadn't been cleaned; dispense change to a customer in a way that might make the recipient feel that his or her hands were considered unclean; put a plate of food on the table with an excessive thump: All these behaviors signaled possible disapproval of their clientele. None were very conducive to customer retention. Would you want to go back to a place that was disapproving of the way you looked? Education made Denny's staffers more aware of their actions in their restaurants and in their offices. In 1997, three years after Denny's first claim, the company had another lawsuit brought against it, by a group of Asian-American students who claimed that they had been discriminated against and evicted from a restaurant after complaining that white customers were being seated before them. Staff at this restaurant had not received the mandatory training in nondiscriminatory practices.

Atlantic Richfield, the oil company better known as ARCO, lists phone numbers of state agencies handling discrimination cases. It both gives employees a road map to the courthouse and incentivises management to act appropriately.

• *How do we hope to change behavior by introducing incentives and sanctions, promoting positive role models, and encouraging consistency of behavior?* One of the surest ways of changing behavior in employees is to incorporate the new behaviors into the ways in which their success is measured and for executives the way that performance contracts, the conditions upon which they get remunerated, are organized. Sanctions or clear deterrents can also be effective to dissuade the negative behavior. Fraud and corruption are usually sacking offenses in many organizations and if applied rigorously can be effective at minimizing fraud. Shell has been a company that has rigorously applied sanctions against fraud. In 1976 it withdrew from Italy for 14 years when extortion demands totaling $4.5 million were uncovered. The general manager was dismissed and Shell decided to no longer do business in that country. Shell's "bribe and you're out" policy is well known as a key part of corporate behavior.

Credit Suisse Bank links its compensation for key executives directly with respect for diversity. ICN Pharmaceuticals' alleged problems of sexual harassment were exacerbated by being an organization that promoted such events as "the best legs contest." These events don't encourage respecting people for their intellect and their commercial contribution.

Monitoring

Monitoring how well we are doing in our efforts is as important to an effective program as is the strategy we deploy. Monitoring can involve structured research, technology-led ideas such as call monitoring, incident analysis, or very simple informal opinion surveys. Our attempts at monitoring need to cover these areas:

• *How are stakeholder perceptions of reputation being monitored?* We need to ask stakeholders if they perceive a difference in the way a company behaves with regard to the principles toward which it aspires. If we set out to be known as a great place to work because of the way we provide transferable skills and knowledge to employees, then we should know if our employees notice our efforts. Our firm wins "employer of the year" and "most favorite company" awards where employees state that the quality of learning they receive is one of the reasons they rate us highly.

At Denny's, customers and employees were encouraged to phone a special free telephone hot line prominently displayed in each restaurant to comment on the company's fight against discrimination. Calls were monitored for suggestions and improvements on how the company could continue to improve.

• *How are changes in corporate behavior being monitored?* Changes in behavior shape the way in which a company responds to its principles of corporate responsibility. When our London office decided to embark on Project Seedcorn, it invited employees to submit ideas for community projects for sponsorship by the firm. We wanted staff to feel involved in these programs, which had previously been managed and owned by a small group of senior partners. Over time the applications began to increase, first as a trickle and then later as a flood as more and more people began to take an interest. Community affairs adviser Anne Wolfe also monitors the behavior of senior management toward allowing local community groups to use facilities at the London office for events and educational activities. She says, "A few years ago there would have been questions asked about young men in earrings and strange hair or Rastafarians in woolly hats hanging about in the atrium. Today it's all seen to be part of this firm giving up valuable space for community groups to use in education, fundraising, or welfare projects."

In other examples executives may wish to monitor weekend working or late-night working to see if employees are sacrificing time with their families on a consistent basis. Examples of work behavior by executives are also important. Clara Freeman, the first woman to be on the board of Marks and Spencer, a company where more than 70 percent of employees are women, makes it a point of going home at 6:30 every evening to signal to employees that family life is important to her and to the company.

The rigor with which supervisory staff carry out regular appraisals is another behavior which may need to be monitored if an organization is trying to act fairly toward employee performance. We publish on notice boards the names of managers who have not completed their staff appraisals. It's an effort not only to monitor behavior, but also to publicize inaction.

Reinforcing attitudes toward training is another area. Five years ago we set out to change behavior toward education and training in our practice. Consultants would frequently cancel their place on a course at short notice if client duties dictated. Their decision not to attend would often be supported or even initiated by their manager. Education was becoming sidelined. Peter Davis, the partner in charge at the time, set out to change things. He asked that he be kept informed of all cancellations on a weekly basis and those authorizing the cancellation were required to give their reasons. At the same time he also stated his support for education and said that he would take a dim view of repeat offenders. Attendance improved overnight.

• *Are we achieving our agreed actions?* The actions that are agreed to by an organization need to be acted upon. Key milestones need to be monitored and those who were charged with completing activities called upon to account for their responsibilities. All this is merely professional program management as applied to building a plant or constructing a software system; why shouldn't its application be just as effective in managing reputation?

• *How do we monitor our continuous improvement?* Japanese management practices pioneered continuous improvement in the 1980s, with each business reporting the number of employee suggestions that had been logged and the percentage that had been taken up. The fact that the company was monitoring the process of continuous improvement was in itself a strong signal to employees that their comments and ideas were valued. In the United States, 3M monitors the amount of employee and management time devoted to innovation; 15 percent of employee time can be dedicated to this activity on self-selected projects.

EFFECTIVENESS AND BUSINESS RESULTS

What's most important of all are the results that follow from these management processes. (See Figure 7.5.) One of the early failures of the Baldrige model was that it failed to recognize the business results being produced by companies with great processes. Sometimes we might have a great process, but it can be inappropriate in terms of timing or the nature of business we're in. The business results are the final check to assure ourselves that what we are doing is improving shareholder value, keeping

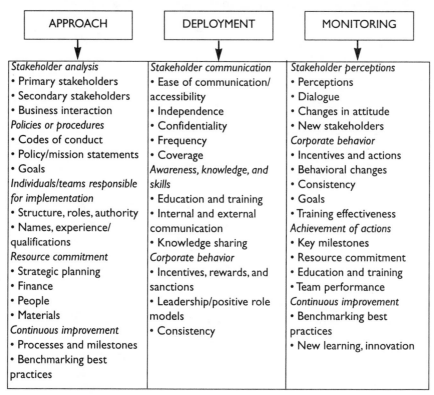

APPROACH	DEPLOYMENT	MONITORING
Stakeholder analysis • Primary stakeholders • Secondary stakeholders • Business interaction *Policies or procedures* • Codes of conduct • Policy/mission statements • Goals *Individuals/teams responsible for implementation* • Structure, roles, authority • Names, experience/qualifications *Resource commitment* • Strategic planning • Finance • People • Materials *Continuous improvement* • Processes and milestones • Benchmarking best practices	*Stakeholder communication* • Ease of communication/accessibility • Independence • Confidentiality • Frequency • Coverage *Awareness, knowledge, and skills* • Education and training • Internal and external communication • Knowledge sharing *Corporate behavior* • Incentives, rewards, and sanctions • Leadership/positive role models • Consistency	*Stakeholder perceptions* • Perceptions • Dialogue • Changes in attitude • New stakeholders *Corporate behavior* • Incentives and actions • Behavioral changes • Consistency • Goals • Training effectiveness *Achievement of actions* • Key milestones • Resource commitment • Education and training • Team performance *Continuous improvement* • Benchmarking best practices • New learning, innovation

Figure 7.5 *The Three Key Reputation Management Processes*

139

customers loyal, motivating employees, building our trust with the community, and attracting the best business partners.

A word of warning, though: We can get measurement fatigue. It's important to measure only what's really important to achieving the key principles in your framework. Decide on those key measures and watch them with eagle eyes. If, for example, you are committed to promoting fair trade, then measure the number of times fines have been levied upon you for infringement, and commit to a reduction. If the occurrence of those fines doesn't fall significantly, then question the effectiveness of your deployment or indeed the approach you have employed.

If you're committed to providing a fair compensation, then check the effectiveness of the key measure: staff retention. (See Figure 7.6.) Of course, along the way you have to measure the salaries you pay in comparison to industry benchmarks, fringe benefits, and the health plan.

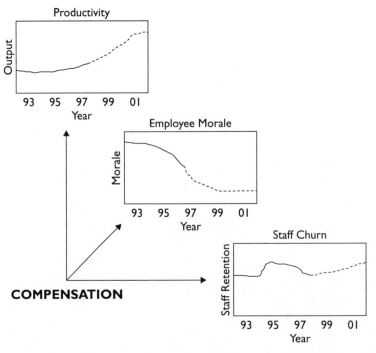

Figure 7.6 *Effectiveness Indicators (Breakdown)—Compensation Principle*

Table 7.1 Self-Evaluation—Compensation Principle

Step	Score (0–10)		Self-Assessed Rating
Approach	8	All policies and procedures agreed. Resources assigned. People appointed.	Excellent
Deployment	7	Policies communicated. Good level of understanding.	Excellent
Monitoring	7	Regular monitoring of pay scales and compensation packages.	Excellent
Effectiveness	3	No clear improvement in morale or in staff retention.	Poor
Overall rating			Moderate

We have now been through the steps you need to take to assess the importance of a principle and to implement a program to address that principle. Evaluation of how you stand today with regard to that principle is carried out by comparing this model to how well you have executed each of the steps just described.

This is where self-evaluation comes in—truthfully scoring yourself for each of the key steps. (See Table 7.1.) In this case, the organization has excellent processes but its poor rating on results drags its overall rating down to moderate. It must find out why. In the next chapter we will look at how to use the model in more detail.

Rosy and Rupert supply some extra tailwind to the flight of "Assurance Framework One."

CHAPTER 8

THE REPUTATION
ROUTE MAP

I've been a private pilot for a number of years and it has become a passion. What I love about flying is the sheer adventure of never finding any set of circumstances identical to any previous journey. On one occasion the weather might favor us with beautiful blue skies and a helpful tailwind; on another, unfriendly cumulus clouds and a strong headwind may make life difficult. One moment we may have uncrowded skies with a friendly air traffic controller; another moment we may encounter a surly ogre of a person harassed by the plethora of airplanes which all want to be at the same place at once. Add to that an infinite set of other variables such as route traveled, the mechanical state of the airplane, and the condition of its avionics, and you have a most interesting admixture of circumstances to keep most private pilots like myself on their toes and provide for endless hours of après-flying talk.

Deciding what you do after you have carried out an assessment of where you stand with regard to the reputation assurance framework is a bit like plotting a course before setting off on your journey. Some principles will have very little opposition from any of your stakeholders and may in fact provide you with a tailwind to help you along. The effort and the resources you require for implementing policies and procedures may be minimal. Other principles may come under opposition from some of your more powerful stakeholder groups.

When Disney decided to extend its equal opportunity policies to gays, Southern Baptists launched a boycott. Some of Disney's customers clearly didn't like the idea of Disney treating all its employees equally. Principles like these are like headwinds that need more energy and resources to overcome. Knowing about them beforehand, though, would help in planning for extra resources and setting expectations: It would be just like my knowing that a 20-knot headwind means I have to carry more fuel on board and extend my expected journey time.

TAILWIND PRINCIPLES

Tailwind principles are those which an organization does well instinctively. They may be part of the culture of its founders or be a reason for its distinctiveness. Ritz Carlton has a reputation for meeting customers' expectations, Hewlett Packard is great at providing its employees with transferable skills, Coca-Cola does a fantastic job at raising the economic power of the citizens of Atlanta where it is based, and GE can provide a competitive return for its shareholders with its eyes closed. Tailwind principles are those which are part of the culture and get us well along our route, making building reputation quicker and easier.

As an illustration of this, look at the superior performance of the companies in Table 8.1. Each company distinguishes itself in its sector, providing total returns to investors above the average for the sector, by being distinctive in one or two stakeholder principles.

Table 8.1 Tailwind Principles and High Performance

Company	Area of Distinction	Shareholder Returns 1997–1998	Shareholder Average Returns (Sector)
Southwest Airlines	Employee development	68%	61% (Airlines)
Dell Computer	Partner cooperation	216%	24% (Computers)
Wal-Mart	Customer guarantees	75%	26% (General merchandise)
BP	Society and environment	23%	14% (Oil and gas)
Campbell Soup	Shareholder governance	47%	43% (Food)

Source: Fortune, Financial Times, 1998

- In 1997–1998 Dell Computer's total returns to investors were a staggering 216 percent, compared with a 24 percent average for its sector. These results cover one year, but it is important to note that performance remained consistent over many years. We see Dell, the personal computer (PC) supplier, being the top performer in its sector by having forged innovative partnerships with its partners and suppliers. Whatever Dell does well is usually due to its partners. Those factors include the responsiveness of its supply chain, the quality of its machines, the development of new technologies, and the battle to stay highly cost-competitive. The company has for many years fostered equitable relationships with its suppliers and believed in high levels of disclosure of its future strategic investment plans.

- Over the same period BP provided total returns to its shareholders of 23 percent compared to the average for its sector of 14 percent. BP-Amoco has also outperformed its sector by separating itself from other energy companies on its social and environmental policy. It was the first to announce that it would be withdrawing from the Global Climate Coalition, an energy-company-led initiative that seeks to oppose reductions in carbon emissions. It engaged in dialogue with the two main activist NGOs—Greenpeace and Friends of the Earth—and responded by announcing that it would begin to build a significant renewable solar energy business as its contribution to reducing its income dependence on carbon-based fuels. Its CEO, John Browne, was the first oil company executive to be asked to address a major Greenpeace conference.

- Wal-Mart, another good performer in the general merchandise sector, provided shareholder returns over the 1997–1998 period of 75 percent against an average for the sector of 26 percent. The company has long distinguished itself by offering price guarantees to its customers. Wal-Mart has worked hard to maintain these guarantees by keeping its operational costs to a minimum and by ensuring that no other competitor can match it on value. It vigorously promotes these values to its customers by showing how its price points compare with other general merchandisers, and it keeps a regular price watch to ensure that its guarantee is never undermined.

145

• Southwest Airlines' returns to investors in 1997–1998 were 68 percent, compared with a sector average of 61 percent. This was significantly ahead of the 1987–1997 period when returns were 29 percent, double the sector average of 14 percent, outstripping its bigger rivals such as American Airlines. Last year Southwest received a *Fortune* magazine award as the favorite place to work by its employees.

• Campbell Soup, the food company, provided returns of 47 percent over the 1997–1998 period against a sector average of 43 percent, and at approximately twice the sector level over 1987–1997. Campbell Soup has prided itself on its good corporate governance in protecting and conserving shareholders' assets. It has one of the most balanced boards of nonexecutive directors and external oversight of any company in its sector.

These companies have taken a view that focusing on a particular set of principles in a stakeholder grouping would give them a tailwind toward high performance. In other words, focusing efforts on one critical stakeholder area can be more effective than trying to distinguish an organization in a number of areas.

In these examples, the choices for differentiation are not surprising. BP went public on the environment at a time when there was rising concern in society about the potential effects of greenhouse gases: El Niño, the Kyoto agreement to limit emissions, record levels of urban air pollution necessitating car bans in cities such as Paris and Mexico City. By taking such a high-profile and responsive stance on the global warming issue, BP found that environmental activists and the media began to distinguish between BP and the other oil companies that were still arguing that there was no link between carbon emissions and the effect on the environment.

Southwest Airlines' focus on employee values came about from the realization that any company in the service sector needed to recruit and retain employees who were highly motivated and incentivised to work for the company: "Happy employees lead to happy customers" was a philosophy ingrained in the company's values. While other airlines put their employees through military-style organization with uniforms, strict hierarchy, and a management-knows-what's-right ideology, Southwest did the opposite. It encouraged empowerment, gave workers a greater share in success, and fostered a more relaxed style of dress and behavior. Customers loved the airline and gave it the highest satisfaction scores. As competitors suffered from strikes and low morale, Southwest continued to prosper.

In the case of Dell Computer, the company was aware that in the fast-commoditizing world of the PC, flexibility and committed suppliers were all-important to success: They had to feel part of the company. While others had chosen partnerships with suppliers which relied on more adversarial relationships, Dell chose a virtual organization which made the suppliers an integral part of it. Suppliers knew they had to get products shipped in record time and at the least cost, and that new lines had to be developed and introduced before competing products established a foothold. While competitors struggled with bloated corporate overheads unaffordable in this highly competitive sector, Dell's virtual organization of close partnerships paid off.

Wal-Mart took the view that in the general merchandise sector, value was the most important thing it had to demonstrate consistently to its customers. Its reputation had to be built on a price guarantee that would take the problem of shopping around away from its customers. To be trusted as the providers of the greatest value, the company had to demonstrate that it had the lowest cost of supply, that its supply chains were low on inventory but responsive to customer needs, and that it could easily beat any other competitor on price.

The Campbell Soup Company established that in the food sector it couldn't get ahead in the usual areas of product differentiation. Most of the leading players already had big brands that had been around for decades. But Campbell did take the view that while most of their competitors' top management ran cozy clubs with relatively little accountability to shareholders, it could establish an organization that offered transparency. It set about recruiting more nonexecutive directors, greater independence on remuneration committees, and by far the greatest oversight of its strategy and future plans. In the past 10 years this approach has paid off as Campbell has outperformed the sector by providing twice the returns for its investors.

CHANGING WINDS

While flying a route, the trained aviator is aware that winds do change from time to time. What was a good tailwind might abate and provide less advantage than before. The wind might change direction and you have to plan your route accordingly. Continually being in touch with your stakeholders is like being a good aviator being in touch with the weather. As stakeholder concerns shift according to economics, demographics, or politics, companies need to tune in to the principles that might give them the advantage others have failed to notice.

One word of caution, though. Just because a principle ceases to become a differentiator doesn't mean you stop doing it. It's more that stakeholders don't need reminding of your conformance to those principles. Most airline passengers don't want to be continually reminded of the safety of the airplane they're flying in; punctuality and service may seem to be more important. But if there is some horrific accident, like ValuJet, they will want that assurance.

Dell has now begun to look at its relationships with customers to see if an increased focus in this area will continue to give it an advantage. By dealing directly with its customers, it has established more information about them than other computer suppliers, which tend to deal through extensive links of intermediaries. Before BP began to distinguish itself through environmental principles it worked on putting together one of the industry's most innovative partnerships with Mobil in Europe. In its early days Southwest Airlines put great emphasis on customers and meeting their expectations, things that it can now do as a matter of course.

HEADWIND PRINCIPLES

Headwind principles are the ones that slow us down. The constant pressure to provide for a sustainable world acts as a drag on a natural resources company like Shell, which needs to increase its hydrocarbon reserves to continue to be a viable business in the eyes of the stock market. Nestlé has to continue to defend its position of selling infant milk substitute in developing countries. Boeing's defense contracting business must be extremely careful about who it supplies arms to, and GE's chemical business needs to work hard to allay fears that its processes might harm the environment.

Denny's has found its headwind principles in implementing a nondiscrimination program. The action by a group of Asian students in 1997 for being discriminated against must have set back the good intentions of the company two years after it began its initiative. But many companies like Denny's need to be aware that they operate in societies where not everybody signs up to a corporate value. Part of the challenge in headwind principles is changing corporate behavior.

Headwind principles require extra thought, extra effort to work with stakeholders to understand their concerns, and extra attention to detail to assure concerned parties that the company respects their feelings. The organization needs to allow for greater investment of resources to take on these headwind principles. It's just like taking on board more fuel to do the same journey. Headwind principles are not a differentiator; they merely limit the company to operating at only acceptable levels. But failure to be aware of or respond to these headwind principles could set a company back. Typical problems could be a costly strike by employees, a consumer boycott leading to falling revenue, refusal to grant approval for a key facility, or poor-quality products from suppliers.

BANANA SKINS

Part of good route planning also requires a pilot to allow for unplanned events—one of your engines cutting out, or the destination airport being fogged in unexpectedly. Having an alternative airport to divert to along the route may save lives. What if for some reason one of your company's oil tankers does run aground and spill its contents into the sea? What if one of your managers is reported to be systematically harassing female employees? What if the government of a country in which you are a major investor does turn ugly and begin persecuting its citizens? What if thousands of bottles of the drinks you produce are found to contain carcinogens?

Good route planning doesn't help avoid banana skins along the way but it helps you to react appropriately when you do slip up.

GETTING STARTED

Getting started is the most difficult thing in any major program. There is always a good reason why you need to put off the event. That's why I find it's best to bring in the reputation assurance framework at the beginning of a planning or budgeting cycle, when most organizations have to begin to submit their plans for meeting next year's sales targets, their requirements for capital expenditure, their need for resources, and so on. Planning for your reputation is no different.

The reputation assurance framework is a good way to begin the process of identifying the people in the organization who may be involved in the evaluation and the preparation of action plans to meet the reputational targets for the coming year. Shareholder principles may best be addressed by the CFO's office, the secretariat, and the general counsel. The customer principles should almost certainly involve people with marketing and sales responsibility, and employees are best handled by human resources personnel.

Partners—and that includes suppliers, alliance, and joint venture partners—usually need to be addressed by a range of people with responsibilities in procurement and operational management. The details will depend on the nature of the partner relationships. I find that some companies have complex multiple joint venture and alliance relationships, while others prefer to do business largely as wholly owned entities. Natural resource companies usually have many joint venture relationships, which often are the source of hidden areas of risk to reputation, since these business relationships tend to be more difficult to control than those businesses which are operated according to principles dictated by the corporate center. Rio Tinto is one of these companies that are frequently under attack in situations where it maintains only an equity interest. Many of these organizations are now looking to the reputation framework as a means of performing the necessary due diligence before agreeing to a commercial contract.

Many of the principles relating to society could come under the responsibility of corporate affairs. But there is also an increasing tendency for business managers to begin to take more of an interest in the way their business conforms to some principles such as raising the economic standards of the community in which they trade. BP's business unit managers have obligations to increase the economic welfare of the citizens of Cuisianna in Colombia, and these are enshrined in their performance contracts.

There are a few specialist and technical areas that deal with the environment and health and safety which will require the relevant people assigned to safeguarding the organization in those areas. It's difficult to be precise about how many people should be involved in carrying out all these evaluations. At its simplest level one or two and at its most complex any number could be involved. Remember that the framework is designed to assist all those dealing with issues and principles to apply a common structured process to the way they work through a program. I find that at any one time most businesses are dealing with only one or two significant headwind principles that require their utmost attention and vigilance. Examples are Denny's working on its fight against discrimination, Nike overcoming concerns on the alleged use of child labor, or Monsanto and Novartis defending health and safety concerns regarding the use of genetically modified foods.

HOW DO YOU APPLY THIS IN LARGE CORPORATIONS?

Very large organizations will be made up of different businesses in various geographic regions. Each business has characteristics which make certain principles more important to it and others less so. Geography is also highly relevant. Operating in the People's Republic of China will require more emphasis on principles related to, say, human rights, while the same business in the United States could take human rights for granted.

As a result, in large corporations we need to segment the organization into a number of clusters or assessment groups. (See Figure 8.1.) Each one of these contains a certain homogeneity of constituency and line of business issues. By accident or design, I find that these clusters correspond quite well to entities that carry a profit and loss accountability.

HOW DO WE STACK UP?

The initial assessments are best done by individuals working through the principles for which they feel they have either direct or indirect responsibility. They would answer the questions we posed earlier as faithfully as they can, indicating where the organization stands today and what actions they might take to improve in the coming year. An honest response to those questions can help them break an industry-wide consensus about how they should operate—a consensus that could keep them from skillfully waltzing with the raptors. Each responsible officer should provide evidence to justify his or her claim about how well a principle is adopted. Evidence can usually be given in the form of documentation such as a policy on a particular procedure or even

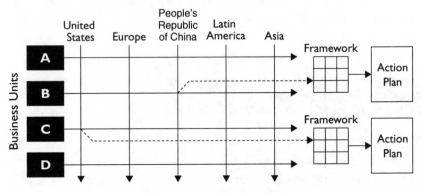

Figure 8.1 *Large Corporate Evaluations*

videotapes of people giving their views. Resources, committees, finance allocated, or people appointed are good examples of tangible evidence.

The managers deemed to have been responsible for each principle then get together for a planning retreat and over a couple of days jointly review their existing position, determine the actions they need to take, and reach a new and more up-to-date consensus on the reputation plan. I have found these retreats to be a valuable forum for members to debate and challenge each other's position on each of the principles. This is the time when any inconsistencies in a self-assessment are ironed out. One person might claim that his or her communication program on, say, sexual harassment has been a great success. Others in the team may challenge that assumption as recipients of that communication. Debate on the importance of key principles and the issues relating to them is vital in resolving the prioritization of resources. Figure 8.2 describes a typical running order for a reputation planning retreat.

- *Why are we doing this?*
    What have we achieved in the past year—rational ethics or just good business? What do the business leaders think? What do our key constituencies say?
- *Prioritizing the principles*
    Which are the most important policies for our organization? How do we justify these priorities based on discussions with constituencies?
- *How do we stand?*
    How do we rate today on each of these principles? Are we being fair in our assessments? Have we got the results and the evidence to back up these claims?
- *Goals going forward*
    What do we want to achieve? What are the target ratings for each of the principles?
- *Actions and resource requirements*
    What do we need to do to achieve these targets? Who takes responsibility? What resources do we need?
- *Do we believe in what we are doing?*
    Standing back, do we believe we will have a better organization if we achieve our goals? How do we help each other? How do we convey this to the people who aren't here?

Figure 8.2 *A Reputation Planning Retreat*

THE ROAD MAP

A road map is a document that communicates both the short- and the long-term direction of the organization. It should embody the key actions to be taken and the goals and targets for each of the critical principles. A road map recognizes that a company is on a journey toward building its reputation and signals to its stakeholders that direction. Limits to resources and the time required for changing culture dictate that some values will require a number of years to implement. That's what we saw with Denny's, where two years after it began its nondiscrimination program, the staff in one restaurant still hadn't received the word or been properly taught and were accused of discriminating against a minority.

The road map should have an indication of the company's current position, the goals it wishes to set for the coming two to three years, and the actions it will take to achieve those goals.

The reputation road map in Figure 8.3 shows how an organization can develop an action plan with targets in each of the stakeholder categories. In this example, the company has assessed itself as poor in the two categories of society and partners. It must therefore allocate resources to improve its reputation in the first year. Some of these initiatives will take longer to implement than others, and it is clear that in, say, the case of developing its human rights policies it has allocated a period of three years to develop, implement, and monitor this program. Conversely, in its shareholder category the actions to increase nonexecutive directors and redesign reporting can be implemented in relatively short order of under a year.

Customers are a relative strength for this company as it assesses itself as excellent and hopes to keep it that way. Those are what we called the tailwind attributes, the ones which help us along and distinguish us from competitors. The company has decided to continue to review its satisfaction monitoring and the awareness of its product guarantees. Continually keeping these stakeholders under review is a good idea. It ensures we

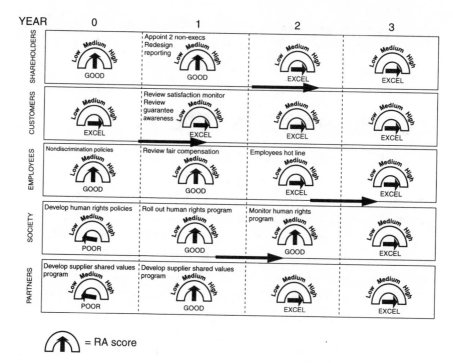

Figure 8.3 *The Reputation Road Map*

don't take anything for granted and will take opportunities to improve our reputation.

REPORTING

In Appendix A we have shown an example of a report on how a company conforms to its principles of reputation. Public reporting is catching on. Partly, it's buoyed by pressure from shareholders. It's also a way of telling stakeholders the various actions a firm is planning to take to improve its reputation. Reports on reputation must not be glossy public relation covers for shoddy practice. They should actually reflect how well you think you're doing, and the areas where you think you could do better. I would strongly advise companies to perform a thorough evaluation of their own reputation performance using the reputation assurance framework. It is important that you know your own weaknesses before you go public.

MECHANISMS FOR ENGAGEMENT

Companies use several channels for engaging their stakeholders—from the formal town hall meeting for employees, which usually means bad news, to the annual general meeting for shareholders, to the consultations with nongovernmental organizations. The style and format of these mechanisms usually depend on the basis of the relationship. With suppliers, for example, a relationship is more formal and contractual with written and legally binding obligations. Engagement therefore is usually more formal, regular, and documented. At the other extreme, there are informal or implied relationships with stakeholders, often people with whom the company has never interacted before, and who need to be engaged in a way that encourages them to contribute in dialogue. A company's greatest challenge is finding ways of determining the degree to which the various constituencies which claim to represent these informal relationships truly reflect broad opinion. Figure 8.4 describes the different channels of engagement.

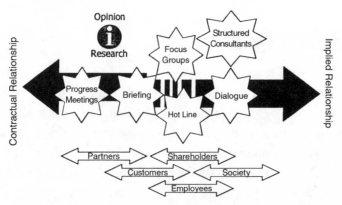

Figure 8.4 *Mechanisms for Engaging with Stakeholders*

Consultations with nongovernmental organizations have become a favorite mechanism for corporate engagement. Some of these consultations may take the form of informal dialogue while others may be more structured, sometimes lasting over a couple of days and involving a number of representative groups. These consultations are a valuable way of identifying concerns and debating the ways in which a company can and should respond.

For example, the representative of an environmental group may challenge an oil company to reconcile its attempts to reduce carbon emissions from flaring and other production activities with the vigor of its exploration activities. How do you justify increasing your capacity to produce hydrocarbons on the one hand, while also trying to decrease the effects of hydrocarbon emissions? The oil company might argue that energy is vital to economic activity and that it sees itself and its 100,000 employees playing a key role in increasing that economic activity. Replacing reserves is a key measure of the market value of an energy company and secures the future of its employees. Consultations help both sides see each other's arguments.

Dialogue on key issues can also help to air concerns and at the same time document each group's stance on an issue. One such dialogue, which has now been published, is the interactions among Amnesty International, Pax Christi, and Shell over the company's role in Nigeria and their reaction to a human rights crisis. Letters, interchanges, and areas of agreement between the parties did much to bring the difficulties to the surface and find potential areas for resolution.

Hot lines using 800 numbers were used initially as consumer complaint channels; their success has now spread to their application for employees. Hot lines give people easy access to the company. They can be independent channels to protect the identity of the user and they have the immense benefit of allowing the company to track the pattern and frequency of calls. This allows an organization to get to the root of problems early by tracking trends in the type and nature of calls. Call measurement can often be useful to assess the effectiveness of the hot line. Could Mitsubishi's problems of sexual harassment have been picked up a lot earlier with an effective independent hot line to track complaints?

The Internet, too, has become an efficient means of collecting comments and feedback from a global community of stakeholders. One can watch issues escalating on the Internet into widespread campaigns as users search for other like-minded individuals who share their concerns. The power of this medium is only just beginning, but no global corporation can ignore its potential as a source of valuable information on what a wide constituency of stakeholders feels about the company. Tracking Internet-based communication could become a full-time occupation for communications managers.

Focus groups have been used in consumer research for some time, and their use continues in engaging the views of stakeholders. Focus groups are valuable in cases where an exploration of issues uncovers greater insights than direct interrogation. Questions such as, "Do you think that this company was wrong to invest in Burma?" may only result in a positive or negative response. It's more valuable to find out why people feel that the decision was wrong. Focus groups are good mechanisms for doing this and for uncovering fears, uncertainties, and vulnerabilities that cannot be expressed through other channels. Many observers of stakeholder engagement see Britain's new Labour party's widespread popularity resulting from the extensive use of focus groups. Their use is recommended for customers, employees, and societal stakeholder groupings.

Opinion polls have been used for mass consumer research and they are helpful in gauging intentions and views which can be encapsulated simply and clearly. They are also useful for capturing a snapshot of these views that need to be tracked over time. Their use in measuring the effectiveness of campaigns or actions taken by the company can give direct feedback on their effectiveness. Their weakness is that the responses can be heavily influenced by what is fashionable at a given time and may not provide a robust basis for significant action. But if that's taken into account, they can be fruitful for customers, employees, and partners. More formal relationships existing between, say, suppliers or shareholders take place in regular intervals, usually as private briefings or contract meetings. They serve the dual purpose of facilitating not only a two-way dialogue but also the building of trusting relationships.

These are only guides as to how one could engage with stakeholders. As communication experts have found, companies that engage in these dialogues will find they can be a constant source of innovation.

In 1992 Procter & Gamble's management ranks were a male bastion. Here was a company led by men that sold leading brands of feminine personal products from sanitary napkins to beauty products. It was men who decided brand strategies for products such as diapers and detergents bought by homemakers, nearly all of whom were women. These men were doing a good job; P&G had brand leadership in many markets, but company CEO John Pepper did wonder if they could do better with more women at the top who had more firsthand experience of using some of these products.

But it was another reason which completely convinced Pepper and his team that they had to correct this gender imbalance. They discovered that they had a deleterious talent exodus. P&G had a human resources tracking system to monitor the performance of its employees and to help identify star performers early on in their careers. An analysis showed that of every three of their star performers who left the company, two of them were women. The company could not afford this exodus of talent in the long term. Something had to be done to arrest this flow.

Put simply, P&G was recruiting great people. It was funneling resources to help them deliver their potential to a point, and then for some reason they upped and left. Now, there was probably a perfectly simple reason for this which P&G could do very little about: These were women who reached that time of life when they wanted to start a family and wanted to pursue their future as homemakers rather than business builders. But further analysis proved this not to be so, since 95 percent of the women leaving were going on to other jobs, some of them with even higher levels of stress and effort involved. There must be another reason.

To tackle the problem, P&G set about using something the company was very good at—marketing. Lesson 1.01 in marketing is "understand the customer." So P&G set up the "advancement of women task force" and began to interview women who had left the firm, women who were considered valuable to the future of the company. And some interesting facts began to emerge.

To begin with, many of the women being interviewed were hearing for the first time that they were considered valuable to the future of the company. Nobody had told them before. But perhaps most importantly they told the researchers that they felt put down by men, trampled over. And the main cause was that the female consensus-building style didn't fit well in the traditional P&G command-and-control model. The men made decisions fast, had a more aggressive style, liked turning up the heat to make people feel uncomfortable, didn't accept mistakes quite so readily, and ignored difficult unspoken issues.

Here was the answer to the female talent drain. The huge male presence stifled women. To correct the imbalance, the task force decided to employ the technique of setting market share targets. They wanted to achieve a market share of at least 40 percent women in management, up from the 5 percent levels in 1993.

Meaningful communication is a key part of a marketers' box of tricks, and the task force chose an innovative way of communicating in a program called Mentor Up. This was a reverse form of mentoring as it encouraged women to discuss the program with their male bosses in an effort to encourage the bosses to think about women's issues affecting the company's future. They were relying on the most powerful form of marketing communications known to brand managers—word of mouth.

Now the exodus has stopped; women make up about 30 percent of general managers, and P&G's executive committee now has its first woman member. The company has shown that marketing techniques of engaging consumers used to sell soap can also be used to address a severe gender imbalance.

INDEPENDENT VERIFICATION

I have previously emphasized the importance of self-assessment, and how a company needs to begin by truthfully examining its position with regard to the key reputation principles. The reasons for this, we argued, were that an organization needed to feel that self-assessment was part of good management practice. The better you did it, the better run your company would be. But this isn't enough to satisfy many activist groups who are still deeply suspicious of business. That's quite understandable given some of the gross abuses of the environment, the exploitation of employees, the abandonment of customers, and the mass fraud of investors' capital. As a result, many organizations will be faced by calls to "prove to me that you are reputable."

More specifically, these calls for verification will be based around key issues such as child labor. There is no point in companies such as Nike, Gap, and Adidas telling activists that they have just decided that self-assessment is the answer to their alleged use of children by subcontractors. Activists and NGOs want proof, and the only proof they are prepared to accept is a thorough verification process, carried out by an independent third party.

There are two highly contentious phrases in that last sentence, and I do not want to diminish their importance. Firstly, the concept of a "thorough" verification process is one that is open to endless debate. In some cases, though, standards are emerging that most activists would deem to be acceptable for their cause. One example is the SA8000 standard we referred to earlier. Certification by the Forestry Stewardship Council is another standard, this time for sustainably managed timber, that is finding widespread acceptance. The Coalition for Environmentally Responsible Policies (CERES) has also developed principles aimed at environmental protection. This is an area where you need to work with other companies in your industry and establish which standard appears to be acceptable. You don't want to take on the full cost or the effort of developing your own. Customized standards can be expensive to verify. It's much better when verifiers can visit a factory or site only once on behalf of a number of companies, using the same standard, and then share the cost out among the companies involved. The United Kingdom–based Ethical Trading Initiative is an alliance of the major supermarkets and retailers, NGOs and trade unions, committed to identifying and promoting good practice in the implementation of codes of labor practice.

Standards for specific issues or principles are being developed all the time. A good stakeholder consultation process will soon bring you to an answer as to which standard would be best to adopt. Clearly the choice will depend on its acceptability to your company as well as to the primary stakeholders and activists. When Andrew Young carried out his verification for Nike, NGOs objected to his lack of a thoroughness in approach. So standards can be important.

The second area of contention is the choice of the "independent" verifier. This is a difficult area, perhaps more difficult than your choice of standard. Independent verifiers cannot have any ax to grind on the principles or issues involved. They must be good interpreters of the standard and have a good nose for finding out the truth. That rules out many activist groups and NGOs, since they have far too much invested in the issues to offer real objectivity. The Council for Economic Priorities, for example, which developed the SA8000 standard, does not offer verification. It is pleased, however, to put you in touch with agencies that will carry out verification to the standard. So, beware of individuals or nonprofit organizations that offer verification services. Check their independent credentials and check their suitability to your stakeholders. These are difficult areas, but then we didn't say waltzing with those raptors was easy.

THE LEARNING ORGANIZATION

We have of late been finding out how great organizations learn to offer outstanding service, recruit the best employees, and deliver superior results.

Companies that have been around for decades have adopted a culture for doing these things well by getting their values from founders, from preceding generations of employees, or from an entrepreneurial leader. We see this in Richard Branson, the founder of Virgin, a British group involved with airlines and financial services, to name just two of their many diverse activities. Branson phones customers personally to apologize for getting them late to their destination, distributes prophylactics to help stop the spread of AIDS, and has even launched a crusade to keep the streets clean. Many believe that Virgin's reputation is based on Branson and his various high-profile activities.

But what happens when Branson goes? What happens if some of the allegations of his sexually harassing female employees are found to be true? Where does Virgin go then?

Reputation assurance is a framework that allows companies to learn how to behave and act in accordance with the principles of reputation. It's for those organizations that don't have the advantage of having had generations behind them which inculcated a culture of trust. It allows organizations to learn how to conform to all those principles and learn to do them well, together.

I'm a terrible speller. Before the days of Microsoft's wonderful spelling checkers, I'd ask out loud around my office area if anyone knew how to spell a certain word, or if, say, "bizarre" had an "e" at the end. Sometimes no one could help, but usually there would be at least one or two people who would confirm that, yes, it did have an "e" or, yes, they had a dictionary and could look it up. Even the most difficult words were not beyond the ken of Ethel, the wonder speller.

Companies are like that when it comes to implementing reputation principles. There is always a business or a small group of people like Ethel who have been operating some of the principles in ingenious ways. Everyone could learn from them. A retail unit in New Brunswick may have found out how to work together with the community to preserve the livelihoods of local shopkeepers. A manufacturing unit in Chicago may have worked out a way to get employees from diverse backgrounds to work as a high-performing team. A chemical factory in Houston may have a unique solution to recycling exothermic energy emissions. More often than not, however, this knowledge is kept hidden for years without anyone else in the organization finding out. Wouldn't it help if these good ideas could be spread more effectively?

The reputation assurance framework is a good device for getting an organization to learn how its different constituent parts approach, deploy, and monitor the principles. Organizational learning takes place when one part of the organization can compare itself with another, as when a distributor in New York can compare itself with a similar unit in Los Angeles. How does it compare on employee policies? How does it compare on meeting employee guarantees?

The framework allows you to make these comparisons at a glance. But it also does more, for it allows you to look at *how* the best examples succeed. For example, your New York distributor might have worked out a good way of communicating with its employees via an intranet, and used discussion groups as a means of picking up on key issues as they emerge. Perhaps employees were concerned about the inflexibility of working times, and felt that other employers were offering their employees greater latitude in start and finish times. This could have been picked up and incorporated into new policies so that employees today could work flexible shifts. Other distributors could also consider using such intranet-based discussion groups, and benefiting from better staff retention and morale.

By using a common framework, the whole organization can compare its diverse operations more readily. Learning readily happens when there is such close comparability, and other branches of the firm can see in detail how principles are implemented. Encouraging people to share their knowledge is easy. People are instinctively proud of what they do. They want to talk about their experiences, especially if there is some peer group, or even better, some company-wide recognition of their innovation or hard work.

And why stop at confining learning to within your organization? It's possible to use the same framework to compare yourself with other organizations within your own industry. If you are concerned about anticompetitive behavior, then you can go outside the industry. Find partners that want to learn together, and agree to use the reputation assurance framework as a basis.

It's a bit like benchmarking, only now you have a common basis to compare the way you go about addressing the principles. Benchmarking, in my experience, burns up a lot of time by frequently making comparisons which have no value to your business, simply because there isn't this common basis to make effective comparisons. Learning through common frameworks is a lot more useful.

"This approach can lead to a sudden loss of support in the market."

THAT COULDN'T
HAPPEN HERE

In earlier chapters, we've seen a number of examples of great companies stumbling on reputational issues, the raptors attacking ferociously at every instant. How could reputation assurance help prevent some of these instances of organizational maiming? Let's review our list of lessons learned and see how we can avoid them.

WHO'S IN CHARGE AROUND HERE?

In a number of cases we saw that various officers in the company would join together to try to cover up misdemeanors. Reputation was an afterthought, and ego and face-saving got in the way. I suggested that although reputation was a responsibility of all individuals, there still needed to be one individual with senior executive powers, responsible to the board for corporate reputation. The chief financial officer is responsible for ensuring finances are in order; the vice president for marketing ensures that the brand is maintained; but who's looking after the reputation of the company?

It's true that the CEO has the eventual reputation responsibility, but that's together with a million other things. A reputation officer would have a full-time occupation, if an organization managed its principles in the way that we have discussed in this book. A chief reputation officer would have the following responsibilities:

- To agree to the priorities of the reputational principles annually.

- To commission research and to manage the stakeholder consultation dialogue.

- To ensure that appropriate communications and education with all stakeholders are conducted on aspects of reputation.

- To be responsible for ensuring that all parts of the company carry out reputation assurance self-assessment checks as part of an annual planning cycle, and that appropriate actions and plans are prepared to protect vulnerable areas.

- To engage suitable external verifiers who can validate the extent to which self-assessment matches reality.

- To prepare external reports on reputational values.

- To be the person who decides how to deal with a major reputational crisis.

Many companies already have ethics officers, but in many organizations these positions are more related to compliance with the law than the advancement or protection of a wider interpretation of reputation. These positions are also low in the decision-making hierarchy of companies, which means that these officers have very little in the way of influencing or operational powers.

For the chief reputation officer to have teeth, the position should be a senior board-level appointment. The CRO should have a hand in evaluating all major investment decisions to enter new markets, developing new mainline products, and arguing for resources to battle against those headwind principles we discussed in Chapter 8. It helps if the CRO is a seasoned operations manager who has proven credentials in running a business and commands respect among peers.

INDEPENDENT AUDITING

An independent auditor with no ax to grind, no face to save, no ego to massage, can help diffuse problems before they become bigger or the subject of a major cover-up. Suppliers complaining of coercion, employees claiming harassment, and customers concerned with deception are all areas where independent checks help. It's human nature to try to cover up your mistakes. This reflex gets really dangerous, though, when the reputation of an organization is at stake.

There are two levels of independent auditing. The first of these is an *internal* auditor who has been given clear autonomy to act independently and, hopefully, report directly to the chief reputational officer. Internal auditors have carried out an important role for years in organizations, but have been primarily responsible for financially related auditing. In some organizations that's one of the best jobs to have and in others the worst. The reputation assurance framework offers internal auditors the opportunity to redefine their responsibilities and to address an emerging and important need. The independent auditors would be the first line of assurance that the principles are being applied consistently across the firm.

The second line of assurance comes from an *external* auditor. The job of an external auditor is made much easier with a good internal auditing capability. The external auditor would be an experienced individual who sees how reputational principles are being applied in other organizations. An external auditor can make comparisons between your company and others more easily. Above all, the auditor has a reputation for independence and impartiality to protect.

Firms like mine have begun to be asked by companies to use their auditing competence to provide the backup, external audit of reputation. It is my belief that the most effective way for external auditors to operate is to audit the extent to which management and employees have adopted principles of reputation. The framework described in this book is our first attempt to define an auditable process for reputation assurance. I am sure it will go through a number of iterations before we have a generally accepted standard. The use of a framework based on quality management principles was intended to facilitate the adoption of this technique by a wide cross section of companies that have already implemented quality management techniques.

VALUES TO ACTIONS

Statements of corporate values run the risk of going the way that mission statements went over the past decade. No one knows them, employees are highly skeptical, and anyway, they don't quite see how it all fits in with the everyday job of getting on in the company. The reputation assurance framework we described is designed to put action and meaning behind value statements. It's not enough having well-articulated principles. The framework asks you to think about policy or procedures to support a principle, to communicate them, to educate people as to what it all means, and to monitor corporate behavior. Do all those well, and you're on the road to a great reputation.

As one example, with clear goals on equal opportunities we've become more aware that we have a real shortage of women partners. We now look more closely at our new admission candidates for promising women who have had a good record with the firm. More people are asking that if there is a man and a woman of equal ability and we have only one position that we take the woman. Goals and targets make those value statements more meaningful.

The framework is also part of a regular planning process with specific actions encouraged to address the approach and deployment of principles. These actions are communicated to stakeholders so that everyone knows the organization's intention to implement principles and it doesn't turn into a well-kept secret. The actions will hopefully begin to manifest themselves in policies and procedures. Eventually, we hope, they will be reflected in improved reputation assessment scores.

We need to do more than merely follow targets and actions, however. As Texaco showed, we also have to change behavior and attitudes. We do this through education but also by showing positive examples. Our CEO, Jim Schiro, and his chief operating officer, Woody Brittain, regularly work at a soup kitchen in New York. It gives the rest of the organization an important signal that corporate responsibility extends all the way up.

DO THE RIGHT THING

We saw that simply responding to regulation didn't advance the reputation of a company. Regulation creates a level playing field where either side has an equal chance of winning. But competition is about choosing your own playing field where the slope is in your favor. To choose your own field you have to be first in the game. Going beyond regulation and doing what you think is right for your stakeholders helps you create your own playing field. While others are waiting to respond to regulatory recommendations on corporate governance or other matters, you are streaming ahead with your own standards, which exceed federal recommended guidelines. You are leading the way.

Going beyond regulation is also important for a global organization. If you trade around the world, you will inevitably find yourself in countries where regulation is less developed than back home. But there is a growing expectation that companies need to implement common values wherever they trade in the world. There is an acceptance of an international code for reputation. Partly it's buoyed by world trade, and partly by rapid communication. Why should Chinese employees, for example, be granted fewer human rights than, say, their European counterparts, simply because the government of the People's Republic doesn't insist on those rights?

The reputation assurance framework helps you do the right thing for your stakeholders through the generic principles. Treating all employees equally applies anywhere in the world. You don't have to wait for regulation in that country to observe that principle. Respect intellectual property wherever you are, even if the local government secretly encourages traders to break international law.

PREVENTION RATHER THAN CURE

We saw a number of examples where the investment in management time, let alone the financial penalties to cure a reputational problem, could be highly damaging to a company. Throw in the harsh treatment meted out by the Federal Sentencing Guidelines, and a reputation crisis, arising from a class action on harassment or from infringing the intellectual property of suppliers, could begin to hurt the company for years.

Reputation assurance is that apple a day that can help you avoid catching a cold, or, worse, the deadly influenza of a Chapter 11 bankruptcy. Implementing policies and procedures in accord with the framework would minimize the occurrence of a major crisis. When a product is reported to be causing harmful side effects, frontline teams know that the cases have to be quickly and rigorously followed up on. You have to assume that customers are telling the truth and see how their health can be fixed quickly. It's better to fix the problem early, before that cold spreads and you contract something fatal.

Stakeholder dialogue is also a good way of getting to problems and concerns before you see them first on CNN. Beginning to have consultations as a regular management process across the company network is like starting to waltz with the raptors that had previously attacked your business. While you're waltzing, you're keeping their attention. With the extensive efforts of Shell to engage their stakeholders and the acknowledgment of their case that they have won from previously angry NGOs, a crisis now would be highly unlikely. If it did occur, it could be dealt with quickly through this new relationship.

AVOIDING COVER-UPS

Reputation assurance is an open process. To begin with, you have publicized your action plans, as well as the principles to which they relate. Your priorities for action have been agreed upon. There are independent checks. You annually publish how well you are doing with regard to your principles. Someone's going to have to be very devious or foolish to want to cover up any major breach of those principles.

Cover-ups escalate quickly once a company executive says publicly, "It wasn't the company's fault." A whole denial machine has to go into action to defend that statement, which if untrue is going to be damaging at some point in the future.

ONE SIZE DOESN'T FIT ALL

Respecting local laws and culture is important in order to implement a good reputation. You can't afford to ram your corporate values down people's throats. Take into consideration values from different groups' own visions of what's right and wrong. Consultation and dialogue with stakeholders help to identify those areas where you need to adapt to local conditions while keeping to your corporate principles.

Threatening to apply boycotts to countries whose companies employ children was damaging to some 30,000 children in Bangladesh involved in the production of clothes. This was a desperately poor country where everybody worked if they could, regardless of age. Some companies working with local NGOs and activist groups had begun to evolve solutions that included the children in a working routine but also provided them with access to educational facilities—all this helping to regenerate an economy where the average wage is less than a dollar a day.

We saw how keeping men's and women's living accommodations separated by intimidating prison-like barbed wire, and a strict "in by six" routine were necessary to assure society that men and women were not engaged in relationships outside marriage. It's something Western societies are far less concerned about but was of the highest importance there.

Reputational assurance is not about compromising your principles, but rather adapting the way they are implemented.

WHO'RE YOU WALTZING WITH?

McDonald's got into real trouble in Cleveland by negotiating with the wrong people to find black franchisees. Equally, the unions you are dealing with might not truly represent the interests of your employees. In some countries, they may be just as corrupt as the police force and the judiciary. Add to that cranky activists or Internet activists who claw away at your reputation, and you have a wide range of constituents to engage. But the quicker you get waltzing, the quicker you're going to find out who to avoid.

John Elkington, author of the fine book *Cannibals with Forks*, describes nonprofits and NGOs in eloquent marine-life terminology. "Killer whales" are highly intelligent organizations that can adapt quickly and use coercive fear as their weapon. They are unpredictable, like operating in deep water, and can operate over large distances. Although "dolphins," on the other hand, are equally creative and adaptive, they can help fend off sharks, and are definitely the sort you want to cultivate. "Sharks" are of low intelligence, attack undiscriminating targets, and attack in packs, while "sea lions" are friendly, enjoy a spectacle, play in safe waters, and get eaten occasionally by the sharks or killer whales.

There are many reputable NGOs that will advise you on the relationships you should be cultivating (we list some of them in Appendix B). Their mission statements describe who they are, and what they stand for. How many do you know? How many know your organization, and are planning their next attack?

CHANGING CORPORATE BEHAVIOR

Reputation assurance has all the components of a change management program with foundations in quality management. The best reputation programs are those which reflect genuine corporate behavior by employees and managers. Corporate behavior is part of the reputation assurance framework. Both incentives and sanctions are an important blend of a carrot-and-stick approach to bring about change: For example, anyone involved in fraud walks, no matter how big a superstar they are; regional managers who make a positive contribution by improving the local economy in which they operate, however, get rewarded with a chairman's bonus. Role models are also encouraged to show employees that principles are not just words.

In many cases companies need to overhaul their measurement and incentivization packages. The salesperson needs more than mere revenue targets, the purchasing manager needs to be rewarded by life-cycle costs, and the claims department of an insurance company needs to be measured by the level to which claims are settled.

The great British pensions misselling bonanza, which cost the industry $18 billion, came about because salespeople were targeted with selling as many pensions as they could, without due regard for the integrity of their product. They didn't care that the unfortunate middle-aged woman who purchased a policy was giving up something very valuable for something which wasn't. They didn't have the time or they just didn't care about only selling policies to people where it would genuinely benefit their circumstances.

If a company is serious about encouraging employees to enjoy time with their families, then managers need to lead by example. I know successful executives who make a virtue of describing how they get home for their children's bedtime story, or attend their kids' annual school play.

REPUTABILITY OF NEW PRODUCTS

New products must not just pass technical checks. They should also pass the reputability test, with the reputation assurance framework as its test bed. Is this product going to meet customers' expectations? Is your advertising and communications a faithful representation of what you are selling? Can you realistically fulfill the written or implied guarantees that go with the product or service? And perhaps the biggest failing of them all: Does the company have a good channel of communication to monitor mass consumer acceptance and take-up?

If those gas tanks keep exploding on the new automobiles you introduced, you need to act without delay. If customers are leaving because you took away a product they always loved and gave them something new which they don't like, bring the old one back quickly. These are some of the common failures of new products and services that the reputability check will help minimize.

SURF RAPTORS

Organizations can't ignore the Internet. It's a powerful means of communication with stakeholders, as well as a means by which stakeholders communicate with each other. Good corporate web pages with all the information you need to inform and to encourage comment are de rigueur. The sloppiness of a corporate web page reflects a company that is out of touch and that does not want to reach out and communicate with its stakeholders.

Also, equally important, is Internet surfing, to watch out for people who have views about you and who are using the cheapest public broadcast system of them all to vent their anger about you, who want to tell the world's other 200 million Internet users to watch out for you, and who might be gradually building a campaign to bring you down. Surfing is much cheaper and quicker than scanning press or media comment.

THE TRUST BUSINESS

Reputation assurance helps build trust with stakeholders. The principles are your corporate dashboard of the things you need to constantly monitor to ensure that trust. Sometimes your eyes will be glued to a few principles on that dashboard, just as a pilot may watch the fuel gauges like a hawk at the end of a long flight when running to the end of the plane's endurance. Other times, you may scan all of them, to ensure that all's well and that no trouble spots are developing. Stakeholders will also want to know how you fulfill those principles, in different levels of detail. All this is about building trust in your business.

Once trust is broken, it's hard to repair.

PARTNERS AND SUPPLIERS

When partnering or outsourcing some of your operations you are passing on trust to the companies you do business with. The reputation principles should be those which your partners sign on to. This means that the assurance techniques should also be part of the relationship you have with these organizations. Your success in maintaining your reputation is highly dependent on your suppliers maintaining theirs.

The reputation assurance framework should be included in discussions with partners and they could also be used as a means of selecting the ones you want to work with. Ask key suppliers to tell you how they respond to the principles in their organization. Do they have a reputation report? What do their action plans look like?

THE PROGRAM'S DO'S AND DON'TS

Here are some of the things that readers can take away for their own firms.

Do's

• *Do be honest and open about your communications with stakeholders.* Sustainable reputations are not about building up a perception which you cannot match with reality, so don't make statements you haven't validated previously and you may not be able to deliver on. No one likes to find surprises one didn't know about, so say where you think you could do better and by all means promote all the good things you do. Be like Levi Strauss, which admits that China uses forced labor and doesn't have a great labor record but that the decision to invest in that country will give particular emphasis to bringing change. Be like the

United Kingdom's high-performing Co-operative Bank, which admits that its equal opportunity policy isn't producing more women in management and that it hopes to address the issue with a number of actions. Be like BP, which asks that stakeholders accept that it is primarily a hydrocarbon-based energy company which needs to explore and increase its reserves but at the same time it will do all it can to operate in the most environmentally sustainable way it can.

• *Do talk to your stakeholders.* Know who they are, involve them, find out what their concerns are, and allow yourself to be moved. They say that listening is the best form of communication. Use focus groups, hot lines, and research-based surveys. Listen to the opinion formers as well as the followers. Watch behavior; actions do speak louder than words. Be like PepsiCo, which withdrew from Burma after it listened to college students who disapproved of their investments in that country. Be like The Gap, which listened and then responded with ethical sourcing programs.

• *Do sell the idea throughout the organization.* Tell your managers and your employees why reputation management is important and why it is necessary for everybody to work together on such a program. It's something you do rather than have done to you. Be like Ritz Carlton, the company that encourages its employees to deliver corporate promises and guarantees of great service to the highest standards. Be like Southwest Airlines, which makes its employees proud to work for a company with the highest reputation in the industry.

• *Do link good reputation processes to business results.* Show how your fair compensation schemes are producing improved productivity, higher morale, and less employee churn. Be like Ernst & Young, which reduced staff attrition by promoting women-friendly employment policies. Be like Ben & Jerry's and show how your local sourcing initiatives have helped raise the purchasing power of the local community and helped take market share from competitors that don't.

• *Do base reputation management on action.* Make it part of a regular planning process. Make it bottom up from the ideas and suggestions of employees and their supervisors to senior management. Make it like financial planning or sales targeting. Make it business as usual. Be like the Body Shop, which plans to implement new principles every year, tell its stakeholders about them, and allow the company to be audited.

• *Do have evidence ready if you're attacked.* Show evidence of action plans, resources committed—all the things that go into your reputation report. Be ready to defend your position with concrete results and evidence. Meet emotion and frustration with facts.

If BP or Monsanto are criticized on environmental grounds, they can honestly show that they've been monitoring pollution levels, talking with the chief nonprofits concerned, and giving sufficient training to the operating staff who are responsible for controlling pollution. Any charges of overpollution are more likely to be rebutted that way: either by being proven erroneous or by being accepted as just a onetime fault.

• *Do measure as much as you can.* Be like DuPont, which doesn't aim for workforce diversity alone, but regularly measures how well it's being achieved. That way shortcomings are registered—and fixed—in advance of complaints. Or be like BMW, which is expert in doing thorough environmental audits and measuring the impact of each production stage.

• *Do focus on the key items for your stakeholders.* If they're concerned about labeling on food, find out which aspects; the list can be quite long. Keep finding out, because their concerns change frequently.

So much for samples from the positive side—showing what's good to do. There are also notable failures that illuminate what to avoid:

• *Don't try to mask your failings with a public relations exercise.* Your audience is likely to be extremely savvy, and cynical, and will see through it. Don't use glossy brochures that extol the virtues of all the good things you do without providing balance with all the areas you could be doing better. Use some humility in your corporate communication and cut down on the traditional smug arrogance associated with PR.

• *Don't shut out unwanted or unreasonable views.* We saw that before deciding how to dispose of its huge Brent Spar oil-storage rig, Shell checked that it was observing all suitable government regulations. But the company didn't pay attention to environmental activists who were seemingly against any disposal method. Their attitude seemed illogical, but it's what could have given early warning of an important public sentiment and helped Shell avoid the bad publicity and boycotts that arose when it went ahead with its disposal scheme. Be sensitive to anger and frustration being vented against your company, and try to find out the root cause of that anger and frustration. You may find it isn't your company that is causing it but rather the people you associate with.

• *Don't promote your moral superiority.* Doing that laid the Body Shop open to attack for having the slightest falling off from perfect standards. When a journalist charged that one of its suppliers was using animal tests on products, the story was avidly taken up by the press. A company that had been more modest about its goals wouldn't have been such a glaring target. Better to say that your position is purely stakeholder-driven and that you are going to do all in your power to address stakeholder concerns.

• *Don't make the measurements you're imposing too complex.* Rather, show that the measurements can encourage ways of working better. Be like the chemical companies that introduce pollution control measures from the start of the planning cycle, so that production processes are more efficient than they would be otherwise. Too much measurement clouds your judgment as to why you're doing things in the first place. Don't be a slave to the numbers. Look at process as well.

• *And above all, don't have policy imposed solely from the top down.* As we see throughout the book, exhortation by the CEO alone has very little effect. Only when the reasons for the change are widely understood—and well-geared measurements are in place throughout the firm—will the necessary changes take place.

"I only asked a perfectly innocent question on the corporation's handguns policy."

QUESTIONS

AND ANSWERS

I n this final chapter I'll attempt to answer all the questions I usually get asked about reputation assurance.

Q. *Stakeholder theory has been around for years. What is different about your approach that would make it work better?*

A. Stakeholder theory is definitely not new thinking, but the thought that old ideas are not good ideas is fallacious. We used stakeholders as a framework to group together the wide range of reputation principles. Many of the companies we were working with, or which had good programs of their own, were familiar with the idea of stakeholders. I also like the idea that there are a number of different constituencies that have a stake in an enterprise. Some, like employees, have to work for that stake, and others, such as the community, have it handed down to them by previous generations.

Concentrating on stakeholders also seemed a good way of breaking down the responsibility for dialogue within the corporation. The CFO, or someone in that team, had the job of regularly keeping in touch with shareholders. Marketing and sales had the responsibility of keeping the lines of communication open with customers. External and public affairs officers were there to hear from society and government. Human resources managers had to keep their ears to the ground to listen for employee concerns, and purchasing had a similar role for suppliers.

Our categorizations of the five stakeholder groups are very broad. Most companies will need to break them down further, to suit their needs and the issues which are prominent in their business.

Q. *You haven't mentioned ethics much. Isn't this all about ethics?*

A. I guess it all depends how you wish to look at things. Suppose you were a Quaker in the 19th century, and you believed that slavery was morally repugnant, and that you would do all you could to oppose it and obliterate the practice. On the other hand imagine you were William Wilberforce, immersed in the day-to-day operations of commerce and business, and believing that slavery was not in the best interests of society or in the long-term interests of business. Both points of view got you to the same answer: We need to abolish it.

I see business ethics as the Quakers' way of looking at values and principles. Reputation assurance is more like the Wilberforce approach, of looking at the long-term sustainability of a business. Both are compatible, but it's looking at the issue through different eyes.

I can be a deeply religious person and believe that it is wrong to kill people or to steal from them, yet equally I can come to the same conclusion as an agnostic. Reputation assurance is agnostic on ethics, but comes to many of the same conclusions.

There is another point. Unfortunately, in the United States ethics has become closely associated with legislation. In Europe, any government minister who seems to put his head above the parapet and claim to be executing ethical policies is instantly mauled by the raptors who think otherwise. Many ethics officers spend most of their time digging their corporations out of minefields of malpractice. Few can say they have the time for selling the strategic advantage of ethical business to senior management.

Reputation assurance is an attempt to take the agnostics' view and encourage senior managers to take an emerging code of good business principles seriously. This is because it leads to a better deal for all stakeholders and ultimately to shareholders and senior management themselves.

Q. *How can you recommend companies to take on such a program without a financial justification? Is there a clear one?*

A. There are many studies that claim a direct correlation between companies which have invested in social and environmental responsibility programs, and superior economic performance. I have found many of these studies to be less than rigorous in their approach, and believe that most skeptics could drive a truck through the research.

Why is this? Here is where you need to apply common sense, a little bit of observation, and an eye to the future. Common sense tells you that good businesses rely on quality processes and attention to detail. Why should the reputational principles be any different? Good businesses—those referred to as blue-chip companies—consistently deliver results with a minimum of risk. They do this by keeping in touch with what's happening in both their inside and outside worlds. Reputation assurance is about keeping in touch with a wider world, because we believe the set of relevant influences is broadening all the time.

A little observation tells you that many of these blue-chip companies have been able to perform so consistently because they have observed the principles which have been especially important in their market. These have varied from strong supplier partnerships to good employee relationships. If most companies did half as well with their employees as Southwest Airlines, SAP, or Marks and Spencer they would be performing much better.

Reputation widens the search for other principles that would lead to better performance. Even blue-chip companies can often do better by taking on areas where they have weaknesses.

And lastly, looking to the future we see a changing set of societal expectations, the likes of which we have not seen before. We see communications enabled by staggering advances in technology, which creates a more global community of activism. And we see business getting bigger and more embroiled in partnerships with governments. None of these conditions have prevailed in this combination before. Any retrospective evaluation of the effectiveness on shareholder value is trite, and probably a waste of time.

It's like an investor saying, "Show me the track record of investing in the new growing markets of China or Brazil and then I'll consider it." These markets don't have a track record, because the conditions which augur well for the future are different from the past: more liberal government, less corruption, more deregulation, and so on. Reputation assurance is like those new markets or new products. They don't have a track record and you just have to look at the trends going on and act. Of course, you need to put in process and measurement to ensure that you are making some progress and not blowing away your resources.

Q. *Reputation assurance sounds very procedural. Where is the passion and evangelism that generally accompany such programs?*

A. Have you ever been to a seminar where the speaker blew your socks off with mind-numbing rhetoric and argument? Have you then gone back home and discovered a few days later that there was very little you could remember about the talk, except that you were moved? Reputation assurance won't get you to that emotional peak which comes from outstanding oratory and a good cause. But the method will tell you what you should do next.

If you are going to act to enhance your reputation, then you need to go about it in the way you undertake any major change program. Some bits might seem unnecessarily arduous and labored, but they are necessary if you are going to put substance behind the expressions of caring about your stakeholders. You will need evidence to back up your claims and measures to show if you are improving. Feeling good is not good enough.

> "This is what you write. What is it you do?"
> —*Thilo Bode, Head of Greenpeace International*

Imagine that you're the CEO, and you've made your impassioned plea to your Kansas employees about the need for corporate responsibility among all employees. Let's even suppose that they're impressed with what they hear. What happens when you hop back on the corporate jet back to headquarters? You need to leave behind a framework which employees can work with to meet your aspirations—preferably the same framework all over the company.

Q. *How do you get teams working together to build reputation in a company?*

A. There are several levels where team working can operate in building reputation. The management team needs to agree to the principles and the key issues affecting stakeholders, as well as the actions that need to be taken to assure the firm's reputation. They do this by a truthful examination of how they stand today with regard to how their stakeholders see them and how they see themselves. They then agree on certain actions to take away to their organizational units for cascading down through the company. The human resources manager may take away the entire area of employee-related actions on diversity and build a team to establish and execute that policy. The head of marketing develops the principle related to respect in advertising, and so on. Soon everybody in the organization is affected in some way in the reputation program.

Q. *It's not clear to me if the framework is a guide to structuring an organization's efforts in protecting risk, or if it's a rigorous checklist for reputation assurance.*

A. I would hope it is both. Look at Figure 10.1. You can be in one of four places with regard to any of the principles of reputation.

Say you are in the top right-hand quadrant, where your efforts to project a good reputation closely match the reality inside your organization. This might mean that you make a big play on safety and reliability of your production facility; the accident record looks impressive, procedures have passed ISO certification, all employees have safety and reliability drummed into them all the way from their induction on. The external perception in the community in which your plant is based is also good. Citizens believe that you are not a hazard to them or to the employees who

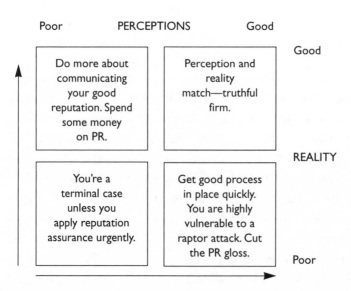

Figure 10.1 *How You Stand with Regard to Applying Reputation Assurance*

work there, many of whom are their husbands, wives, sons, or daughters. It's good work. Keep it up.

How about if you are in the bottom right-hand quadrant? People think you are a safe installation because you provide jobs in the community and they are prepared to believe your publicity. But in reality, you have a number of flaws in your safety management: no independent certification, accidents not being reported (so as not to blemish a clean record), and safety frequently being compromised. Here you are vulnerable because your publicity exceeds the reality in the organization. Whistle-blowers or disgruntled employees could blow away your facade of good safety. You need to put resources behind establishing better processes and building up reality.

Being in the top left-hand quadrant is a nice problem to have. You merely have to get better at telling the community the good news. If you're in the bottom left-hand quadrant, however, then it's hard times ahead. You're going to have to take some immediate action, tell the community what you are doing, and invite them to check that you are meeting your promises.

In these four examples we see how the framework can help you check on where you need to allocate resources to assure your reputation. It also tells you the type of resources you might need and trawls through an integrated framework of all the key stakeholder principles. But it does more: It ensures that you have all the essential steps in place, just like any quality program.

Q. *The model seems to be very internally focused. Shouldn't it include a survey of what stakeholders think?*

A. The model is a check on whether you have been rigorous in your thinking and have executed your ideas well. It asks you if you have surveyed stakeholders and if those perceptions have been taken into account and then asks you to provide evidence in terms of data, trends, and actions. This is a self-assessment model.

It relies on you to take responsibility for your reputation. Part of that is checking with the external world and seeing what others think of you.

We don't see it to be the job of independent verifiers to conduct stakeholder perception studies. Stakeholder identification, research, and analysis is the job of the organization. Each part of the company has its own set of stakeholders and relationships.

Q. *Quality management has become unfashionable of late. It's seen to be laborious and overladen with procedures. Are you sure this is a good model for reputation?*

A. All management techniques and processes have to change as we learn how to use them. Perhaps quality management also has to evolve and change. In some ways, management seems to have taken quality concepts and refined them further. But few people would argue about the key components of good quality programs. I have little reason to doubt their applicability to reputation assurance. (See Table 10.1.)

The first of these components is comprehensiveness. A good quality program must include all the activities of the company and not simply, for convenience, exclude some bits either because they're in the "too difficult" category or because they're far too embarrassing to talk about. What credibility would a quality

Table 10.1 Comparing Quality Management and Reputation Assurance

Quality Management	Reputation Assurance
Comprehensiveness	Integrated framework
Comparability	Generic principles
Inclusivity	Stakeholder model
Continuous improvement	Reappraisal
Communication	Disclosure

progam have if it didn't monitor defective products returned by customers? Equally, what credibility would a reputation program for a nuclear-powered energy plant have if the management chose to stay silent about the safety record?

The second component is comparability. Any system of assessment is worthless until you can compare it with what happens around you: in the rest of the company, as well as in other companies in your industry and in the world at large. This also applies to reputation. If you were flying Aeroflot as a Russian in the 1980s, before the collapse of the Soviet Union, you would have thought that flying with passengers standing in the aisles and sitting in seats without working seatbelts while, worse still, the pilot let his 10-year-old son fly the plane, were all part of the joy of flying. You'd have been wrong, but you found out only when you looked over the wall and boarded an American Airlines jet to New York. We have designed the reputation principles to be generic so that they are comparable across a company's diverse operations and across industries.

The third component is inclusivity. Quality systems have to include all employees in the organization. In just the same way, reputation assurance has to include all stakeholders who have a part in the organization.

Continuous improvement is the fourth component of quality. You cannot stand still; systems must evolve and get better. You need to continue to raise the barriers of achievement in this tough Darwinian journey toward maintaining a good reputation. These past few years you worked hard to combat the use of child labor. Next, you're going to have to tackle some tougher human rights abuses by your partners. The process is not static. It's continually evolving to match societal concerns and expectations.

Communication is the final quality component. Without clear communication, quality systems fall apart. You must tell your stakeholders what you're doing and feed back to them what they think of you. People who bought Saturn automobiles liked the openness of the company—the way it published J. D. Power's surveys of the cars and told customers and employees the areas where it needed to do better. Good reputation is also built on open communications with stakeholders and honestly showing them your report card.

So we see that quality management is common sense. It's just good management. So is reputation assurance.

APPENDIXES

RETAIL INTERNATIONAL

REPUTATION

REPORT 1998

This is the second reputation report from Retail International. Our first report, published last year, provided a framework for establishing our actions and priorities. It also gave us an opportunity to assess our position on reputation, with regard to the complex constituencies who either directly or indirectly interact with us.

This year's report goes further, giving us a chance to provide evidence of our progress in achieving the highest standards of reputation in our global organization.

WHO ARE WE?

For the reader who might be new to our organization, we are a transnational corporation dedicated to retailing food and household consumer goods and services. Our origins were in groceries retailing, but in the last 10 years we've widened our product range, following market development opportunities. Our revenue comes from the following broad categories: groceries, 56 percent; household goods, 26 percent; financial services, 18 percent. We are quoted on three major exchanges: the NASDAQ, FTSE, and Nikkei.

OUR LAST REPORT

In our last report we assessed ourselves as an overall "good" on the reputation assurance (RA) framework. (See Figure A.1.) We believed that we had good ratings for principles relating to shareholders and cus-

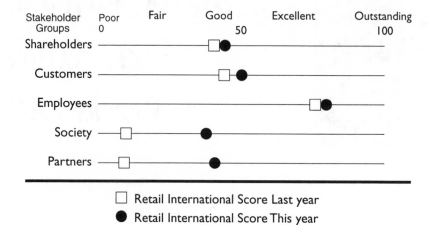

Figure A.1 *Reputation Index*

tomers and scored "excellent" for employees. But we had some considerable work to do in improving our ratings for societal and partnership constituencies. In our last report we set out how we expected to invest resources, to improve there, as well as to maintain our ratings in the other groupings.

THIS YEAR'S REPORT

We believe that we have been successful in achieving our aims over the last year and now have a more balanced set of reputational values. While we continue to distinguish ourselves in the employee category, we now have good assessments in all four stakeholder groupings. Greater dialogue with local communities, alliances with local suppliers, and our program of engaging with schools have helped improve our scores.

In keeping with our reporting standards we have given auditors full access to the assessment records, and this report is validated by them. We also follow the standard format of reporting by each stakeholder principle, giving the status of actions being taken, and recording our effectiveness scores.

SHAREHOLDERS

Through a process of briefings and focus groups we have come to the conclusion that our shareholders are greatly concerned with some principles and less concerned with others. *Respecting shareholder concerns* was the key principle they ranked as being the most important at the time, and we have put in place a program to respond to this. (See Figure A.2.)

Principle 1: Providing a competitive return
(level of concern: moderate)

For the last five years we have outperformed the market by an average of 18 percent with regard to total returns to shareholders. We exceeded the NASDAQ composite by 16 percent, the FTSE by 15 percent, and the Nikkei by 23 percent. Most buy-side analysts consistently gave us a buy recommendation throughout the last year. We rated ourselves as excellent. Our discussions with institutional investors and individual shareholders conducted through our web pages have not logged any major issues of

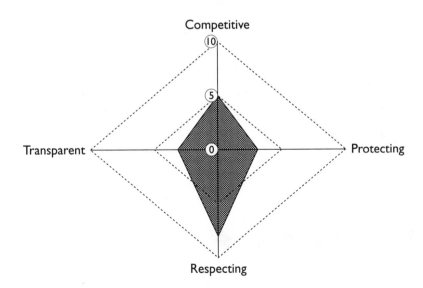

(0–3 low concern, 4–6 moderate concern, 7–10 very concerned)

Figure A.2 *Shareholder Concerns*

concern. A full description of our financial performance can be obtained from our web site on www.Retail.com.

We anticipate that the continuing Asian economic crisis will affect our income in that region. As a result we have taken the following actions in accordance with RA.

ISSUE

Reducing group impact of Asian slowdown (level of concern: high).

APPROACH

Our regional economic forecasting unit believes that overall retail spending in our product sector will decrease by between 15 percent and 20 percent. Our good reputation in the region would reduce those effects to about 10 percent. We have appointed a task force to manage the slowdown in a way that minimizes the impact on group earnings, but at the same time doesn't damage our avowed commitment to the region.

DEPLOYMENT

The task force is investigating ways that operating costs can be reduced while the economic slowdown continues. A personal letter has been sent to all staff and management in the region by the regional vice president. Local town-hall meetings with staff have also been held to explain Retail International's response to the situation. Staff have been asked to submit ideas for cost reduction to help the company get through the coming year of falling sales.

MONITORING

Activity-based costing systems are being introduced to give greater transparency of cost in key areas such as energy, distribution, and inventory management.

KEY BUSINESS RESULTS

The two critical business result areas are sales and operating margin. The challenge for the business is to maintain operating margins in the light of falling sales. (See Figure A.3.)

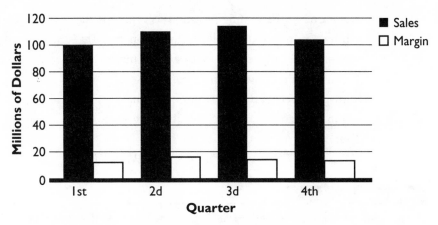

Figure A.3 *Sales and Margins*

HOW ARE WE DOING?

On the basis of the anticipatory actions taken and the deployment of those actions we have assessed ourselves as "good." In next year's report we will be able to determine the success of those actions and hopefully achieve an "excellent" rating.

Principle 2: conserving and protecting assets (level of concern: low)

We have continued to observe the best in practice in corporate governance procedures and our balance of nonexecutive directors to full-time executives; the governance of our remuneration committees has been continually under scrutiny.

Principle 3: respecting shareholder concerns (level of concern: high)

We began our first report because of a concern, expressed by a number of our shareholders, that they wanted to see evidence of our performance with regard to our relationships with partners, as well as our ability to work within the communities in which we operate. We have continued to rate this issue highly, and our continued dedication to the RA framework won us support from our shareholders at the last annual general meeting.

> "As one of the leading protagonists urging Retail
> International to publish a reputation report, I
> would like to go on record to express my admira-
> tion for the way this company has responded
> imaginatively and speedily to instituting a reputa-
> tion assurance process and publishing their first
> report. . . ."
> —*Jane Brady, CEO, Public Services Pension Fund*

APPROACH

We have adopted an integrated framework that combines all the key principles of reputation with our constituencies. Our goal has been to get all
our asset managers to buy into the use of the RA framework. We believe
that a common framework will facilitate comparisons between our different asset units and enable the sharing of experiences. At the center we
have assigned a full-time team of three people who are charged with the
effective roll-out of the RA program. The leader is a senior director who
had previously been involved with our Hong Kong operations. She reports to the main board. Her goal is to establish RA policies and to improve our reputation according to a set of measures, which are yet to be
defined.

DEPLOYMENT

We have communicated our wish to publish a reputation assurance report
to all our employees and investors and nongovernmental organizations
(NGOs) with which we interact on a regular basis. We have set up training
in reputation assurance techniques, and all retail branch managers, human
resources managers, buyers, and marketing team leaders are now required
to attend.

MONITORING

Our internal auditors have been trained in the RA process and they act as
an internal resource for monitoring the implementation of the framework.

In addition, our external auditors have been asked to validate the accuracy of the effectiveness measures, and to act as an external independent verifier of our observance of the RA processes.

EFFECTIVENESS MEASURES

By the end of last year all three regional management teams in North America, Europe, and Southeast Asia had received training in the RA framework. Over 80 percent of participants who attended recorded higher than 70 percent levels of satisfaction with the training and in postattendance assessments, 60 percent recorded the lessons learned as having been "very useful" in applying it to operational problems. (See Figure A.4.)

CUSTOMERS

Our customer-related principle evaluations for this year have increased slightly in the range of a "good" rating. We have a history of providing good customer service and our loyalty programs continue to help us maintain our market share despite a price war and significant cost cutting in many of our markets.

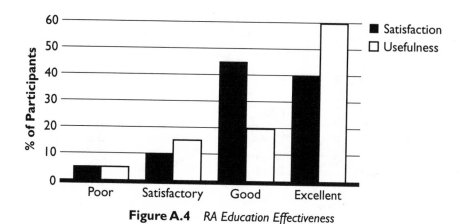

Figure A.4   *RA Education Effectiveness*

Principle 4: Meeting customer's reasonable expectations
(level of concern: high)

We continue to research customers' expectations of our company using opinion research, exit interviews, and focus groups in all our key locations. Last year one key issue that had been consistently highlighted was the area of food labeling. (See Figure A.5.)

ISSUE

Labeling of food origin (level of concern: high).

The outbreak of bovine spongiform encephalopathy (BSE) in cattle in England, the intensive farming of animals, and the introduction of genetically modified soya crops have caused many consumers to ask for products to be labeled in a way that allows the consumer to choose products according to their origins. It has not always been possible for us to source products that have clearly traceable origins in the way that consumers are now demanding. We have therefore had to instigate special action to accommodate their expectations.

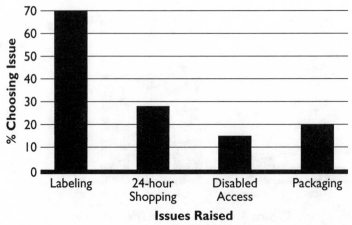

Figure A.5 *Customer Expectations*

APPROACH

We adopted a policy of "honest labeling" giving consumers product information in the key areas in which they continued to express concern. After discussions with our key suppliers, procedures for this year were instigated to adopt traceability criteria for all cattle that ended up on our shelves. All poultry that are farmed in nonintensive techniques, as defined by industry standards, would be identified as such. The previous practice of produce carrying erroneous labeling such as "farm-fresh" would be discontinued. We would endeavor to put pressure on our suppliers to introduce labeling of all products that contained genetically modified soya. There have been considerable complexities in implementing this policy and we have set ourselves a two-year deadline to fulfill our obligations.

DEPLOYMENT

We have distributed leaflets in stores telling customers about our "honest labeling" policy and encouraging them to write back to us with comments on the program. There is a free phone number and a web site. We also have communicated our customer concerns to our suppliers, and encouraged them to incorporate traceability criteria into their food production methods. We have sought to publicize model farms and include them in our own promotional literature. We are also offering financial incentives such as low-cost credit loans for suppliers who will conform to our standards.

MONITORING

We employ independent inspectors from outside the local area to visit our suppliers and verify their conformance with our standards. In the past we have found local veterinarians have not been able to provide the degree of independence that we would have liked. We also monitor the number of suppliers that apply for accreditation to our standard.

EFFECTIVENESS MEASURES

To assess the effectiveness of our program we have measured the impact on sales of the products most affected by the "honest labeling" campaign. Sales volume of beef and poultry had begun to improve three months after the program began. Sales of lamb and fish which benefited marginally in the first two quarters declined slightly as customers returned to beef and poultry. (See Figure A.6.)

Principle 5: Meeting customer guarantees (level of concern: low)

We have always operated a no-quibble guarantee on all products sold at our stores. At no time in the last few years has this been an apparent concern to our customers. We have clear policies and procedures on the return of all defective goods sold. Our staff are fully empowered to re-fund and deal with customer complaints in a way that they feel to be most appropriate. Our price guarantees on all household goods and branded merchandise have helped us maintain our market share. We continue to be successful at promoting the value proposition to our customer base.

Principle 6: Respect in marketing and advertising (level of concern: moderate)

Our marketing department has developed advertising guidelines for agen-cies to ensure that none of our reputational principles are breached in any of their campaigns. We take great pains to make sure we do not cause any

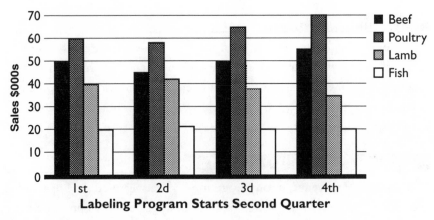

Figure A.6 *Product Sales Trend*

offense to any group on the basis of their gender, race, or culture. To help this, we have a penalty clause incorporated in our agency contracts to recover the cost of any claims from offensive materials. Our complaints have been insignificant in this area, but we continue to give this principle only a "moderate" rating because of the potential damage offensive campaigns could do to our business.

EMPLOYEES

Retail International has believed in and practiced the philosophy that employees are our greatest asset. In our last report and in this one, our employee principles have given us the highest ratings at the top end of the "excellent" range. We employ 45,000 people on three continents and we have achieved a consistent level of staff morale worldwide. Our levels of remuneration, training, and employee involvement in the development of our business give us an active differentiator in the tough, highly competitive world of retail.

Fortune magazine rated us the 19th most favorite place to work in America and we have won the European Foundation for Quality Management award for the most favored employer for two years in succession. (See Figure A.7.)

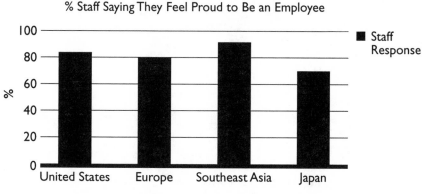

Figure A.7 *Proud to Be an Employee*

Employees' values have always featured highly in our management style, and our ratings for both years of this report have put us in the upper end of the "good" rating. Last year we surveyed our employees internationally to determine which of the RA principles they were particularly concerned about for the coming year. Questionnaires were handed out to them at the end of a video briefing by our CEO announcing last year's results to staff.

The results, illustrated in Figure A.8, show that *employability and transferable skills* and *equality of all employees* featured as principles of high concern, while *fair compensation* and *suggestions and complaints taken seriously* featured as moderate concern. We've allocated our resources to the implementation of principles accordingly.

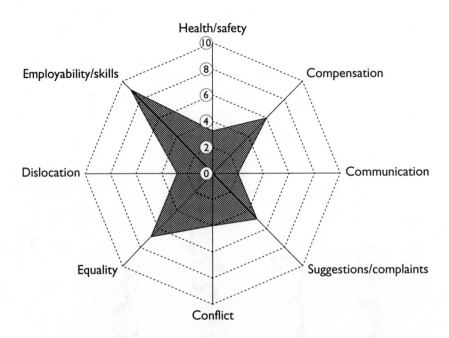

(0–3 low concern, 4–6 moderate concern, 7–10 very concerned)

Figure A.8 *Employee Levels of Concern*

Principle 7: providing transferable skills and employability

APPROACH

The finding that skills acquisition was given higher priority than compensation was a revelation to us. We published a policy and mission statement three months after the survey and set goals for transferable skills training. We appointed Ted Epstein, a visiting professor at Harvard, to oversee our management development program. We have also commissioned a consultants' report on training and development of all employees. (See Figure A.9.)

> "Retail International is committed to the development and training of all staff to enable them to have the skills needed to maximize their potential in the jobs market. We want to employ people who are highly valued by our competitors and who feel valued by us."
>
> —*Justin Peoples, Director of Human Resources,*
> *Retail International*

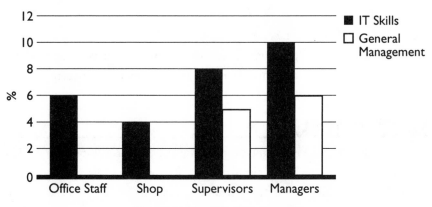

Figure A.9 *Skills Development*

DEPLOYMENT

Two pilot courses were run earlier this year and their initial assessments were good. Training programs combine computer-based learning, classroom sessions, and learning in action. This form of learning has been developed using the latest thinking on the subject and the technique we've deployed is known as "accelerated learning." The program is being launched worldwide in three languages.

MONITORING

In order to gauge the effectiveness of this program, participants are regularly being asked to evaluate themselves and the quality of the materials, teaching methods, tutors, and relevance to their longer-term employability.

BUSINESS EFFECTIVENESS

In the last quarter the number of business improvement ideas from staff and managers rose by 200 percent. Most of the new suggestions relate to cost improvement ideas, which if implemented could improve our margins by a further 10 percent. Other suggestions relate to customer service and loyalty program initiatives, and their impact is still being evaluated.

Principle 8: respecting labor rights (level of concern: high)

Our employees are drawn from a wide cross section of society and we have had a policy of equality of opportunity for all employees regardless of sex, marital status, disability, race, or ethnic origin. Recent cases of sexual harassment and racial discrimination in other companies have been heavily profiled in the media and this has raised our employees' concerns in this area. (See Figure A.10.)

APPROACH

We reacted quickly to reexamine our policy and have developed a fresh set of guidelines that have been circulated to all employees. We reviewed our old policy and came to the view that we needed to go beyond treating all employees equally, and rather try to fully appreciate their diversity. Our thinking has been influenced by a number of management thinkers and

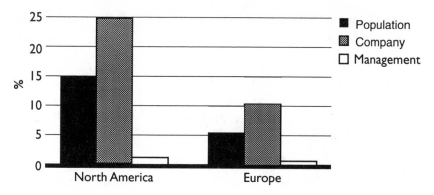

Figure A.10 *Ethnic Diversity in Retail International*

experts in the field of diversity. It's a more appropriate policy for today's world, since this company needs to take in influences and expertise from a range of different cultures and ways of thinking.

DEPLOYMENT

We have been explaining our new policy to management and employees. Workshops on diversity have been run for managers to show how diverse teams can perform better than homogeneous ones in an international company like Retail International. Managers are being encouraged to learn at least one other language than their native tongue. Supervisors, who frequently are responsible for employees from several different races, cultures, and nationalities, are being asked to promote a "buddy" program among their staff. The program encourages staff to adopt a buddy who might be of a different race or nationality and to learn about some of the positive attributes of that person's origins. The company newsletter, "Shopfront," has carried a number of appreciations of staff members and their buddies.

MONITORING

Monitoring of our diversity in terms of ethnic and gender mix began last year. We have yet to implement monitoring of employees with disabilities. Our ethnic mix correlates well with regional population statistics. On average, in North America and Europe we employ more minorities than are officially recorded in the population, but our levels of minorities in management are significantly lower. In Asia we have yet to begin the monitoring of ethnic diversity.

We employ more women than men overall in the company, but we have a poor record of matching that gender spread when it comes to managers. We hope that our diversity program will address that imbalance, which currently weighs considerably in favor of men. These figures have been collated for the first time in the history of the company, and they have clearly highlighted the situation for employees and management. Our goal is to double the existing level of female managers over the next four years.

BUSINESS RESULTS

We hope to witness a reduction in turnover of staff as a result of our diversity program. Although our overall annual turnover of 18 percent in the North American market is considerably lower than the industry average of 29 percent, most of that turnover comes from female employees, and in the senior and supervisory grades the turnover doubles. We aim to reduce overall turnover to 10 percent.

Principle 9: Suggestions and complaints taken seriously
(level of concern: moderate)

We implemented a free phone hot line for employees two years ago, and calls to the facility have continued to increase. The first calls were overwhelmingly complaints from employees about unfair treatment, workplace bullying, and alleged fraud by employees. Last year we reported how an independent task force had been charged with following up on all complaints, and we are pleased to report that two years after its implementation the balance of calls have swung in favor of suggestions. Total call rates are also up since we began. (See Figure A.11.)

Principle 10: Fair compensation

One of our founding principles is to provide a fair compensation to all employees for a fair contribution by them to completing the activities to which they are assigned. We have standard job evaluation processes and our

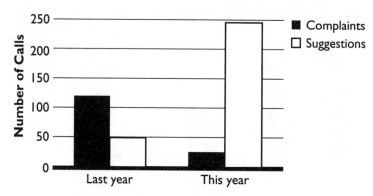

Figure A.11 *Employees' Calls to Employee Hot Line*

salary packages are positioned to be around the median for the retail sector. It is our policy to always pay above the minimum living wage in any
country in which we trade. We continue to monitor salary levels and extend our benefits package according to changing social and environmental
needs. (See Figure A.12.)

Other employee principles

Our other principles of *health and safety in the workplace, honesty and
openness in communication, handling conflict sensitively,* and *sensitivity in dislocation* were rated as being of low concern for the current year. These
principles are still important to us and form the foundations of good
employee reputation. We continue to monitor our accident record and
we are always reminding ourselves to keep our communications with
staff honest. When conflicts with employees do arise, there are well-
tried-and-tested procedures in place to assure them of sensitive and fair
treatment.

SOCIETY

Over the last year we have held a series of consultations with nongovernmental organizations, community groups, government representatives,
and nonprofit organizations. Of some surprise to us, there was considerable agreement both geographically and between these groups as to the

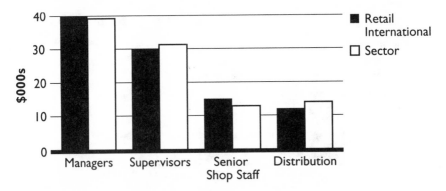

Figure A.12 *Salary Comparisons*

priorities we need to place on the RA principles. Our rating on the RA framework last year was "poor" and we set out to establish a "good" rating; we have achieved this, thanks to the considerable dedication of our staff. (See Figure A.13.)

Principle 11: Making an economic contribution and raising the purchasing power of citizens

Retail International has been under some criticism by local trade organizations and chambers of commerce for the effect it has had on local businesses and community trade in the area around one of our stores. Here we believe we have a genuine conflict of interest between our commitment to bring our customers the best prices for our goods, to deliver outstanding customer service, and to preserve local trade and commerce.

In many instances small retailers and producers are unable to offer the scale economies which we can afford, nor do they offer the range and choice which we can carry as a global retailer. Customers are inevitably drawn away from local stores, not by predatory pricing for which we are accused, but by the strength of our offer. It is with this challenge in mind that we have embarked upon a program to begin to redress the damage which we are aware is being done to small tradespeople.

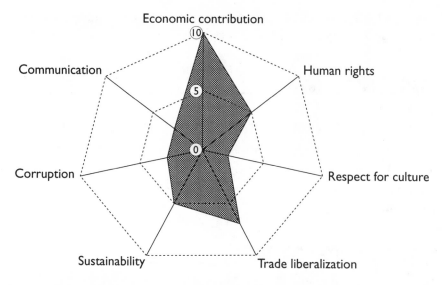

(0–3 low concern, 4–6 moderate concern, 7–10 very concerned)

Figure A.13   *Principles of Importance to Society*

APPROACH

Last year we began a "buy local" program where we offered customers the choice of buying local produce at special sections of the store. Groceries sourced from local suppliers were promoted with the names of the village or county in which they were produced. These products were allowed to compete side by side with often cheaper, nationally or globally sourced items.

DEPLOYMENT

The program was well publicized in local press advertisements, and local traders were targeted with flyers to tell them how to get in touch with Retail International buyers and qualify for the "buy local" displays. Store staff were briefed on the campaign and told why the company had decided to embark on it. Some stores have made their local products range available on a local store's web site to provide daily customer communication on what might be available at a particular store. Customers have often been disappointed because of the very limited range which small suppliers can carry. Locally produced honey sells out in minutes and smoked salmon from a well-known smokery sells out in the hour.

MONITORING

We monitor customer satisfaction with the program and run regular opinion surveys with local suppliers. We found that 70 percent of suppliers feel that their businesses are healthier since the program started, but 25 percent still think they are worse off. Customers, too, have expressed their satisfaction, with 55 percent of customers at our pilot sites saying that they would rather buy local produce if it were available.

BUSINESS RESULTS

Within six months of introducing the program on five pilot sites, customer satisfaction levels have risen by on average 10 percent. Average expenditure per customer had risen by 5 percent, and gross margins were up 1.5 percent. The pilots have undoubtedly been successful and we now are embarking on a plan to roll out the "buy local" campaign in 100 stores.

Principle 12: Promoting human rights
(level of concern: moderate)

Two years ago Retail International completed negotiations with the Myanmar government to establish a retail outlet at a site in the center of the capital, Yangon. No sooner had the official press release been issued than the outcry began, first from activist groups such as Amnesty International and later from customers and shareholders writing to us with their objections. The incident showed us how out of touch we were with the way society felt about the situation in that country.

We withdrew from our contract within six months. Now all new investments have to be subjected to a stakeholder analysis to determine the levels of concern from societal groups, and we investigate whether those concerns can be accommodated. In the case of the government of Myanmar, we could not get any assurances that the human rights situation would improve in the short to medium term.

Our support of human rights is embodied in many of our principles and the inset describes our policy.

Human Rights Policy

- We engage in human rights issues when making business decisions.
- We have regular consultations and dialogue with groups that defend human rights.
- We educate our managers and employees, particularly those working in regions where abuses are more common, of how to resolve some of the more complex human rights dilemmas.
- We monitor human rights violations in the countries in which we operate.

Principle 13: Supporting sustainable development and conservation (level of concern: moderate)

Ecological conservation has been identified as a principle of moderate concern in our areas of operation. However, as there were significant business benefits derived from our "more from less" campaign two years ago, we continue to give this principle a high operational priority.

APPROACH

Our policy may be summarized as follows:

- Reducing energy consumption.

- Reducing waste.

- Increasing the use of ecologically sound packaging.

- Minimizing the impact of transport on the environment.

- Phasing out the sale of products that do harm to the environment.

DEPLOYMENT

Our policy has been communicated to all staff, suppliers, and customers and they have been asked to comment on how well we measure up to our policies. Specific business improvement workshops now consider how to cut our energy bill and reduce packaging of products without forfeiting their safe handling. Last year we ran a successful campaign in 30 locations where we contracted with local bus operators to run a neighborhood free transport service to our stores. We estimate this cut the number of weekday car journeys by 15 percent. Our suppliers have been asked to submit proposals over the next year to reduce the packaging on products and to increase the recyclability of materials.

MONITORING

We have now instigated energy monitoring systems that help each store track its monthly energy consumption. All services were included in this system.

BUSINESS RESULTS

Our energy costs in all sites which have now implemented our policy have fallen by over 20 percent. Managers believe that a 30 percent reduction on the levels of two years ago is achievable. If this were to be implemented across the group, it could produce $20 million of savings.

Other principles

The principles that were of lesser concern were *transparency in communication, respecting local laws and culture*, and *avoidance of illicit operations and corrupt practices*. Once again, these principles, although of low concern to our societal stakeholders, are an integral part of our values. We continue to communicate these values to our employees and partners and we monitor occasions when we would appear to violate them. However, for this year we have not sought to engage in specific programs that address these principles.

███ PARTNERS ███

Partners are the category of stakeholders that include our suppliers and joint venture partners. We have reviewed the principles which concern them most via contract discussions, relationship reviews, and quality audits. Their views are reflected in Figure A.14.

Principle 14: Choosing similar values

One of the reasons why this has appeared as a principle of great concern was a series of allegations made last year by a human rights group in the People's Republic of China claiming they had footage of prisoners stitching garments that had Retail International labels. The prisoners were in "reeducation" camps where they had to work in forced labor conditions and were paid about $1.50 a week. We followed up these allegations with our subcontractors operating in the region, and to this day have not au-

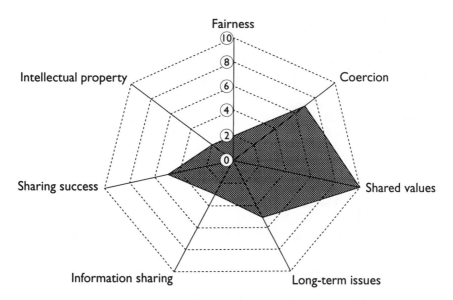

(0–3 low concern, 4–6 moderate concern, 7–10 very concerned)

Figure A.14 *Principles of Concern with Partners*

thenticated the allegations. But they were significantly damaging for our reputation nonetheless, as garment sales plunged 35 percent in North America, where press and TV reports gave the story the greatest coverage.

APPROACH

We have had to review all our relationships with suppliers in the aftermath of that event. We have found that our Southeast Asian suppliers have complex hands-off arrangements with other subcontractors. Work gets passed down an endless chain of agents. This makes it very hard to control the conditions under which our garments are manufactured. Our policy has now been clarified to include a strict condition that requires all subcontractors to agree to abide by a similar set of values for our employees. Human rights is a nonnegotiable part of those values. All hands-off arrangements have to be agreed to by the buying organization.

DEPLOYMENT

Buyers have been made aware of our "clean clothes" campaign and their performance contract with the company includes a component for ensuring that this policy is followed. We have also discussed the policy with all our suppliers and asked them to confirm that they can adhere to the guidelines without any impact on pricing.

MONITORING

We have adopted the Council for Economic Priorities standard for monitoring, SA8000, and inspectors have been appointed to carry out inspections of all suppliers in accordance with the standard.

BUSINESS RESULTS

Since introducing the standard, return rates for garments have fallen, implying an improvement in the quality of these products. We have also monitored the overall purchased goods prices and found that they are unaffected by these arrangements. The downward currency movements of Asian markets admittedly may hide some of these price effects. (See Figure A.15.)

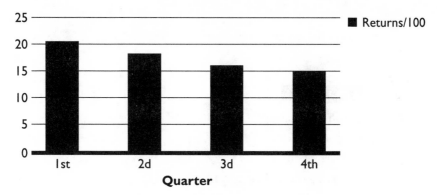

Figure A.15 *Garment Returns per 100 Purchases*

Principle 15: Coercion-free dealings (level of concern: high)

Buyers in the retail general merchandising sector have historically had a poor reputation with suppliers. Buyers have been remunerated for accessing the cheapest sources of products in significant quantities. At times they have used the purchasing power of a large corporation, and the relationships have been decidedly one-sided in favor of Retail International. We recognized that our reputation with suppliers was important in the long term if we were to continue to expand our operations and carry the burden of product development, inventory management, and running an efficient product replenishment supply chain. Our opinion survey of suppliers showed us to be poor in regards to fairness and building trust. (See Figure A.16.)

APPROACH

We set about building trust with suppliers with a redefined policy of engaging with them to identify how we could build trust to foster long-term relationships. In our new policy, supplier costs and profit margins are taken into account, as indeed are considerations as to whether the supplier company can be enhanced as a going concern on the basis of our relationship. Our buyers have to make it their business to assure themselves that the deals that we reach do not disadvantage suppliers.

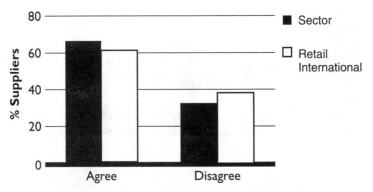

Figure A.16   *Retail International Treats Its Suppliers Fairly*

DEPLOYMENT

Buyers' performance is now based on a combination of their cost price performance, access to markets, and their supplier record. We promote an annual Retail International Partners Forum in a major conference location to encourage suppliers to talk about their experiences and to suggest how their partnership with us could be enhanced. Last year's first such conference in Las Vegas was a tremendous success; this year's is planned in Bermuda. Our CEO gives a keynote address at each forum and lays out our strategic plans for the coming year.

MONITORING

We have engaged an independent firm of opinion researchers to audit the degree to which our relationship is seen to be fair and noncoercive. This is an anonymous survey and we measure the way that our suppliers see us in relation to our competitors. This survey is used to monitor buyer performance.

BUSINESS RESULTS

The occurrence of stock-out situations has fallen.

Over the last year we have taken the decision to outsource more of our activities to third parties and the areas we have favored for outsourcing are information technology and communications. We were persuaded by the fact that organizations that specialize in technology would be better providing us with this support. We have found that the best way to enter into an outsourcing arrangement with our selected partner, Technology Solutions, is to set up an alliance to become foundation partners for new retailing systems for the next decade. An area that has become of concern since our last report has been allegations by some of our branded goods suppliers that we have been retailing goods which are modeled as lookalike products. Our suppliers feel that their intangible assets are not being respected.

Principle 16: Respecting intangible assets

Many of our partners today invest heavily in branding to differentiate their products from competitors' and it is up to us to respect those investments. (See Figure A.17.) Recently we procured jeans at highly competitive rates, which utilized many of the design concepts of some of our more up-market

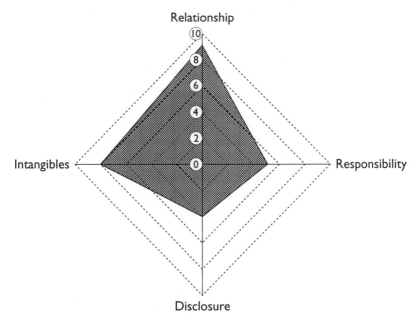

Figure A.17   *Relative Importance of Outsourcing Partners*

branded goods jeans suppliers. Suppliers claimed that customers were buying these jeans under the mistaken assumption that they were buying branded goods. We put in place a program of clear display labeling to differentiate these products.

We have invited suppliers to approve our displays and to monitor the impact on sales data.

THE AUDITORS REPORT

Our approach to auditing this report is to verify that Retail International has used the RA process in a substantial part of its operations worldwide. We have also verified that the key effectiveness measures published in this document are accurate and reflect the principles to which they have been associated.

We also verify that the RA process of self-assessment is a robust and valid way for a company to assure its reputation. The process of assuring the importance of each principle, the approach, deployment, and monitoring is a component of standard quality management. The structure of reporting and grading achievement in each stakeholder category is also part of a systematic and uniformly applied process.

On the basis of our agreed audit processes we are satisfied that this report gives an accurate and balanced view of Retail International's reputation with its stakeholders.

Nongovernmental

Organization (NGO)

Mission Statements

JAPAN

ASIAN HEALTH INSTITUTE FOUNDATION (AHI)

AHI's motto is "sharing for self-help." Based on the Christian faith, which teaches that people must love their neighbors, AHI seeks to assist communities in shifting health priorities to community-based health care. Founded in 1980, AHI is committed to supporting the marginalized peoples of Asia. AHI works with other NGOs for human resource development through participatory training programs. These training programs provide opportunities for middle-level workers from organizations throughout Asia to enhance their capacities, as community organizers and trainers on health and development issues, and as facilitators for people's organizations involved in community-based action for health and development (CBAHD). Further, AHI promotes networking among participants and their organizations to strengthen NGO institution building and overall effectiveness.

CONSUMERS UNION OF JAPAN

To protect and promote consumer interests, and also to promote international cooperation among world consumers in order to cope with the overwhelming work performed by the TNCs.

JAPAN COMMITTEE FOR UNICEF (JCU)

The Japan Committee for UNICEF is established to support the work and goals of UNICEF, including the pursuit of the goals and principles contained in the United Nations Convention on the Rights of the Child and the 1990 World Summit for Children Declaration and Plan of Action. JCU undertakes advocacy activities and organizes appropriate fund raising campaigns for UNICEF's programmes of cooperation. Advocacy and fund raising encompasses activities such as education for development, media relations, promotion of adequate financial contributions to UNICEF on the part of the government, and all other activities undertaken in the spirit of UNICEF's policies.

NIWANO PEACE FOUNDATION

To contribute to the realization of world peace and the enhancement of culture by promoting research and activities, based on a religious spirit and serving the cause of peace, in such fields as thought, culture, science, and education.

OISCA-INTERNATIONAL

Established in 1936, OISCA-International has been working on agricultural development in rural area in Asia and Pacific region. We built 21 training centers overseas and four of them in Japan, where trainers are taking agricultural and industrial courses. Twelve training centers overseas out of 21 are managed by OISCA Alumni Association, who have graduated from OISCA training courses. Other than human development, we are keening on environmental conservation since 1980s, such as reforestation and environmental education. OISCA-International received the UN ECOSOC Category I Consultative Status in 1995 and the Earth Summit Award from the United Nations in 1993.

PACIFIC ASIA RESOURCE CENTER (PARC)

The main goal of PARC is to bring about fundamental change in the "North-South" divide and work to create a society where people can live together in mutual solidarity. In attempting this, PARC informs and educates the public on various issues, in particular, environment, poverty alleviation in Southeast Asian countries, gender awareness, and social development.

RURAL ASIA SOLIDARITY ASSOCIATION (RASA)

The aims of RASA are to cooperate with people in developing countries seeking development of their lives, and simultaneously to reflect our lives in Japan.

WORLD CONFERENCE ON RELIGION AND PEACE (WCRP)

Since its founding in 1970, WCRP has been dedicated to promoting co-operation among the world's religions for peace, while maintaining respect for religious differences. WCRP is a global movement, with over thirty national chapters and members in over one hundred countries. Accredited by the United Nations, WCRP engages in vigorous peace-promoting initiatives throughout the world in cooperation with other religious, development, and UN agencies. Throughout its history, WCRP has worked to share, among religious leaders and representatives, knowledge of the sanctions and traditions each religion has for Peace and Justice; identify common religious commitments and principles conducive to the Peace of the human community; and undertake "Actions for Peace."

EAST ASIA (EXCEPT JAPAN)

AMNESTY INTERNATIONAL PILIPINAS

Amnesty International Pilipinas is a nonprofit, nonsectarian, unpolitical organization which works in solidarity with Amnesty International sections worldwide for the welfare of all prisoners of conscience and all those who have suffered the violation of their human rights. Amnesty International Pilipinas works to uphold human rights through education and information campaigns as well as other activities which raise awareness among the youth and the general populace. This organization works both in the national and international levels.

CENTER FOR COMMUNITY SERVICE

The Center promotes agrarian reform, sustainable agriculture, and rural development by establishing models, building NGO-PO capacities, and creating positive development environments through networking.

GROWTH WITH EQUITY IN MINDANAO PROGRAM (GEM)

The GEM Program intends to accelerate economic growth in Mindanao, and helps assure that the benefits of growth are widely distributed among the people of Mindanao. GEM works with producers' associations and co-operatives, NGOs, chambers of commerce, local and national government agencies, small and medium scale businesses, financial institutions, donor agencies, and others working to bring about equitably distributed economic growth in Mindanao.

HARIBON FOUNDATION

Haribon's mission is to conserve the biodiversity and integrity of ecosystems in the Philippines. Haribon's objectives are to promote community-based management, to undertake scientific research to aid conservative programs, and to raise public awareness on the environment and create a constituency through membership.

INSTITUTE FOR ECONOMIC STUDIES, RESEARCH & DEVELOPMENT (LP3E)

TNCs should promote/encourage the development of small industries, especially in rural areas, through subcontracting and other ways of conducting strategic alliance. TNCs should help the government of the host country (in this case, Indonesia) in the effort to reduce imbalances of national development, such as through the establishment of factories in less developed areas (in Indonesia's case, in the east part of the country). TNCs should also encourage "the right of working."

INSTITUTE FOR NATIONAL DEVELOPMENT STUDIES (LPN/INDES)

The mission of our organization is to support sustainable development through policy, gender, policy advocacies, and public opinion. The objectives are to provide the government with a strong analytical framework on important development issues; contribute to solving the problem of poverty; and contribute to the development of human resources in Indonesia.

INSTITUTE FOR SOCIAL AND ECONOMIC RESEARCH, EDUCATION & INFORMATION
(Lembaga Penelitian, Penddkan dan Penerangan Ekonomi dan Sosial) (LP3ES)

The Institute promotes the advancement of economic and social sciences that will help foster the sociocultural development of the Indonesian people through research, education, and information activities. It provides a contribution to more integral development of the human resources of Indonesia, particularly to assist the young generation in preparing themselves for the socioeconomic challenges of their own future by improving knowledge and understanding of development problems of Indonesia among the public, and promoting international cooperation with national and international organizations which have common objectives.

JESUIT VOLUNTEERS PHILIPPINES FOUNDATION, INC. (JVP)

Mission: To form a community of men and women who are able to live the Ignatian spirituality through service, simplicity, and solidarity by being agents of change in order to help build a sovereign society of peace and freedom based on social justice, people's participation, and authentic Filipino values.

Objectives: To recruit and send volunteers to assist other agencies which share the JVP vision, especially those with greater need; to provide information and support programs that enhance the volunteers' knowledge, skills, orientation, and spirituality for more effective service; to build local communities to deepen the JVP vision in the life of its former volunteers by providing venues for involvement in social transformation; and to establish partnerships and linkages to promote volunteerism.

KAUSWAGAN SA TIMOGANG MINDANAO FOUNDATION

Kauswagan's present program is to assist small entrepreneurs stabilize, even expand, their income-generating projects by lending them money for added capitalization. Our objective, therefore, is to create as many entrepreneurs as possible within the reach of our resources. We do not want to create mendicants or beggars. We want to form small enterprising businessmen and women. At present, we assist some 400 struggling entrepreneurs. We wish to reach more by our loans.

PAN PACIFIC AND SOUTH EAST ASIA WOMEN'S ASSOCIATION (PPSEAWA)

The purpose of PPSEAWA is to strengthen the bonds of peace by fostering a better understanding and friendship among women of all Pacific and Southeast Asia areas, and to develop cooperation among women of these regions for the study and development of social, economic, and cultural conditions.

PHILIPPINE DEVELOPMENT NGOs FOR INTERNATIONAL CONCERNS (PHILINK)

Philink is a consortium of Philippine development nongovernmental organizations (NGOs), NGO networks, people's organizations, and issue-based grassroots groups working for equitable, participatory, and sustainable development. Philink counts among its members two of the most vibrant national NGO networks in the Philippines, with a combined base of 120 affiliates; a national federation of provincial peasant organizations; and eight individual NGOs with independent concerns. This brings PHILINK's effective membership to more than 150 NGOs, grassroots POs, and cooperatives all over the Philippines.

PHILIPPINE RURAL RECONSTRUCTION MOVEMENT (PRRM)

Founded in 1952, PRRM seeks to enable rural communities, through a fourfold approach of education, self-government, livelihood, and health, to participate fully in building a democratic sustainable society.

INDIAN SUBCONTINENT

CENTRE OF CONCERN FOR CHILD LABOR

Centre of Concern for Child Labor's mission is to bring improvement in the quality of life of the poor, resulting in increased protection of the rights of children, thus reducing the exploitation of child labor and contributing to strengthen democratic institutions and empower the people. Priorities are: promoting sustainable development; undertaking action research and relief and rehabilitation of child labor, particularly girls; technology; and policy advocacy. We work closely with media and believe in creating political will among others.

CENTRE FOR PUBLIC POLICY AND SOCIAL DEVELOPMENT

To enrich the political process so as enhance its role as the prime mover of public policy and the social transformation of the democratic Republic of India, making it a model for global democracy.

Aims and Objectives: Research, including evaluation and case studies on various facets of constitutional democracy and social development. Setting up think tanks on specific issues of public policy, and bringing out policy profiles covering definition of issues, existing policy and legislative framework, policy options, and implications of alternatives. Rendering advisory services on public policy, social development and organizational reengineering. Providing advisory services on public policy, social development and organizational reengineering. Disseminating policy profiles to the members as well as among the wider public. Organizing workshops, consultations, seminars, and conferences on public policy and management at local, regional, and national levels. Enhancing professional capabilities of the youth aspiring to take to politics as means for advancement of human welfare.

CONSUMER EDUCATION AND RESEARCH CENTRE

Ensuring consumer safety, ranging from safety against explosion of gas cylinders in the kitchen to air crashes in the sky. Public accountability of public utilities (which are monopolies, too). Protect consumers against unfair and restrictive trade practices. Handling individual complaints organizationally which fail through courts. Availing of consumer forum and commission for evolution of tort liability of businesses for defective goods, deficient services, and negligence and unfair trade practices resulting in loss or injury to the consumers.

DEVELOPMENT ALTERNATIVES

The mission of Development Alternatives is to create sustainable livelihoods in large numbers. It does so through technology innovation and
design of more effective delivery systems. The technologies of Development Alternatives are geared primarily to the creation of local jobs and
to the production of goods and services indeed within the local economy. While working within the market system, our endeavor is to build
the capacity of small and micro enterprises to create wealth for the
community by conducting commercially viable and profitable businesses that address basic needs without destroying the environmental resource base.

FRIENDS IN VILLAGE DEVELOPMENT
BANGLADESH (FIVDB)

The organization views the ideal society as a vibrant society based on
justice, equity, democracy, and environmentally sound principles. To
achieve this notion, FIVDB seeks to contribute toward the educational
and socioeconomic empowerment of people. FIVDB follows a varied
strategy to achieve the mission. They are: direct program implementation
in the field, aimed at the building of human, social, and economic capital, and to change society's behavioral aspects so as to make it conducive
for development; extend FIVDB's intervention through building partnerships with other actors in the field of development; and networking,
lobbying, and advocating at the local, national, and international levels in
order to suit the activities FIVDB feels actively contribute toward development.

HUMAN RIGHTS COMMISSION OF PAKISTAN (HRCP)

The mission of HRCP is to uphold and implement the Human Rights
Charter of UNO in letter and spirit. Our NGO believes that all discrim-
inatory laws be banished from our country (Pakistan). We are against eth-
nicity, religious and cultural fundamentalism, gender discrimination,
child labor, death penalty, inhuman treatment of prisoners, discrimination against minorities, state repression and dictatorship, and censorship
of the media.

HUMANITARIAN AGENCY FOR DEVELOPMENT SERVICES (HADS)

HADS believes in true humanistic feelings which can only eliminate the social discrimination and other elements that troubles the sound growth of social harmony and economic atmosphere. Mission and objectives of HADS are: to thrive with ideal manpower on the society through exercise with humanistic, social, and spiritual values, stimulating hidden human quality and in accordance with skill-building practice and methodology; to develop self-reliant village organization of the struggling poor, emphasizing a united effort over wealth and individual agnostic power; and to develop entrepreneurship for the best use of local resources, maintaining ecological balance of the environment and socioeconomic atmosphere.

MADARIPUR LEGAL AID ASSOCIATION (MLAA)

MLAA is a voluntary organizing registered with the government of Bangladesh. Since the emergence of Bangladesh as a new nation, significant gaps in the rule of law and the human rights situation have been apparent. Seeking justice became particularly difficult for the vast majority of the poor and disadvantage people. Thus the objectives of the organization are: to raise awareness of citizens about their fundamental rights; to work for reform of law and the legal system through seminars, research, and advocacy; to raise awareness of the workless about workers' rights under labor laws; to work for women and children's rights; and to work closely with other national and international organizations in the same field.

PEDDIREDDY THIMMA REDDY FARM FOUNDATION

The Foundation aims at securing adequate and appropriate policy support to: promote awareness and self-reliance among the farming communities in tune with liberal democracy and economy, thus making agriculture vibrant and contributing to rural prosperity in the best interests of Indian economy and society; promote awareness, empowerment, and organization of farming communities in tune with liberal democracy, and to help carry information to the farming communities in order to strengthen their organization and to improve farming practices, irrigation systems, cropping patterns, and market access; help secure a rightful place for agriculture in the national economy through decentralized planning and management of the rural economy; promote productivity of the farming sector; help protect and promote farmer's interests as a consumer of agricultural inputs in the storage and transport services marketing facilities and in pricing of their products; and help carry the process and benefits of economic liberalization to the farm sector, thus integrating the agricultural, rural, and unorganized sectors with the process of development, with due concern for equity and sustainability.

RURAL WOMEN WELFARE ORGANIZATION (RWWO)

Rural Women in Development is the main object of RWWO. Our mission statement is as follows: RWWO works for the uplift of women through awareness and participatory development of women, to enable them to successfully pursue the activities met to bring change in their own status.

SARHAD RURAL SUPPORT CORPORATION (SRSC)

The primary objective of SRSC is the evolution of local institutions at the grassroots level for establishing an effective management system so that rural communities can move toward sustainable development. The strategy to achieve this objective rests on the following three essential elements: (1) willingness of the community to help themselves; (2) willingness of the community to improve their socioeconomics conditions and reduce poverty; and (3) honest and reliable leadership willing to help the people.

SOCIAL WELFARE AGENCY FOR VILLAGE DEVELOPMENT (SWAVD)

The development strategies of SWAVD pursue two major goals: alleviation of poverty and empowerment of the people. To achieve these goals, SWAVD prioritize people and their participation in the development process. SWAVD believes that changes in the conditions of the rural poor can only be brought about by developing the rural people and empowering them. The target groups have to become conscious of the basic causes of their poverty and only then will they be able to unite and take part in programs of their socioeconomic uplift. All SWAVD programs and strategies are designed to achieve this purpose. SWAVD programs have been designed to operate multifaceted programs involving mobilizations of vast multitudes of people.

SOCIETY FOR COMMUNITY ORGANIZATION TRUST MADURAI (SOCO)

The SOCO Trust was formed in the year 1982, by a band of young men who were witnesses to the sorry plight of the weaker sections of the Indian society, people denied social justice, guarantees spelled out in the Indian Constitution and the International Conventions and Resolutions and where violation was more a rule than exception. They have not had access to justice and fair play. Therefore, the SOCO Trust, in order to achieve for them what is their legal and constitutional rights, seeks to create access for them to the judiciary, including the apex court of the country, by providing legal assistance. It has also mounted a concerted campaign to protect and promote human rights and to maintain the ecological equilibrium. Among our missions are the ensuring of gender justice and the empowerment of women, and ending the pernicious system of bonded labor.

AFRICA AND MIDDLE EAST

AFRICAN WOMEN'S DEVELOPMENT AND COMMUNICATION NETWORK (FEMNET)

The African Women's Development and Communication Network is a network of grassroots, national, and subregional NGOs working for the advancement of women throughout Africa. FEMNET enables NGOs in Africa to work together to be more effective in their advocacy and programming for gender equity throughout the continent. The basic objectives are networking, communication, advocacy, capacity building in gender and development, lobbying, peace, and conflict resolution.

ASSOCIATION D'ENTRAIDE PROFESSIONNELLE (AEP)

The aim of AEP is to make it possible for people who are excluded from undertaking economic initiatives to be able to realize them. Through its credit system, the AEP helps such people to become active and responsible agents, contributing to the social and economic reconstruction of Lebanon, while preventing them from becoming victims of poverty or having to resort to begging.

DEVELOPMENT INNOVATIONS AND NETWORKING (IRED)

IRED is a global network of peaceable associations and grassroots movements. It seeks to create or support networks of these organizations to fight exclusion and marginalization. IRED acts as a development support service and a facilitator in the areas of policy analysis and advocacy for economic empowerment and democratization.

THE FORUM FOR CIVIL SOCIETY (FCS)

The Forum for Civil Society (FCS) is a nonprofit, nonpartisan, nongovernmental organization devoted to developing democracy, supporting electoral systems, strengthening civic society, and increasing women's participation in all aspects at Yemeni Society. In 1993, the founders of FCS began democracy development in Yemen, coordinating the first domestic monitoring effort in the Arab World. Founding members of FCS were part of an ad hoc committee, the National Committee for Free Election (NCFE), formed to monitor the first Yemeni parliamentary election. With coordination and assistance from the Washington-based National Democratic Institute for International Affairs (NDI), NCFE recruited and trained approximately three thousand Yemeni volunteers to observe the election process in thousands of polling stations all over the country.

Following the election, FCS was formed under the name of the Arab Democratic Institute (ADI) to spread programs of civic education to the Arab World. The positive results of the domestic monitoring project in Yemen stimulated activists from other Arab countries to establish their own democratic institutions. Due to the expansion of democracy institutions in the Arab World, a network comprised of 13 organizations from 8 Arab countries is currently being formed to develop democracy in the Arab World called the Arab Network for Democracy Development (ANDD).

As a response to the formation of ANDD and the dissolution of ADI, FCS was created. FCS will continue concentration in two areas: (1) working at the national level through ANDD, and (2) continuing the work of democracy building on a domestic scale in Yemen.

Since its establishment, FCS has been involved in various programs including election law reform, women's participation, domestic monitoring, coordination of internal observers delegation, voter education, and publishing a civic education newsletter.

KAGISO TRUST EXECUTIVE
Kagiso's mission to contribute to the alleviation of poverty, and to the reconstruction and development of South Africa.

MWELEKEO WA NGO (MWENGO)
MWENGO's mission is to strengthen the capacities of NGOs in Eastern and Southern Africa to articulate and implement a development agenda rooted in Africa experience and analysis. There are five major goals which guide the organization's activities: to promote research, analysis, and documentation within and among NGOs; to enhance the role and ability of NGOs to participate in the policy-making process; to strengthen the technical and managerial capacity of NGO staff; to build the institutional capacity and integrity of NGOs and promote the creation of democratic and accountable structures for decision-making in individual organizations as well as within the sector of the African NGO identity, role, and mission; and to define a constructive civic role and practical strategies for NGOs.

ORGANISATION MAROCAINE DES DROITS DE L'HOMME (OMDH)
OMDH's objective is to protect and promote human rights—civil, political, economical, social, and cultural. It contributes to the consolidation of the state of law, the respect of the independence of justice, and the democratization of the political institutions. OMDH tries to have regular dialogue with the state about human rights problems, and asks to be recognized as a "public utility" association to have the legal advantage of receiving private donations.

EUROPE

ASSOCIATION POUR LA COOPERATION TECHNIQUE (ACT)

ACT works in concentrated areas in Africa, Latin America, and the Philippines. Its mission is to ensure livelihood security through support of the local economy by stimulating local entrepreneurship.

ASSOCIAZIONE CONSUMATORI UTENTI (ACU)

ACU, active over the last 20 years, is an Italian consumers' association having offices all over the national territory and tens of thousands of active members. ACU is a full member of Consumers International, with nonprofitmaking association ONLUS statute. As a consumers' association, independent and nonprofit, ACU's first mission is defense of consumers' rights: satisfaction, redress, education safety, security, information, choice, representation, and environment. ACU actively supports any initiative whose aim is defending civil rights, from a worldwide point of view; hence, ACU participates both to negative actions (boycott, etc.) and to positive actions (fair trade, fair tourism, etc.). Besides being a consumers' defense organization, ACU is an opinion movement toward ethical consumption.

ASSOCIAZIONE ITALIANA AMICI DI RAOUL FOLLEREAU (AIFO)

AIFO, active since 1961, is inspired by the thoughts of the French journalist, Raoul Follereau, also called the Apostle of Leprosy. At present, AIFO supports development projects in 57 countries in three main fields: control of leprosy and primary health care; community-based rehabilitation programmes aimed at persons with disabilities; and children and persons in vulnerable areas (war, refugees, slums, ethnic minorities, etc.). Promotion and strengthening of national nongovernmental organizations is an important part of AIFO's operating strategy, which also collaborates actively with governments and international organizations of the United Nations.

BERN DECLARATION

The Bern declaration works to promote fairer relation between Switzerland and southern countries, in particular in the field of sustainable development.

CONSUMERS INTERNATIONAL

Consumers International supports, links together, and represents consumer groups and agencies all over the world. It has a membership of more than 220 organizations in 100 countries. It strives to promote a fairer society through defending the rights of all consumers, including poor, marginalized, and disadvantaged people, by supporting and strengthening member organizations and the consumer movement in general, and campaigning at the international level for policies which respect consumer concerns.

ERIKSHJAPEN U-DEPAN

Erikshjapen U-Depan is a Christian nondenominational NGO with the aim to improve the lives of children (families) through education and health programs carried out in cooperation with local counterparts in the region of the world where Erikshjapen operates. The fight against poverty and poor health is carried out through specific projects where donations of ordinary women and men are the principal source of funding. Cooperation with a broad base of funding along our policy is welcome and will be for the benefit of the poor of the world.

FRIENDS OF THE EARTH (ENGLAND, WALES, AND NORTHERN IRELAND)

Friends of the Earth International is a worldwide federation of national environmental organizations. This federation aims to: protect the earth against further deterioration and restore damage inflicted upon the environment by human activities and negligence; preserve the earth's ecological, cultural, and ethnic diversity; and increase public participation and democratic decision-making. Greater democracy is both an end in itself and is vital to the protection of the environment and the sound management of natural resources; to achieving social, economic, and political justice and equal access to resources and opportunities for men and women on the local, national, regional, and international levels; and to promoting environmentally sustainable development on the local, national, regional, and global levels. Friends of the Earth International has a democratic structure with autonomous national groups which comply with the guidelines established by the federation. Friends of the Earth member groups are united by a common conviction that these aims require both strong grassroots activism and effective national and international campaigning and coordination. Friends of the Earth International is seen as a unique and diverse forum to pursue international initiatives, taking advantage of the variety of backgrounds and perspectives of its members. By sharing information, knowledge, skills, and resources on both the bilateral and multilateral level, Friends of the Earth groups support each other's development and strengthen their international campaigns.

INTERMON

Intermon is a Spanish NGO for development founded in 1956, which works for poverty alleviation in the Third World by the execution of programs in more than 30 countries in the South. We are members of OXFAM International and EUROSTEP, and we are also a consultant NGO for the ECOSOC.

MANI TESE

Mani Tese was founded in 1964 to implement projects in the South of Italy, and development education and advocacy activities in the North, with local volunteer groups all over Italy. So far it has implemented 1720 projects in Asia, Africa, and Latin America, and a number of initiatives in Italy. It is a member of EUROSTEP and of numerous networks and campaigns relating to different issues. In 1997, Mani Tese was awarded special consultative status at the UN ECDSOC. It produces many informational materials such as books, dossiers, videos, CD ROMs, and a 40,000-copies-per-month magazine.

MISEREOR

Misereor is the Agency for Development-Aid of the Catholic Church in Germany. We support development and human rights work of partners in

Africa, Asia, Latin America, and Oceania, and to a limited extent advocacy and political lobbying on behalf of our partners. Development education and active participation in different campaigns and NGO networks are parts of our mission to work for more justice, especially in North-South relations.

OXFAM GREAT BRITAIN

Purpose: to relieve poverty distress and suffering throughout the world, to educate people about the causes and effects of poverty distress and suffering; and to campaign for a world without poverty, distress, and avoidable suffering. Objectives: support the efforts of poor people, especially women, to secure basic human rights and reduce their vulnerability; respond to urgent humanitarian needs in emergencies, and help poor people to reduce their vulnerability to emergencies; and advocate policy changes with partners to reduce poverty and injustice.

PROGETTO CONTINENTI

Progetto Continenti dedicates its energies to support self-development in poor countries and the work of local NGOs capable of cooperation with local people. Progetto Continenti operates mainly in the fields of health and education. In Italy, Progetto Continenti promotes the culture of solidarity with groups spread all over the country, acting with schools, municipalities, and institutions. Progetto Continenti self-finances its projects; some are cofinanced by European Community. Our NGO is working in Central America (Nicaragua-Salvador-Guatemala) and South East Asia (Cambodia and Vietnam). There is a disruptive presence of TNCs in these countries, especially Asiatic TNCs, that act only by the principle of maximization of profit, regardless of human rights and sustainable development.

SOCIALISTISCHE SOLIDARITEIT (FOS)

FOS supports the organization of indigenous groups of marginalized people in their building up of counter-power, and supports concrete actions (such as health-credit systems and small industries) to that end. FOS has its origin in the socialistic movement in Belgium. It aims to create support al-

liances between trade unions and movements of small farmers in the South
and North in order to build a global network of counter-powers.

SOMO CENTER FOR RESEARCH

SOMO, a center for research on multinational corporations, is a research
and consultative institute. SOMO works for unions and environmental,
women, Third World, and ethical groups. Areas of expertise are development, women/gender, trade (MAI/WTO), workers representation, gar-
ment/textile industry (global), and ethical commerce/consumers.

SÜDWIND INSTITUTE FOR ECONOMICS
AND ECUMENISM

Since 1992 Südwind Institute for Economics and Ecumenism in Sieg-
burg, Germany, has worked on background studies on economic development, in particular the responsibility of the industrialized countries and
TNCs for the developing world. Our main topics today are the Third
World debt crisis, debt for development swaps, women and economy, the
social situation of textile workers in Southeast Asia, the impact of the used
clothes export to Third World countries, and ethical investment. Südwind
has also been analyzing listed companies according to social and development criteria.

TRANSPARENCY INTERNATIONAL

Transparency International is a nongovernmental international organization dedicated to increasing government accountability and curbing both
international and national corruption. It is the only nonprofit and politi-
cally nonpartisan movement with an exclusive focus on corruption. Its
concerns are several: humanitarian, as corruption undermines and distorts
development in many parts of the world; ethical, as corruption undermines a society's integrity; and practical, as corruption distorts the operations of markets and deprives ordinary people of the benefits which
should flow from them.

Transparency International believes that combating corruption effectively and sustainable is only possible with involvement of all the stakeholders in international business and national integrity systems, which

include the state, civil society, and the private sector. Government cannot tackle corruption effectively on its own, other than in highly repressive and ultimately corruptive ways.

Transparency International, through its national chapters, brings together people of integrity in civil society, business, and government to work for systemic reforms at the national and international levels. We do not "name names" or attack individuals, but focus on building systems that combat corruption effectively.

Corruption often transcends the national level. Effectively combating corruption increasingly is beyond the reach of national governments. We work to ensure that the agendas of international organizations, both governmental and nongovernmental, give high priority to curbing corruption. We also shape public policy discussions in various fora to criminalize transnational corruption in an internationally coordinated manner.

NORTH AMERICA

AGA KHAN FOUNDATION CANADA (AKFC)

Aga Khan Foundation Canada (AKFC) is a nonprofit, nondenominational international development agency that promotes sustainable and equitable social development in Asia and Africa, without regard to race, religion, or political persuasion. The Foundation's particular emphasis is on health, education, rural development, and the strengthening of non-governmental organizations.

AKFC is part of the Aga Khan Development Network, a group of agencies established by His Highness the Aga Khan, the 49th Imam of the Ismaili Muslims. These agencies work to improve living conditions and opportunities in specific regions of the developing world, with individual mandates that range from health, education, architecture, and rural development to the promotion of private sector enterprise. All members of the Network share a common objective: to empower people to take charge of their own lives and a hand in the environment. The Network's development programmes emphasize community participation, creation and use of local expertise, rigorous management of resources, use of appropriate technology, and ultimate self-sufficiency.

BREAD FOR THE WORLD INSTITUTE

Bread for the World Institute seeks to inform, educate, nurture, and motivate concerned citizens for action on policies that affect hungry people. It works closely with Bread for the World, a Christian citizens' movement of 40,000 who advocate specific policy changes to help overcome hunger in the United States and overseas.

CANADIAN CATHOLIC ORGANIZATION FOR DEVELOPMENT & PEACE (CCOD&P)

CCOD&P was founded by the bishops of Canada in 1967 with the mandate of international solidarity. It supports socioeconomic development programs in the south and conducts programs of public education on international justice in Canada.

CANADIAN CENTRE FOR INTERNATIONAL STUDIES AND COOPERATION (CECI)

The goal of CECI is twofold: to contribute to the advancement of people in the Third World through human resources and funding; and to promote international development that is sustainable and which involves local participation. The Objectives of the Organization are the following: to fully involve Canadians in international development as co-operants, and to prepare them to be effective development agents in the Third World and Canada; to provide support to the Third World partners in their efforts to cope with their biophysical, socioeconomic, and cultural environment; to take part in the ongoing exchange of ideas on international cooperation; and to educate the Canadian public towards building equitable relations with the Third World.

CANADIAN UNIVERSITY SERVICES OVERSEAS (CUSO)

CUSO is a Canadian organization which supports alliances for global social justice. We work with people driving for freedom, self-determination, gender and racial equality, and cultural survival. We achieve our goals by sharing information and human and material resources, and by promoting policies for developing global sustainability.

CARE

CARE's reason for being is to affirm the dignity and worth of individuals and families in some of the poorest communities of the world. We seek to relieve human suffering, to provide economic opportunity, and to build sustained capacity for self-help. CARE has programs focused in micro-enterprise, agriculture and natural resource management, water and sanitation, post-conflict resolution, girls education, primary and reproductive health, and emergency relief.

CARE CANADA

CARE Canada is a member of CARE International, with projects in 60 countries reaching 45 million people each year. CARE supports efficient and professional emergency aid and long-term development focusing on poverty alleviation and building of civil society.

CENTER OF CONCERN

Founded in 1971 at the initiative of the United States Catholic and the Society of Jesus, the Center of Concern is an independent, interdisciplinary organization engaged in social analysis, theological reflection research, education, and policy advocacy. Guided by a global vision and a commitment to "read the signs of the times" and respond, the Center, through all its activities, seeks to promote a global community where people-centered development and a just distribution of the world's resources are acknowledged as enhancements of every human's being-in-common.

The Center holds consultative status with the United Nations and in the past three years has played a leadership role at the UN World Summit for Social Development (Copenhagen), the UN Fourth World Conference on Women (Beijing), the UN/FAO World Food Summit (Rome), and the UN Conference on Human Settlements—Habitat II (Istanbul).

The Center of Concern is a nonprofit, tax-exempt organization incorporated in Washington, DC. Its annual budget is raised through a combination of contributions, earnings from the sale of publications, lectures and consultations by staff members, and grants for specific projects from foundations and other organizations.

CO-OP AMERICA

Co-Op America, founded in 1982 as a national nonprofit organization, provides the economic strategy, organizing power, and practical tools for businesses and individuals to address today's social and environmental problems. While many environmental and social action groups choose to fight important political and legal battles, Co-Op America is the leading force in educating and empowering our nation's people and businesses to make significant improvements through our economic system. Some activities include the Green Business Program, the Consumer Education and Empowerment Program, the Corporate Responsibility Program, and the Sustainable Living Program.

FRIENDS OF THE EARTH

Friends of the Earth is dedicated to protecting the planet from environmental degradation, preserving biological, cultural and ethnic diversity, and empowering citizens to have an influential voice in decisions affecting the quality of their environment and their lives.

HUMAN RIGHTS WATCH

Human Rights Watch conducts regular, systematic investigations of human rights abuses in some seventy countries around the world. Our reputation for timely, reliable disclosures has made us an essential source of information for those concerned with human rights. We address the human rights practices of governments of all political stripes, of all geopolitical alignments, and of all ethnic and religious persuasions. Human Rights Watch defends freedom of thought and expression, due process, and equal protection of the law, and a vigorous civil society. We document and denounce murders, disappearances, torture, arbitrary imprisonment, discrimination, and other abuses of internationally recognized human rights. Our goal is to hold governments accountable if they transgress the rights of their people.

Human Rights Watch began in 1978 with the founding of its Europe and Central Asia Division (then known as Helsinki Watch). Today, it also includes divisions covering Africa, the Americas, Asia, and the Middle East. In addition, it includes three thematic divisions: arms, children's rights, and women's rights. It maintains offices in New York, Washington, Los Angeles, London, Brussels, Moscow, Dushanbe, Rio de Janeiro, and Hong Kong. Human Rights Watch is an independent, nongovernmental organization, supported by contributions from private individuals and foundations worldwide.

THE INSTITUTE FOR AGRICULTURE AND TRADE POLICY

The Institute for Agriculture and Trade Policy is a nonprofit, independent research and education organization dedicated to fostering economically, socially, and environmentally sustainable communities and regions. Its main program activities include food, environment, trade, and globalization.

INTERFAITH CENTER ON CORPORATE RESPONSIBILITY (ICCR)

ICCR is a North American association of nearly 275 Protestant, Roman Catholic, and Jewish institutional investors, including denominations, religious communities, pension funds, foundations, and diocese and health care corporations. These investors believe that to be responsible stewards, they must work to achieve much more than a financial return on their investments. They utilize religious investments and other resources to change unjust or harmful corporate policies and practices, challenging the powerful role corporations play in the use or misuse of the Earth's human and physical resources. ICCR members also make alternative investments to promote economic justice and development in low income and minority communities.

ICCR's members hold corporations accountable using the power of persuasion backed by economic pressure from consumers and investors. They sponsor shareholder resolutions; meet with management; screen their investments; divest stock; conduct public hearings; publish special reports; testify at the United Nations, Congress, and state and local legislatures; and sponsor actions such as letter-writing campaigns, prayer vigils, and consumer boycotts.

Issues addressed include sweatshops; the environment; global warming; land mines and other weapons; affirmative action; equal employment opportunity; U.S. and foreign debt; economic development; access to pharmaceuticals and health care; tobacco; maquiladoras in Mexico and Central America; sustainable living wages; human rights in Burma; fair employment in Northern Ireland; and global codes of conduct.

INTERHEMISPHERIC RESOURCE CENTER

The Interhemispheric Resource Center, founded in 1979, is a research and policy studies center that produces popular education materials, policy reports, periodicals, and books about current economic and political issues, especially those that concern U.S. foreign policy in this hemisphere. Our projects reflect our belief that political and economic reform is necessary in the United States. Similarly, we believe that U.S. foreign policy and U.S. international economic relations should be reshaped to support a global economy that fosters broad development for all nations, political systems that are more participatory, and environmentally sustainable economic growth. We are committed to a global integration that raises socioeconomic conditions; breaks down traditional ethnic, national, and religious barriers to cooperation; leads to the disintegration of patriarchal institutions, consciousness, and practice; and promotes cross-border and interorganizational collaboration. In an increasingly interconnected world, the mission of the Interhemispheric Resource Center is to provide information and analysis that encourages the general public, community leaders, and government officials to stand behind policies and reforms that increase social and economic justice throughout the world.

LAWYERS COMMITTEE FOR HUMAN RIGHTS

Since 1978, the Lawyers Committee for Human Rights has worked to protect and promote fundamental human rights. Its work is impartial, holding each government to the standards affirmed in the International Bill of Human Rights, including the right to be free from torture, summary execution, abduction and disappearance; the right to be free from arbitrary arrest, imprisonment without charge or trial, and indefinite incommunicado detention; and the right to due process and a fair trial before an independent judiciary. The Committee conducts fact-finding missions and publishes reports which serve as a starting point for sustained follow-up work within three areas: with locally based human rights and lawyers activists; with policy makers involved in formulating U.S. foreign policy; and with intergovernmental organizations such as the United Nations, the Organization of American States, the Organization of African Unity, and the World Bank.

The Committee's Refugee Project seeks to provide legal protection for refugees, including the right to dignified treatment and a permanent home. It provides legal representation, without charge, to indigent refugees in the United States in flight from political persecution. With the assistance of hundreds of volunteer attorneys, the Project's staff also undertakes broader efforts including participation in lawsuits of potential national significance to protect the right to seek political asylum as guaranteed by U.S. and international law.

OXFAM CANADA

OXFAM-Canada, founded in 1963 is a nonsectarian, international development agency working with over 125 African, Latin American, and Caribbean partner organizations to develop self-reliant and sustainable communities. We aim to improve people's basic living conditions through supporting their organizations as they work to overcome poverty and powerlessness. Our current programmes focus on food security, health, and democratic development.

In Canada, OXFAM-Canada works on development education, public awareness, and community development. We also speak out on behalf of our project partners on human rights issues, on questions of government aid policy, and on policies at the World Bank and in other international forums.

SAVE THE CHILDREN (SC/US)

In 40 countries around the world and in 14 states across the United States, Save the Children helps people learn to help themselves through projects that address interrelated problems and promote self-sufficiency. Save the Children especially focuses on early childhood education, preventive health care, and economic opportunities, including sustainable agriculture and natural resource management and family support. Women are a major focus of Save the Children's work. Through their multiple roles as economic producers, primary care givers, and community managers, women play a leading role in development. Save the Children programs endeavor to increase women's options to break intergenerational cycles of poverty and assure a better quality of life for future generations.

THE SYNERGOS INSTITUTE

Synergos is an independent, nonprofit institute dedicated to developing effective sustainable solutions to overcoming global poverty. Synergos works with government agencies, corporations, individuals, and the non-profit sector to strengthen the support and cooperation communities receive from civil society, government, and the private business sector.

WOMEN'S ENVIRONMENT & DEVELOPMENT ORGANIZATION (WEDO)

WEDO is an international advocacy network actively working to transform society to achieve social, political, economic, and environmental justice for all through the empowerment of women, in all their diversity, and their equal participation with men in decision-making from grassroots to global arenas. WEDO organizes the women's caucus at the United Nations, monitors implementation of UN conference agreements by governments, and runs an Action for Cancer Prevention global campaign that focuses on environmental health.

WORLD UNIVERSITY SERVICE OF CANADA (WUSC)

WUSC is a network of individuals and Canadian post-secondary institutions who believe that all peoples of the world are entitled to have access to knowledge, skills, and resources necessary to develop enduring societies.

WUSC's mission is to foster sustainable human development and human rights in a global context through education and training, active and participatory research into development issues, and internationally-oriented programs.

WORLD VISION CANADA

TNCs need to be committed to providing solutions to complex issues. We recognize that they are in a position of high visibility, but they must be more proactive. Child labor is more complicated than a simple "yes" or "no." In many countries, children need to work, but child labor must be controlled so that they can get an education. TNCs can be a very effective advocate as they pursue higher standards. NGOs and TNCs have things to offer each other. It will only work if they have some overarching values that they hold in common.

WORLD WATCH INSTITUTE

World Watch Institute, founded in 1974, is an independent, public policy research institute. Our reason for being is to foster the evolution of an environmentally sustainable society, one in which human needs are met in ways that do not threaten the health of the natural environmental of the prospects of future generations. We seek to achieve this goal through conducting interdisciplinary nonpartisan research on emerging global environmental issues, the results of which are disseminated throughout the world. In a sentence, our mission is to raise public awareness of global environmental threats to the point where it will support effective policy responses. The beneficiaries of our work range from individuals who use our research to guide their political actions or make life-style choices to large organizations, such as national governments, large and small businesses, international development organizations, UN agencies, and nongovernmental groups.

LATIN AMERICA AND CARIBBEAN

ALFORJA PROGRAMA REGIONAL COORDINADO DE EDUCACION POPULAR

Alforja's main objective is to strengthen the participation, negotiation, and management capacity of the civil society on the economic, social, political, and cultural fields through regional programs of popular education and communication. Its immediate objectives are: help NGOs and popular organizations to improve their capacity of planning, systematization, and evaluation of their education and training programs, as well as their strategies of local development; help grassroots organizations to improve their capacities on collective decision making and their representation capacity before communities, municipalities, and unions in order to democratize their structures and organizative methods; favor the knowledge, exchange, and systematization of innovating experiences related to community participation, construction of local power, and social-economic management with the aim to formulate integral development proposals within a regional perspective; make possible the didactic access to information and analysis elements about prioritized topics of regional reality, making emphasis on the ideas, experiences, and proposals of the popular sectors; and consolidate the organization capacity, strategic programming, and incidence on the civil society of Alforja's network.

ASOCIACION PRO DERECHOS HUMANOS (APRODEH)

APRODEH is one of the principal human rights NGOs in Peru. For its work in the promotion and defense of these rights, its director, Francisco Soberón, was the recipient of the 1997 Human Rights Watch award. In the last few years, APRODEH has developed a program for the promotion and defense of economic and social rights. Within this program, one project is related to the activities of TNCs (Shell, Texaco, and Mobil) and their impact on the rights of indigenous peoples.

ASOCIACION INTERSECTORIAL PARA EL DESAROLLO ECONOMICO Y EL PROGRESO SOCIAL (CIDEP)

The Intersectorial Association for Economic Development and Social Progress is an institution for human development. Its social responsibility is to work for education for development by generating formal and informal sustainable educational opportunities that will promote a permanent process of change and participation for men and women and the betterment of their quality of life. Goals include: developing sustainable educational opportunities with a gender perspective to contribute to the improvement of the quality of life of social sectors; developing programs to guarantee the continuity and social rentability of the community; and proposing policies and strategies that will incite innovation and development of the local and national educational system in order to favor the social sectors of our country.

CENTRO BOLIVIANO DE INVESTIGACION Y ACCION EDUCATIVA (CEBIAE)

CEBIAE is a social development, Christian, and ecumenical institution specializing in education that formulates and puts into practice proposals destined to influence the definition of public policies in education to improve the quality of education for children and youth. For this purpose, taking advantage of its institutional capacity, CEBIAE develops educational research; innovative methodologies in centers for education; communication and informational proposals in education; processing and production of informational document; and reflection, analysis, proposal, and consensus construction activities. CEBIAE works closely with with: students, teachers, parents, and education centers and member institutions of the Bolivian Network for Education Information and Documentation; educational communities; Catholic, Methodist, and Lutheran churches; state organisms; private social development institutions; labor unions; grassroots organizations; municipalities; prefectures; and other institutions linked to the education sector. In legal terms, CEBIAE counts on Supreme Resolution No. 185649 of December 22, 1997, where it is recognized as a center of "educational research and action inspired on Christian principles."

CENTRO DE APOYO PARA EL MOVIMIENTO POPULAR DE OCCIDENTE, A.C. (CAMPO)

CAMPO's mission is to foment social processes that will encourage change in the relations between men and women, seeking equity between the sexes, and, in particular, the empowerment of women as an indispensable condition to achieve gender justice. Its objectives are: to achieve the creation or consolidation of economic and income generating alternatives for poor women and their families in order to improve their quality of life, recognizing their peasant production logic and attending to the preservation of the natural environment; and to emphasize in our work those actions that seek a change in the power relations between men and women, mainly through our direct intervention with women, without neglecting our presence in mixed spaces. CAMPO offers professional services to women's organizations so they can consolidate themselves as enabled entities, exercise their full citizenship, and, as such, act upon the day-to-day life of townships and municipalities.

CENTRO DE EDUCACION Y CAPACITACION CAMPESINA DEL AZUAY (CECCA)

CECCA seeks to propitiate the integral and sustainable development of the poverty groups with which it works, especially in the rural areas. It seeks to propel democratic processes in which the participation of all is guaranteed. It works to eliminate any type of discrimination by sex, race, age, creed, or class. It develops training for the defense of the environment and the rational use of natural resources. Its basic objective is the search for justice and equity.

CENTRO DE EDUCACION Y CAPACITACION INTEGRAL HUMANA MAURA CLARKE (CECIM)

CECIM is a nongovernmental organization of Christian inspiration and of non-exclusive social function. We aspire to create cooperative relationships with TNCs so they may come to contribute to the human and socioeconomic development of our communities.

Our mission is to contribute to the socio-educative development of children, youths, and adults of the communities of Ciudad Sandino, Managua. With our work, we seek to promote an ample participation of the members of the community in different projects and programs, to impel activities that will improve education and culture, labor skills, and economic earnings, and thus create progress and the construction of citizens with full knowledge of their rights. Our objectives are to contribute the search of economic and social alternatives of local character.

CENTRO DE ESTUDIOS Y DIFUSION SOCIAL (CEDIS)

CEDIS's mission is to support the efforts and initiatives of the rural population, especially the indigenous, to improve their living conditions through the strengthening of their organization, their cultural identity, and their economy. CEDIS stresses impulse education, communication, and production projects that promote community participation by creating self-sufficient food production units, incorporating agroecological principles, and giving special attention to the equitable participation of women.

CENTRO DE INFORMACION Y DESARROLLO DE LA MUJER (CIDEM)

To contribute to the development and the equal treatment of women in society, particularly in popular sectors from a gender perspective.

CENTRO DE INVESTIGACION Y PARTICIPACION DEL CAMPESINADO (CIPCA)

CIPCA's goal is to promote balanced and democratic rural and regional development in the Grau region (Northern Peru). Its mission is to channel its professional and technical capabilities towards the elaboration of proposals that will make the successful and sustainable incorporation of the most marginal sectors into the dynamics of the modern economy, and thus their democratic participation a viable option. Its institutional design combines direct intervention strategies in the rural areas with information processing, radio communication, and regional concertation. Its activity is production and transfer of knowledge and abilities.

THE REPUTATION
ASSURANCE
FRAMEWORK

The Framework

Stakeholders	Context	1. Stewardship	2. Environment
	A. Shareholders	1A • Ensure a competitive return. • Conserve, protect, increase assets.	2A • Promote environmentally sustainable investments.
	B. Customers	1B • Meet all guarantees. • Meet reasonable performance expectations.	2B • Promote environmentally sustainable products and services.
	C. Employees	1C • Fair compensation. • Respect labor and human rights. • Show sensitivity in dislocation. • Invest in employees' future. • Avoid corrupt practices.	2C • Foster environmental responsibility in the workplace.
	D. Society	1D • Respect culture and law. • Promote human rights. • Contribute to local economies. • Promote fair trade. • Show sensitivity in dislocation.	2D • Protect the environment.
	E. Partners	1E • Foster equitable relationships. • Foster responsibility in stewardship.	2E • Foster environmental responsibility.

3. Health and Safety	4. Communication
3A • Promote healthy and safe investments.	**4A** • Disclose relevant information. • Respect significant requests.
3B • Promote health and safety in products and services.	**4B** • Disclose relevant information. • Respect significant requests. • Respect customer privacy. • Respectful marketing and advertising.
3C • Provide healthy and safe working conditions.	**4C** • Disclose relevant information. • Respect significant requests. • Respect employee privacy.
3D • Promote the health and safety of society.	**4D** • Disclose relevant information. • Respect societal concerns.
3E • Foster responsibility in health and safety.	**4E** • Disclose relevant information.

Principles Matrix

| STEWARDSHIP | ENVIRONMENT |

Shareholders

• *Ensuring a competitive return*
(providing shareholders with a
competitive return based on optimum
balance of financial and nonfinancial
measures)
– Managing key financial drivers.
– Paying liabilities; reporting other transactions.
– Takeovers/mergers.
– Restructuring.
– Competition/cartels.
• *Conserving, protecting, and increasing assets*
– Corporate corruption, fraud and illicit assets,
conflicts of interest, ethical issues.
– Board governance (composition, behavior,
compliance with codes).
– Risk and crisis management processes.
– Treatment of all shareholders.

Shareholders

• *Promoting environmentally sustainable
investments*
(practices, procedures, products, and services
which minimize environmental impact)
– Screening investment for environmental risk.

Customers

• *Meeting standards and guarantees*
(ensuring products and service meet external
standards and guaranteed levels of
performance and facilities appropriatel
measures to address dissatisfaction)
– Conditions/procedures for meeting
standards and guarantees.
• *Meeting reasonable expectations of
performance*
(ensuring that perfromance of the product/
service meets the customer's expectations
and facilitates appropriate measures for
dissatisfaction)
– Continuity of supply.
– Future pricing policy.

Customers

• *Promoting environmentally sustainable
products and services*
(products/services are representative of firm's
environmental principles)
– Life cycle approach to limiting use of natural
resources.
– Restoration of used natural resources.
– Customer education in environmentally
sound use of products and services.

HEALTH AND SAFETY

Shareholders

• *Promoting healthy and safe investments*
(fosters investment in healthy and safe
practices, procedures, products and
services)
• Screening investment for health and
safety risk.

Customers

• *Ensuring health and safety in products and
services*
(ensure that products and services perform
to the highest standards of health and safety)
– Product and service stewardship (limiting
health and safety risk).
– Recall policies.
– Customer education in healthy and safe use
of products and services.

COMMUNICATIONS

Shareholders

• *Disclosing relevant information*
(provision of truthful and timely information
affecting shareholders/future performance)
– Fair communication with respect to future
value.
– Accessibility.
• *Respecting significant requests*
(requests for information that are not in conflict
with the interests of the organization should be
honored)
– Addressing all requests (shareholder
resolutions).
– Open channels of communication and
reporting.
– Soliciting feedback.

Customers

• *Respect in marketing and communications*
(provision of truthful and timely information
affecting customers)
– Unfair pressure/coercion.
– Sensitivity.
– Information about competitors.
– Fair communication on products and services.
– Product labeling.
– Accessibility.
• *Respecting significant requests*
(requests for information that are not in conflict
with the interests of the organization should be
honored)
– Addressing all requests.
– Ensuring open channels of communication.
– Soliciting feedback.
• *Respecting customer privacy*
(all use of information and communications meets
customers' reasonable expectations of privacy)
– Confidentiality of data.

Appendix C

Principles Matrix (*Continued*)

STEWARDSHIP	ENVIRONMENT

Employees

- *Providing fair compensation*
- – Fairness of wage compensation and benefits.
- – Equality of pay.
- *Respecting labor rights*
- – Freedom of association (union activities).
- – Freedom of religious and political expression.
- – Bullying/harassment.
- – Equality/discrimination (ability, age, gender, and race).
- – Child labor.
- – Forced labor.
- *Anticipating and handling conflict sensitively*
- – Strikes.
- – Security threats.
- – Litigation.
- *Sensitivity in dislocation*
- – Facility closure and relocation.
- – Downsizing.
- *Transferable skills and employability*
- – Sustainability of employment
- – Participation in corporate success.
- – Training and development.
- *Avoiding corrupt practices*
- (Business practices discourage the following corrupt activities by employees)
- – Gifts and gratuities (receiving and giving).
- – Political contributions/lobbying.
- – Procurement arrangements.
- – Insider trading.
- – Industrial espionage.

Employees

- *Fostering environmental responsibility in the workplace*
- (Fosters personal/professional environmental awareness and responsibility)
- – Energy efficiency and management of resources.

HEALTH AND SAFETY	COMMUNICATIONS

Employees

• *Providing healthy and safe working conditions*
(Ensures working conditions promote physical/mental health and safety of employees)
– Health and safety in the working environment.
– Security of employees.
– Promoting healthy behavior.

Employees

• *Honesty and openness in communication*
(Provision of truthful and timely information affecting employees)
– Fairness in communication of information affecting employees.
– Accessibility.
• *Respecting significant complaints and suggestions*
(Requests for information that are not in conflict with the interests of the organization should be honored)
– Complaint management.
– Suggestion schemes and feedback.
– Open channels of communication.
• *Respecting employee privacy*
(All use of information and communications meets employee's reasonable expectations of privacy)
– Confidentiality.

Principles Matrix (*Continued*)

STEWARDSHIP	ENVIRONMENT

Society

• *Respecting and promoting human rights*
(Business goals and operations are compatible with internationally recognized standards for human rights)
– Political engagement.
– Impact of security arrangements on local community.
– Respecting and promoting rights of indigenous communities.
• *Respecting culture and law*
(Sensitive to local culture, law, and international law)
– Religious and cultural traditions.
– Language diversity.
– Land transfer/purchase arrangements with local community.
– Opening new facilities.
– Local community development.
• *Contributing to economic power of citizens*
(Promoting healthy local economies through investment)
– Purchasing power of individuals.
– Economic sustainability of local market.
– Opening new facilities.
• *Promoting fair trade*
(Promotes trade which is sensitive to needs of local economies)
– Nonmonopolistic practices.
– Respect of intellectual property.

Society

• *Sustainable development and conservation*
(Business goals and operations are compatible with the highest standards for environmental protection)
– Sustainable development.
– Environmental restoration and compensation.
– Environmental risk reduction.
– Resource utilization.

Partners

• *Fosters equitable relationships*
(Promotes longevity, stability, and fairness in relationships with partners)
– Stable partnerships.
– Fairness and coercion-free dealings.
– Sharing in success.
• *Respects tangible and intellectual property*
(Insuring that partners' rights and revenues are protected)
• *Fosters responsibility in stewardship*
(Fosters relationships with partners who aim to meet the highest standards of stewardship)
– Choosing those who share similar values.
– Compliance with global standards.
– Sanctions.

Partners

• *Fosters environmental responsibility*
(Fosters relationships with partners who aim to meet the highest standards of environmental responsibility)
– Compliance.
– Sanctions.

HEALTH AND SAFETY

Society

• *Promoting the health and safety of society*
(Business goals and operations are compatible with the highest standards for the health and safety of the general public)
– Managing dangerous practices.
– Compensation.
– Disaster response.

Partners

• *Fosters responsibility in health and safety*
(Fosters relationships with partners who aim to meet the highest standards of environmental responsibility)
– Compliance.
– Sanctions.

COMMUNICATIONS

Society

• *Disclosing relevant information*
(Provision of truthful and timely information affecting society)
– Fairness in communication of information affecting society.
• *Respecting societal concerns*
(Business activities respect the concerns of society)
– Addressing all concerns.
– Open channels of communication and reporting.
– Soliciting feedback.

Partners

• *Disclosure of relevant information*
(Ensures communications with partners and between partners and third parties meet highest standards of corporate responsibility)
– Fairness in communications.
– Soliciting feedback.

263

Effectiveness Indicators

STEWARDSHIP	ENVIRONMENT

Shareholders

• *Ensuring a competitive return*
Key Performance Indicators
− Return on investment.
− Total investor returns (current and forecast).
− Share price relative to sector and trends.
− Number of, and support for, shareholder resolutions.
− Actions by regulator legal autorities and success rate.
− Public comment through media.
• *Conserving, protecting and increasing assets*
Key Performance Indicators
− Number of, and support for, shareholder resolutions.
− Actions by regulator and legal authorities and success rate.
− Public comment through media.
− Board turnover (forced/planned terms of office for nonexecutives)
− Reports to board on corporate responsibility.
− Profile of board composition.
− Satisfaction of nonexecs (induction, information).
− Independence of nonexecs (selection, composition, terms of reference).
− Profile and turnover of shareholders (individual/ethical funds and employees).
− Speed/effectiveness of sanctions.

Shareholders

• *Promoting environmentally sustainable investments*
(Fosters investment in environmentally friendly practices, procedures, products, and services)
Key Performance Indicators
− Quantity of investments accepted and rejected on the basis of environmental criteria.
− Results of external reports/inspections commissioned by board/senior managment.
− Quantity of environmental incidents/damage/risks.

HEALTH AND SAFETY

Shareholders

• *Promoting healthy and safe investments*
Key Performance Indicators
– Quantity of investments accepted and rejected on the basis of health and safety criteria.
– Trends in health and safety reporting (and response) to board/senior management.
– Results of external reports/inspections commissioned by board/senior management.
– Quantity of health and safety incidents.

COMMUNICATIONS

Shareholders

• *Disclosing relevant information*
Key Performance Indicators
– Number of shareholder documents distributed.
– Record of meeting commitments.
– Number/turnout proxy ballots.
– Number of briefings by CEO and resulting market activity.
– Attendance at AGMs.
– Number of hits on the web site.
– Clarity and accessibility of information (by facts/survey/awards).
– Trends in reporting.
– Public comment through media and response.
– Trends in shareholder feedback.
• *Respecting significant requests*
Key Performance Indicators
– Number of actions taken on significant shareholder resolutions (minority and institutional).
– Number of communications with investor relations and resulting market activity.
– Results of shareholder satisfaction survey (individual, institutional, specialist).

Effectiveness Indicators (*Continued*)

STEWARDSHIP	ENVIRONMENT

Customers

• *Meeting guarantees*
Key Performance Indicators
− Customer retention.
− Customer complaints.
− Demonstrated conformance with customer-supplied product specifications.
− Customer satisfaction with claims procedures.
• *Meeting reasonable expectations of performance*
Key Performance Indicators
− Customer retention.
− Market share.
− Customer satisfaction.
− Demonstrated reduction in customer requests/concerns.
− Demonstrated utilization of survey results in product/service improvement.
− Number of awards.

Customers

• *Promoting environmentally sustainable products and services*
Key Performance Indicators
− Results of changes in customer behavior.
− Results of customer incentives for adopting environmentally sound behavior in use of products and services.
− Results of life cycle analysis and use of results in design process.
− Restoration statistics and data.
− Number of campaigns and boycotts.
− Results of environmentally related customer satisfaction surveys.
− Third-party ratings and awards.

HEALTH AND SAFETY	COMMUNICATIONS
Customers	**Customers**
• *Promoting health and safety in products and services*	• *Disclosing relevant information*
Key Performance Indicators	Key Performance Indicators
– Successful certification and standards.	– Number of complaints and campaigns.
– Efficiency, speed, and success of product recalls and service suspension.	– Results of customer satisfaction survey.
– Results of changes in customer behavior and misuse of product or service.	– Action by regulatory authorities and success rate.
– Number of incidents, claims, complaints, campaigns.	– Clarity and accessibility of information (by fact/survey/awards).
– Results of health and safety related customer satisfaction surveys.	• *Respecting significant requests*
– Third-party ratings and awards.	Key Performance Indicators
	– Number of requests through customer relations and consumer groups.
	– Number of actions resulting from significant requests (from small and large customers).
	– Results of customer satisfaction survey.
	• *Respecting customer privacy*
	Key Performance Indicators
	– Number of complaints and litigation.
	• *Respectful marketing and advertising*
	Key Performance Indicators
	– Number of complaints, campaigns, boycotts, and advertisements withdrawn.

Effectiveness Indicators (*Continued*)

STEWARDSHIP	ENVIRONMENT

Employees

• *Providing fair compensation*
Key Performance Indicators
– Productivity.
– Morale.
– Retention.
– Country/industry pay and benefits benchmarks.
– Attendance rates.
– Results of employee satisfaction surveys.
– Number of applications for each vacancy.
• *Respecting labor and human rights*
Key Performance Indicators
– Results of external audits.
– Third-party recognition/awards.
– Public comment via media.
– Employee surveys/interviews.
– Incidents of noncompliance.
– Claims and litigation relating to labor and human rights abuses.
– Cost of strikes, lockouts, and disputes.
– Level of complaints.
– Disciplinary records (for those in violation of policies).
– Employment profiles (ability, age, gender, and race).
– Attendance records.
• *Sensitivity in dislocation*
Key Performance Indicators
– Quantity retrained and placed in new jobs.
– Quantity of complaints and protests.
– Quantity and results of exit interviews.
– Lawsuits/protests.
– Results of employee satisfaction levels (surveys).
•Investing in employees future
Key Performance Indicators
– Retention (economy/sector trends)
– Participation rates.
– Trends in levels of qualifications.
– Investment in education and training.
– External accreditation.
– Trends in internal promotions.
• *Avoiding corrupt practices*
Key Performance Indicators
– Quantity of and response to investigations and complaints.
– Quantity of requests to the ombudsman.
– Quantity of incentives distributed and sanctions employed.

Employees

• *Fostering environmental responsibility in the workplace*
Key Performance Indicators
– Effectiveness of employee acceptance.
– Quantities of resource consumed.
– Spend in environmental education and training.

HEALTH AND SAFETY

Employees

• *Promoting healthy and safe working conditions*
Key Performance Indicators
– Quantity of incidents, complaints, and litigation.
– Quantity of sickness days.
– Investment in health and safety education and training.
– Employee satisfaction levels (surveys).
– Other data on well-being of employees.

COMMUNICATIONS

Employees

• *Disclosing relevant information*
Key Performance Indicators
– Quantity of communications.
– Results of employee satisfactin surveys.
– Quantity of complaints.
– Awareness and support for knowledge and values (surveys).
– Clarity and accessibility of information (by facts/surveys/awards).
• *Respecting significant requests*
Key Performance Indicators
– Employee satisfaction survey results.
– Quantity of requests (direct, suggestion schemes and through representatives).
– Quantity of actions taken as a result of employees' requests.
– Results of customer satisfaction survey.
• *Respecting employee privacy*
Key Performance Indicators
– Quantity of complaints and litigation.

Effectiveness Indicators (*Continued*)

STEWARDSHIP	ENVIRONMENT

Society

• *Respecting and promoting human rights*
Key Performance Indicators
– Boycotts.
– Public comment and actions.
• *Respecting and promoting humane treatment of nonhuman species*
Key Performance Indicators
– License to operate withdrawn.
– Protest incidents.
– Public comment and actions.
• *Respecting culture and law*
Key Performance Indicators
– License to operate withdrawn.
– Protest incidents.
– Boycotts.
• *Contributing to local economies*
Key Performance Indicators
– Quantity of employment from local sources.
– Quantity of community investment.
– Increased level of economic activity.
• *Promoting fair trade*
Key Performance Indicators
– Legal actions.

Society

• *Protecting the environment*
Key Performance Indicators
– License to operate.
– Incidents.
– Community action.
– Noncompliance, sanctions, and fines.

Partners

• *Fosters equitable relationships*
Key Performance Indicators
– Number of partners.
– Longevity of partnerships.
– Complaints, surveys of partner satisfaction.
– Results of third-party audits.
• *Fosters responsibility in stewardship*
Key Performance Indicators
– Quantity of partnerships accepted, sanctioned, or rejected on the basis of stewardship criteria.
– Quantity of investment in training and education.
– Performance records of partners for stewardship.

Partners

• *Fosters environmental responsibility*
Key Performance Indicators
– Quantity of partnerships accepted, sanctioned, or rejected on the basis of environmental criteria.
– Quantity of investment in training and education.
– Environmental performance records of partners.

HEALTH AND SAFETY	COMMUNICATIONS

Society

• *Promoting the health and safety of society*
Key Performance Indicators
– License to operate.
– Incidents/accidents.
– Public comment and actions.
– Noncompliance, sanctions, fines, claims, and litigation.

Society

• *Disclosing relevant information*
Key Performance Indicators
– Clarity and accessibility of information (by fact/surveys/awards).
• *Respecting societal concerns*
– License to operate.
– Boycotts.
– Noncompliance, sanctions, and fines.

Partners

• *Fosters responsibility in health and safety*
Key Performance Indicators
– Quantity of partnerships accepted, sanctioned, or rejected on the basis of health and safety criteria.
– Quantity of investment in training and . education.
– Health and safety performance records of partners.

Partners

• *Disclosure of relevant information*
Key Performance Indicators
– Results of partner satisfaction surveys and complaints.
– Quality and timeliness of information.

BIBLIOGRAPHY

BOOKS

Black, Andrew, Wright, Philip, and Bachman, John E. *In Search of Shareholder Value*, FT Pitmans, London, 1997.

Dalla Costa, John. *The Ethical Imperative—Why Moral Leadership Is Good Business*, Addison-Wesley, 1998.

Dunlap, Albert, with Andelman, Bob. *Mean Business*, Simon & Schuster, 1996.

Elkington, John. *Cannibals with Forks—The Triple Bottom Line of 21st Century Business*, Capstone, 1997.

Finnigan, Jerome. *The Manager's Guide to Benchmarking*, Jossey-Bass publishers, 1996.

Greising, David. *I'd Like the World to Buy a Coke*, New York: John Wiley & Sons, 1997.

Jacobs, Jane. *Systems of Survival—a Dialogue on the Moral Foundations of Commerce and Politics*, Hodder & Stoughton, 1992.

Loges, William, and Kidder, Rushworth. *Global Values, Moral Boundaries—a Pilot Survey*, The Institute for Global Ethics, 1996.

Love, John. *McDonald's Behind the Arches*, Bantam Business, 1995.

Maynard, Herman Bryant, and Mehrtens, Susan E. *The Fourth Wave—Business in the 21st Century*, Berrett-Koehler, 1996.

McIntosh, Malcolm, et al. *Corporate Citizenship—Successful Strategies for Responsible Companies*, Financial Times/Pitmans, London, 1998.

Mills, Roger. *The Dynamics of Shareholder Value*, Mars, 1998.

Peters, Glen. *Benchmarking Customer Service*, FT Pitmans, London, 1994.

————. *Beyond the Next Wave—Imagining the Next Generation of Customers*, FT Pitmans, London, 1996.

Price Waterhouse Change Integration Team. *Better Change—Best Practices for Transforming Your Organization*, Irwin, 1995.

Reder, Alan. *Best 75 Business Practices for Socially Responsible Companies*, Putnam, London, 1995.

Rosenbluth, Hal, and Mcferrin Peters, Diane. *Good Company, Caring as Fiercely as You Compete*, Addison-Wesley, 1998.

Slater, Robert. *Get Better or Get Beaten—Leadership Secrets from Jack Welch*, Irwin, 1994.

Treacy, Michael and Wiersema, Fred. *The Discipline of Market Leaders*, Addison-Wesley, 1995.

Wempe, Johan. *Market and Morality*, Eburon, 1998.

Zadek, Simon, Prozan, Peter, and Evans, Richard. *Building Corporate Accountability—Emerging Practices in Social and Ethical Accounting, Auditing and Reporting*, Earthscan, 1997.

PERIODICALS

Business Week. "US Trustbusters Crack Down," August 3, 1998.

————. "How Executive Greed Cost Shareholders $675 Million," August 10, 1998.

Economist, The. "A Charter to Cheat," 15 Feb 1997.

Financial Times. "OECD Urges Bribes Action," April 12, 1996.

————. "Can Consumers Change Corportions," May/June 1996.

————. "Ford Settles Dispute over Racism Claim," January 28, 1998.

"Our World Our People—Environmental, Health & Safety Performance Report," Baxter, 1997.

Wall Street Journal. "Corporate Chieftans' Great Moments at Options Trough," August 11, 1998.

CORPORATE REPORTS

Body Shop, The. "Values Report," 1998.

Cooperative Bank, The. "The Partnership Report," December 1997.

Goodworks International, LLc. "Report on the Nike Code of Conduct," 1997.

Shell Report, The. "Profits and Principles—Does There Have to Be a Choice?" Shell International, 1998.

INDEX